A 47,000-Hour Dashboard Adventure—

From Paradise, California, to Royal, Arkansas, and Up the New Jersey Turnpike

Mad
MONKS
on the
ROAD

Jim Crotty
and
Michael Lane

A Fireside Book   Published by Simon & Schuster Inc.
New York   London   Toronto   Sydney   Tokyo   Singapore

FIRESIDE
Simon & Schuster Building
Rockefeller Center
1230 Avenue of the Americas
New York, New York 10020

Copyright © 1993 by Michael Lane and James Crotty

Designed by Bonni Leon
Manufactured in the United States of America

1 3 5 7 9 10 8 6 4 2

Library of Congress Cataloging-in-Publication Data
Lane, Michael.
Mad monks on the road / Michael Lane and Jim Crotty.
p. cm.
"A Fireside book."
1. United States—Description and travel—1981- —Humor.
I. Crotty, Jim, date. II. Title.
E169.04.C76 1993
973.92'0207—dc20   93-22221
                                                           CIP

ISBN 0-671-76797-6

I dedicate this book to my dearest friend in the world, Michael Earl Lane, who understands me better than I do myself. Thanks for the journey Michael—we've changed the world!—Jim

I dedicate this book to the sustaining power of friendship, and to the courage of my friend James Marshall Crotty for enduring our tortured, highly dysfunctional S & M relationship through this journey of life.—Michael

Acknowledgments

We acknowledge the unselfish love and support of all those who opened their homes and their hearts to us on this journey, as well as those who mistakenly opened their kitchens. Their enthusiasm and encouragement reminds us that America still is a land of passionate dreamers who cherish and respect the kings *and* queens of the road.

And we thank, with the deepest and most profound Monkish gratitude, the following friends, who emotionally, spiritually and/or materially made this book possible (in alphabetical order, but with equal importance!): Roberta & Jay Bouma, Joyce Brasch, Michael Burris, Avy Claire, Carol Clark, Holly Comstock, Richard & Beverly Crotty, John Deming, Jane Dystel, Jack Essex, Charles & Mary David Gary, David Hochberg, Gary Luke, Mr. Apple Pi, Jonathan Scheur, Annie Sprinkle, Deborah Sundquist, Cheryl Wagner, Catherine Whitney and, of course, our beloved cats, Nurse, Nurse's Aide and Her Holiness, The Great Dolly Lama.

The McCauley Moving and Storage

truck arrived at eight o'clock on a sunny Friday morning in San Francisco's Castro District. Making a fatal crash into the concrete retaining wall, it sent a thunderous roar up the canyon of Nineteenth Street. Mrs. Klein's gray cat was flattened under the wheels. It was quite fatal.

Michael Monk jumped awake at the thunderous roar, bumping his head on the oven door. One day left to move and the damn electric heat had been cut, forcing the once upwardly mobile and now penniless Michael to sleep beneath his antique Wedgewood stove for warmth. Everything seemed to be working *against* a smooth departure.

Boxes were piled all over the kitchen in an orgy of cardboard, tape and bubble wrap. Some sat half-assembled, a dozen more leaned against the sliding glass door to the patio.

Half-asleep on a makeshift bed, buried in piles of unpacked books, tapes and bags of papers, Jim lay snoring.

Michael reached for the oven door handle to help himself up as Nurse, the cat, leapt from a towering stack of boxes, leaving them teetering dangerously to the left.

"Nurse, no, watch it, stay . . ." The boxes sagged against the wall, spilling precious first editions to the hard parquet floor.

The McCauley team angrily banged on the large front

The meeting of the Monks. (*J. Deming*)

door. The banging entered Michael's skull like a jackhammer.

Michael abruptly stood up, his legs trapped in twisted trousers, and hobbled to the oak door to greet the impatient movers.

"Fifteen tons of dynamite, that's what it's gonna take to get your piano outta here . . . fifteen tons!" Mr. McCauley of McCauley Moving and Storage bellowed in a raspy growl as he stood outside the door in his kelly green overalls, with fifty feet of rope in his left fist and a wooden dolly at his side.

Mr. McCauley had a piano to move.

"This one's gonna cost you, lad. Didn't say they were *outside* now, did ya? When we ran our estimate, we took your stairs to be *inside*. Gonna have to charge you extra, lad, and even more if one of my lads gets hurt."

Behind Mr. McCauley stood five other brutes of similar height and burly build in their green MCCAULEY overalls, sporting crooked smirks and stifled groans. They were casing the joint, smacking gum, chewing on toothpicks, puffing on roll-your-owns, their beady eyes darting left and right. The strong man, a seven-foot Goliath, sneered at the eighty-five wooden stairs that led up to Michael's "Swiss Family Tree House." Meanwhile, the freckled one, the only redhead of the bunch, was taking a leak on the exotic ferns Mike had planted. All six pairs of green eyes were upon Michael, who stood inside the door rubbing his swollen head.

Michael looked at the McCauley team. The McCauley team looked at Michael. They looked like the Irish Mob—big arms, bruises and cuts. Mr. McCauley had a black eye and a missing right finger.

"Like, how much extra?" Michael inquired.

"Double."

Michael considered the dynamite.

Mr. McCauley considered calling the whole thing off until he remembered the retaining wall below. Not to mention the dead cat.

"Listen, we had a little mishap. It got kind of messy down there. I think someone's gonna be mad. You take care of it and we'll stick to our quote. Deal?" Mr. McCauley stuck out his hand, waiting impatiently.

"What sort of mess?"

"It's a dead cat, that's wut it is," blurted the redhead, who'd left his fly open.

"A cat?!" Michael's eyes bulged. He flew through the movers like hot grease, brushing the seven-foot Goliath against the rail, taking the steps four at a time, sliding over the slick, moss-covered stairs, banging his hips at the turns.

Down at the bottom the twenty-foot McCauley truck was angled in off the street, across the sidewalk and into the ivy where it had taken a sizable chuck of concrete off the retaining wall. There at Michael's feet lay a cat. A flat cat at that.

"Oh, thank God, it's the Klein cat," said Michael, picking its flattened remains up by the paws. "Thank God it's not Nurse or Nurse's Aide!"

Mrs. Klein was just then coming out the front door for her morning *Chronicle*. Without thinking, Michael ditched the cat in a trash can before Mrs. Klein started screaming her bloody head off. This time, for a change, she'd have an excuse.

For the first time that week Michael laughed.

Mrs. Klein looked up and cast her predictable morning scowl his way. This was one neighbor he wasn't going to miss.

"Wait till she gets a load of this!" Michael thought as he passed the trash can heading back up.

At the top of the stairs, the McCauley team was bumbling out the door with the upright piano turned on its end.

"Hey, watch it, watch it! The leg's about to . . ."

The glass window on the porch shattered across the ferns,

the sound echoing down the street. *Of course, it had to be the window with the beveled edges and rounded corners,* Michael appraised bitterly, the window he'd replaced only a month earlier when Jim insisted that the water bed be removed. Michael strained to peek inside and could see where the McCauley monsters had removed a white Corinthian pillar to extract the piano and scraped a freshly painted wall. Glass crunched under the movers' feet, each crunch a painful spike into Michael's fragile nervous system.

"Sorry 'bout that, lad, just send us the bill," Mr. McCauley grunted under his breath. "I should never have agreed to this." He grunted some more, attempting to get the piano around another tight corner.

McCauley's men were now heading for the big drop of stairs, but not before they took out the porch's other window with a loud crash, trampling through the ferns as the two lead men slipped on the wet wood.

"Shiiiiiiiit!"

Just then the phone rang . . . *next door.* Michael's phone had long since been shut off. Any minute now the neighbor would be poking his head out the window to assess the latest damage and report back to the landlord. It was the neighborhood buddy system that always seemed to work against Mike and Jim.

"Just get it out of here!" Michael barked at the men in green.

"*Ayyyyyyyyeeeiieeieieeeeeeeee!*" It was Mrs. Klein, letting out a bloodcurdling scream from down below. "My baby, my baby, *who killed my baby!*"

"Michael, Michael, Donald wants to know if they have insurance," the deceptively sweet neighbor asked from next door, phone in hand.

Mr. McCauley's seven-foot giant panicked when he heard Mrs. Klein's anguished wail. His big frame slipped and he fell down the top flight, landing on his back. The piano headed over the guardrail and then got lodged against a eucalyptus tree.

"I hope you have insurance!" Mr. McCauley warned as the other four movers valiantly struggled to pull Michael's upright piano back onto the stairs.

"Who ran over my cat, my baby . . . *you'll pay for this!*" Mrs. Klein curdled the air, her voice getting closer.

"Are they affiliated with Worldwide?" the neighbor asked from next door, still on the phone.

"Mike, where's the pressure cooker?" A puffy-eyed Jim

leaned out the window. "I can't find the pressure cooker. Which box has the kitchen stuff?"

"My cat, my baby—*I'll have your balls!*" Mrs. Klein was advancing up the steps, huffing and sobbing while still managing to puff on a cigarette out of the corner of her mouth, her eyes filled with pure hate and vengeance.

"You sonnabitch, who the hell did this to my cat!" She carried the bloody mess in her left hand like a purse, while still in her dingy housecoat, clutching a Danish with her right hand, the newspaper rolled under her arm.

"Hey, lady, I wouldn't come up here, this is a heavy load!" Mr. McCauley shouted.

"*I want the balls of the coward that ran down my baby!* Just let me have the son of a bitch. I'm gonna sink my teeth into every one of you!" she shrieked toward the Irish lads.

"Michael, Donald wants to know if the insurance covers . . ."

"Someone's going to have to pay for my man . . . ," sang McCauley.

"Gimme that rope, I'm gonna string you all up by the balls . . ."

"Where's the pressure . . ."

"*Shuuuuuuuuut uuuuuuup!* Shut up! Everyone. Shut the fuck up! And get that piano out of here before I take your fifteen tons of dynamite, McCauley, and blow the goddamn block off the map! I don't, I don't want to hear it. Everyone, get moving . . . *now!*"

Michael stood panting at the top of the stairs, foaming at the mouth, his eyes bulging out of their sockets.

All eyes were upon him, waiting for the next explosion.

"But the pressure cooker, where is the pressure cooker . . . ?" Jim's voice trailed, echoing across the street.

By the time the cops led a frothing, hysterical Mrs. Klein back to her house, the McCauley movers had the piano in the truck. Mr. McCauley wasn't happy about the citation for the damaged wall, but that "tall, skinny bloke" had sent the fear of God into McCauley's Irish heart, and so he carted the piano off with his bruised and grumbling men.

Meanwhile, Jim was inside busily stuffing old high-school debate papers into boxes, labeling them by year, as Michael silently threw out the same papers, which Jim in turn recovered and repacked and Michael again threw out and Jim again salvaged. There had been an ongoing battle of the bulge to stick to the plan and discard useless junk and keep to the essentials for the move.

"C'mon, Jim, you don't need this."

"Are you crazy? You never know when I'll be called upon to debate reverse bail reform and pretrial detainers."

The move was not going as planned. For that matter, nothing had been going as planned for nearly a year. And now everyone was in an uproar. Not one friend approved of the departure.

In fact, no one in the entire megalopolis of San Francisco wanted Mike or Jim to leave. That is, no one except Uncle Jack, who was probably the only person in the entire state of California who would breathe a sigh of relief when the self-proclaimed "Monks" finally hit the highway.

Falling off a park bench several months earlier in mid-January, Michael

Monk hopped a cable car making the sharp ascent to Nob Hill, sat down with his purple knapsack underneath, arms folded, and contemplated the San Francisco Bay. The conductor's bell was much too loud, and it was much, much too early. Not a soul was out as the thick fog packed in against the cold steel girders of downtown. Michael planned to catch an hour of sleep in Grace Cathedral and then go knocking at 1242 Sacramento across the way.

Uncle Jack would be rousing himself from another night out with the boys on Polk Street, hunkering over his gourmet coffee and pleasantly surprised but secretly annoyed to see his nephew slumbering up five flights of stairs to his penthouse at such an ungodly hour.

Somewhere near seven A.M. Jack listened as Michael explained why he was trudging the streets with a two-day beard, a knapsack and an old bottle of zinfandel. Suspecting a long explanation, Jack, the consummate gentleman, switched on his answering machine, brought out the coffeepot, took a long drag on a Camel and settled back in his favorite antique chair. Michael anxiously paced about the spacious room that overlooked the Bay.

"Michael, you're looking a bit peaked," said Jack in that

formal tone he usually reserved for his students at City College.

"I know, I know. I must look really bad." Michael shrugged, pausing at the chess board, stooping to move a pawn.

"I should add, quite odorous. What's wrong, did they turn off the hot water again?"

"Well, no, it's not that, Jack. I've been huddling . . . or camping out you might say," said Mike sheepishly.

"Oh, really, this time of year? Where'd you go, Harbin Hot Springs?

"No, not Harbin."

"You've been evicted!" Jack leaned forward to light another Camel. The room brightened from the first rays of sunlight as the fog began to lift from the Bay.

"No, well, not exactly."

"Then what, another bashing? The Castro getting a little too hot?"

"No, things aren't dangerous, Jack. It's just that the nights have been getting a little out of control lately. You might say it's a result of a young man I've met named Jim."

"And who's Jim?" Jack arched his brows, beginning to take interest.

Only nine months earlier down in the Mission District past twenty blocks of sultry fruit vendors, greasy taquerias and sleazy pawn shops, Mike had met Jim at the only dance jam worth its wooden floor. Perched three flights above Mission Street within earshot of the Spanish whores and souped-up low-riders, the Third Wave Dance Studio opened its doors every Sunday night to whatever manic moon child would plop down five bucks for five straight hours of smoke-free, booze-free dance madness.

Michael was an instinctual dancer and was always there. Every Sunday, Mike the dance addict moved his tall, thin frame to any sound that spun on the record machine. Mike was the gazellelike ringleader of a Rainbow Tribe of crazed dancers bopping around the room like a pack of wild bulls, spasmatically moving to spin doctor Gary's lusty eclectic mix.

At a quarter to midnight on April 1 eve two hundred sweating bodies dressed in tie-dye, leotards and leg warmers were pounding the floor. Meanwhile, two inches from the corner, staring intently into a large mirror, stood James Marshall Luke Crotty, the consummate late-eighties macroneurotic Buddha. Living thirty blocks away in SOMA, the bohemian South of Market Area, Jim usually spent his Sunday nights chewing brown rice in a bare room beneath a curtain of clothes. The clothes hung across the window blocking the lights from Hamburger Mary's, where outside the leather daddies did their nightly roundup. Inside, Jim sat chewing. Fifty thousand chews a week gave plenty of time to think. Or, as Jim would prefer, sit.

Jim sat through almost anything, but not alone. He sat with his *zafu*, he sat with his beads, he sat with his wooden clappers, he sat chanting. Jim was your basic monk . . . with a *moktak*.

But on this Sunday, Jim left his own private zendo to perceive Mission Street with a beginner's mind. He followed the beat off the street and up the stairs to check out the vaunted madness of the Barefoot Boogie. Dressed totally in black, he slipped into Third Wave through a side door and took up his pose in the darkest corner. And there in the belly of the chaos he moved with the only dance he knew . . . t'ai chi.

Michael missed nothing. Miss Nothing they called him. Not a hair or piece of lint, dirty look or broken nail got by him. And least of all, a six-foot Buddha all dressed in black staring at himself in the mirror.

Mike danced in the corner up into Jim's face. Jim avoided. Mike leapt like a lizard snaking around. But Buddha Jim was not budging. No incendiary ballroom clown was going to disturb him from his deep *samadhi*. Jim was quietly engaged in studying his form.

But then suddenly the lights came up, and the music stopped. The herd of wild dancers quickly gathered their belongings, and spin doctor Gary packed his tapes. It was time to leave.

"That's when I'd have called it quits, my dear!" Jack was up at the phone now, asking his teaching assistant to take over his first French class at the college. "You always do get involved with these fringe types, don't you. Ever thought of settling for a good old-fashioned clone?" Jack chuckled.

Michael glowered.

"Alright, I don't go for clones, why should you. So tell me now, what line did you use?" said Jack with a smile, hoping to stroke Michael's tender vanity.

After hours, night crawlers always go out to eat. It went with the turf. And just as Mike was leaving, he noticed Jim the Buddha doing what Buddhas do best . . . avoiding contact and reading the bulletin board.

So Mike took a swallow and sized up this budding philosopher from one telling glance that said, "Starved for contact, please knock louder." It was Michael's big chance to say something. All those years of transpersonal growth-out had prepared him for this one auspicious moment.

Michael knocked.

"You want to join us to eat? Downstairs we're all gathering and you're welcome to come." Jim looked up astonished, shrugged, and followed Michael out the door.

Downstairs the bistro was bustling. It was now April Fools' and the fools were in high form. Frappés, freezes and cappuccinos were slurped around the café as if it were the night before Apocalypse. Bleached blonds with nipple rings, process queens fresh from est and those colorful punks down from the Haight were all over the place. It was a three-ring circus without the elephants, but plenty of snakes . . . your basic SF kind of crowd.

Jim and Mike sat transfixed at a table over a cup of herbal tea. The tea belonged to Jim. Mike was sucking on a vanilla shake studying this young Buddha while holding court with his exotic friends from Noe Hill. Mike's new flaming hairdo, a mix between straw yellow and pink grapefruit, was letting off fumes fresh from the bottle. Then again, everyone was fuming. It was a warm Sunday night and fifty sweaty dancers were causing a heat wave in the tightly packed Café La Bohème.

Jim was taking it all in, casting a critical gaze over the crowd, when Michael turned and dropped the latest psychobabble question for the terminally hip: "How's your inner child?"

You could have heard a pin drop. Someone slammed against a tray of glasses and everyone stopped talking just as Michael blurted out the words.

The whole room was laughing. Both at the broken glass and at Michael's question. *Here he goes again, Mike and his inner child. Who's he after now?*

Jim at first dodged the question but then realized he'd found an avid listener and was soon discharging twenty-five years of emotional baggage about debt, Dad, death, and above all, diet.

They spoke long into the night about this inner child. By the time Michael led Jim out the door, down the street and under the moon, they'd said enough to fill the Bay. So Jim retreated to the safety of his rice. Mike fled to his fortress on the hill. And a plan was made to meet the next day.

"That's it. You didn't even kiss?" Jack was surprised.
"He was straight, Jack!"
"Oh, come on, he was attracted to you, Michael!"
"No, he was straight!" Michael tensed on the edge of the couch.
"Alright. Whatever you say. So what happened, did you see him again?"

At 11:58 the following morning began the Saint Stupid's Day Parade. It was a time-honored April Fools' tradition for Merry Pranksters from around the Bay. A freshly manicured Mike appeared, sporting yellow polka-dotted tights, a pea green swashbuckler captain's blouse and a five-foot broad-brimmed sun hat that flexed up in the wind. Jim appeared in his basic black.

Across Market Street and up California the crowd of demented clowns marched below the imposing buildings of the financial district, as the lunching corporate throngs looked on. Tourists were swallowed whole in the raucous street mime. Mike led the way with a wild tambourine, as Jim wondered who the heck this balding madman was. But Mike didn't care. Recklessly abandoned, he kept up his gait on four-inch spiked heels.

Eventually the parade wound its way to the Sock Exchange at the Pacific Stock Exchange. Fast and furious trading ensued for half an hour on the bullish sock market. Socks of every smell, size and shape made the rounds. Even a bra and a teddy made the floor. Jim was hoarding black socks by the barrel. Mike was collecting panty hose by the dozen. Socks, bras, panties and nylons notwithstanding, a loud whistle finally blew and all trading ceased. The proclamation: "Pandemonium rules and Saint Stupid is crowned!" Mike stood clutching his profit of three pink panty hose.

Three hours later Mike led Jim off the street and up the eighty-five wooden steps to his home. Jim's mouth dropped to his knees as he took in the magnificence of Michael's Swiss Family Tree House With a View.

Jim thought he was dreaming. Expecting some cheap dive at the bottom of the hill, this didn't compute in his Buddha brain. *How did this strawberry blond, six-foot fairy swing it?*

Inside the warm oasis Jim was in for a shock. The house,

all eight rooms, all three levels, was as barren as the most pristine monastery. Jim the Buddha wandered casually around the house, marveling at the emptiness.

And then Jim did something peculiar—he made a beeline for the cupboards. Unsolicited, he took it upon himself to sort through every inch of Michael's kitchen—first the pantry and then the fridge—assessing, examining, making note. In short, seeing if Mike was up to snuff.

It didn't make sense. Orange hair, polka dots, high heels, brown rice, seaweed, miso, tofu, soy milk, rice cakes . . . our glamorous goofball was a card-carrying macrobiotic monk!

But despite the austere appearances, Michael lived well. His home was a rare find in the city. One could see the entire downtown skyline, including the Oakland Bay Bridge, China Basin, the Berkeley Hills and Mt. Diablo. It had four freestanding walls, and a private, *sunny* patio—private enough for nude sunbathing, mud baths and lots of massage, which, as it turns out, Jim was quite hungry for.

Jim liked what he saw. Leaving a trail of shattered spiritual illusions, he'd caught the Green Tortoise bus from Boston to start a new life in San Francisco. Standing now in the living room, overlooking the trees and city below, something took hold. There was no logic, no rationale, but four weeks later Jim moved in.

Jack jerked up from his chair. "Moved *in?* He moved in?! How did that lead to that? You're as bad as me."

"I just asked him to move in. He was in this hopeless situation South of Market and I had the space and . . ."

"You thought you could seduce him if he was under the same roof. I know how your mind works, Michael," Jack said wryly.

"Oh, go to hell, I can be charitable. But that wasn't it either. We just both felt good about it, like why not! He had less than me, and you know how little *I* have."

"Must be those pleading eyes of yours, Michael," Jack said from behind a wall of smoke, hoping to lighten up his nephew.

"You're such a cynic!" said Michael, turning his gaze to avoid contact.

"Never said I wasn't. Anyhow . . ."

The move didn't take long. Unpacking his meager belongings in less than an hour, including a change of clothes, a pressure cooker, some Buddhist paraphernalia and boxes

Nurse, our fearless leader.

upon boxes of papers, Jim wasted no time in taking up residence and spent his first week rearranging the cupboards.

Under the watchful eyes of Nurse the cat Jim adjusted to his new improved monastic digs. Nurse, born under a reggae mixing board in the South of Market Area, had the habit of nursing on anything he could get his mouth on, most notably wool sweaters and skin. Jim had both!

Nurse was pondering the latest in a long line of eccentric roommates with the cool demeanor of a junkie in search of a fix. He was especially consumed by Jim's expensive Shetland wool sweater. But Nurse had a long wait. Macro Jim was perpetually cold and never took off the coveted garment.

A few weeks into Jim's stay another stray feline arrived on the scene, one quite different from neurotic Nurse. He wasn't finicky. He could actually sit on a lap without nursing. And he was quite sociable.

Nurse's Aide.

Following the lead of this younger but wiser cat, Nurse suddenly chilled out. Nurse would now sit motionless for hours waiting for nightfall, when he would join the raccoon mafia in their nightly raid of kitty bowls. The new cat's healing effect on Nurse was so pronounced he was named Nurse's Aide.

This new cat and the new monk quickly became best of friends.

"So whose bed has Jim been sleeping in?" Jack always returned to the bottom line.

"We have our own beds. I mean, sometimes we share my big bed. But it's just brotherly love. We're like a cozy little family."

"*We?*" Jack knew better.

"I mean including Nurse and Nurse's Aide."

"Right. The cats." Jack chuckled to himself. "You call that *family?*"

Up by noon, Jim kept busy following his breath, banging out strange Korean chants on his gourdlike *moktak*, and making elaborate plans for his afternoon breakfast ritual, while Michael planned his lunch and the Nurses mapped out their kitty rounds. Everyone had his bag of tricks. But the tricks proved useless when it came to paying the rent. That is, until the arrival of pies.

The whole thing started as a lark. Mike was fond of baking pies when he met Jim. He was a pie sort of guy, whipping up the best pecan, apple, blackberry and pumpkin pies you'd ever smacked your lips into. They were those whole-wheat kind, without sugar, eggs and butter. Jim was hooked on those pies. Mike would have to bake almost two pies a day to keep up with Jim's burgeoning Buddha belly.

Jim began calling them Mike's Love Pies. And the Mike and Jim friendship blossomed in relation to the number of Love Pies on the cooling rack. So Mike's Love Pies began making the rounds to friends, neighbors and other guests.

Emboldened by the early success of the pies, Mike and Jim were now full of ideas. There's more than one way to pay the rent, and Mike and Jim were determined to find it. Jim quit his part-time gig at KQED TV, Mike quit his job with a record company, and the two coyotes began to scheme.

"You quit your job? You quit your job with the record company for *pies?*" Jack was on his feet. Few things got Jack out of his chair, but with this revelation he was shaking his head in total disbelief. "I could understand moonlighting your idea at night, or even a temporary leave, but *quit?* You've got to be kidding!" However open-minded, Jack was still from the old school that placed a premium on a proper well-paying job.

Michael sank into the couch against the wall and took in a few mouthfuls of nuts on the coffee table. Jack was, after all, *right.*

By October, Mike and Jim had fantasies of turning the house into a monastery of a sort. While shopping for Halloween costumes they came across white cotton paratrooper jumpsuits in a trendy boutique on Polk. With their signature jumpsuits, both men simultaneously knew they were now a team, a duo, an order of . . . Monks. Well, Space Monks to be precise. And Space Monks lived in monasteries . . . of a sort.

By November the pies were becoming very popular. The Monks began selling one-week supplies to hungry buyers. A business plan was made for Mike's Love Pies, as well as Jimmy's Pot Pies. An antique four-burner Wedgewood was bought and carted up the backbreaking steps. All the while Nurse couldn't conceive how this was ever going to pay the rent.

By Christmas, the Monks were almost in business with the pies when Gemini Jim came across yet another even *more* brilliant idea . . .

The Cookie!

That was the fatal mistake. Spending his last savings, Mike sprang for a pantryful of natural ingredients. The Cookie was Jim's brainchild, and he took it upon himself to invent the world's most healthy treat. But most of the cookies hit the garbage can. Many others were as hard as rocks and were used as doorstops.

But Jim wouldn't give up. He had become a madman at the ovens, with new cookie recipes constantly brimming in his kooky brain. He was in the kitchen twelve hours a day with a cart full of ingredients. Dough had so taken over the house that not a clean doorknob could be found. Flour was in every room. So long denied the means to engage his lingering natural-food fantasies, Jim was having a very messy field day.

But enough was enough. On a fateful day in late January, Michael came home and found a trail of barley-flour footprints down on the street leading up to the door. He knew he'd had it. The Cookie was chasing the Monks out of house and home.

Pacing up and down the street, Michael could hear Jim railing on the stairs, flinging a burnt batch out the door, banging on the tins and cursing at the oven. It didn't matter what hour it was, what day it was. Jim was consumed by The Cookie. That's when Mike took to the street with a bottle of zinfandel.

"Jack." Michael bent his head before Uncle Jack with a tear in his eye. "We are powerless over The Cookie and our kitchen has become unmanageable."

"You should just give it up. Did he ever bake one that was even edible?" said Jack while stirring his seventh cup of strong java.

"I just can't give it up. The Cookie is what's holding us together. I can't just throw the whole thing out because of a few bad batches."

Jack took another drag on the Camel, pausing to reflect.

"If he's straight, why are you even bothering? Why are you wasting time with your mad Monk? If you let it go any further, you're just asking for a lot of pain, my dear."

"No, he's not straight. I mean, well, he is straight but sort of not. I guess he's in between. But that has nothing to do with it. There's just something about him that I can't shake. Jim, he just grows on you. He's totally mad. I feel we're on a journey together."

"A journey through madness!"

"No! A journey through the unknown."

Michael began speaking from far away inside a little box trying to warm up to asking the question that had sent him to Uncle Jack's in the first place. As he reached into his pocket, out came a rumpled torn page from a newspaper.

"Have you ever squatted all night in an alley waiting for the sun to come up because you can't bear to face a crazy baker who forces you to *taste-test* until you're stuffed with dough?" Michael leaned forward. "Here's a list of bakeries for sale. Maybe if we got the dough out of the house and into a real kitchen, we could make it work." There was a pause.

"Jack . . ." Michael looked at his uncle. "Invest in Cookies and Pies. You'll be our silent partner. You front the capital, we'll run the business. Fifty-fifty, it's half yours."

Jack took a long draw on his last cigarette. He carefully extinguished it and stood up, arching his back, stretching toward the ceiling.

Michael looked on expectantly. Jack turned facing the Bay, thrusting his hands in his pockets.

Uncle Jack never said no. If he said, "I'll think about it," that meant, "Maybe." If he shrugged his shoulders, that meant, "Probably not." But if he handed you a hundred-dollar bill, that meant, "*Absolutely* not. Now don't bother me for a couple of months."

Michael waited.

At the
intersection of Van Ness and Market, Uncle Jack bade Michael good-

bye, shoving a hundred-dollar bill in his hand before hopping into his silver Corvette.

Mike jumped a ride on the Muni to the beach to sleep the day in the sand far from the Cliff House, where tourists wouldn't see him. When he woke, he warmed a jar of organic pinto beans over the coals of a fire someone had left burning by the old bathhouse and took a swallow from his prized bottle of zinfandel. He waded in the surf slightly drunk and stood looking up at the misty night sky wondering why he even bothered living in a house in the first place.

"Why not just live down on the beach with a jar of beans, red hot and working up a taste from the frothy salt air. Is it any worse than being chained in a house with a madcap baker throwing cookies against the wall?

"If there wasn't so much dough in the house, there might still be a place to sleep."

Mike paused . . .

"But who needs a home anyhow? It's just a place to get out of the fog and throw a few parties. For three years I've been sitting in that same house looking at the same immobile view, the same gray skies, listening to the same damn traffic, working my butt off to pay for the privilege, never enough time to go anywhere but Rainbow Grocery or around the block to Dolores Park. What's it worth?" he exclaimed bitterly.

That evening Michael climbed the cold, wet stairs of the Noe Hill Space Monk monastery collecting cookies along the way. At the top he scraped dough off the door to find the keyhole and followed the trail of flour leading up the stairs into the kitchen. There in the middle of the floor lay the doughboy holding a tray of prune walnut squares, his hair dripping with barley malt and a sweet smile of new success on his lips. Michael woke him and told him the news . . . "Jim, we're moving out of here."

"Moving?" Jim jumped up from the floor. "But I did it . . . the perfect cookie!" Jim blurted, spilling the batch across the parquet floor.

"It's too late," Michael declared. "There's more to life than The Cookie."

"But, Mike, I've done it. I've perfected the world's most perfect portable food. No more elaborate meals. No need for a range of supplements. It will satisfy the nutritional needs of people everywhere. They will get whole grains, complementary protein, essential vitamins, minerals and love all in one single treat. George Ohsawa died for this dream, Mike! We can't quit now."

"Jim, look at you. You're a mess, man. You're obsessed! You can't even hold a conversation. Everything revolves around The Cookie. And The Cookie ain't cut'n it."

"Mike, Mike, listen to me."

"No, *you* listen to me. There's no money, *get it? No money.*"

"*What?*" Gemini Jim's other side clicked in. "Whaddya mean?" Jim asked coyly.

"Look, Jim, we're three months behind on rent. I've told you this before."

"No, you didn't. This is the first I've heard of it."

"Where have you been?" The Monks *had been* through this one before. "Look, before we get into a big fight, let me tell you what's happening."

Jim sat stolid and silent.

"The landlord wants us out of here as soon as possible, so he can jack up the rent. He's been *very* patient with us. Either I pay him what we owe tomorrow or we have to leave."

"But what about our monastery, Mike? Our dream for a nontoxic oasis in the city."

"Jim, why try to be healthy in a city when it's so much simpler to just get to the country."

"Yeah, but we're abandoning the dream. How are we going to support ourselves? Where are we going to live?"

"Look, Jim, I've already thought that out. I talked to my old friend John Deming. He said we could come stay at his place until we figured something out. There's no use in staying in the city—we have to work our butts off to find a nice, healthy spot that's way overpriced anyway. I mean, why not hit the road and find a real oasis where you don't have to make an appointment to see a friend. I'm sorry, I've just been in this city too long. It's a haven, but it's also a trap."

"But what about my Adult Children of Catholic Republicans support group, and the S and M Zen Center, and my macropickling class, and our codependent friends? How are they gonna take it?"

Mike cast Jim a direct, sharp scowl. He knew his soul prankster was playing devil's advocate now.

"Jim! We've gotta pack."

Jim let out one of his gargantuan donkey laughs. Trickster Jim loved toying with Mike's earnest Leo nature.

In truth Jim already understood. He knew the Monks had hit the top of the fun curve and were ready to take the precipitous slide down. The Cookie, the monastery, the city, were but symbols of Buddha Jim's lingering attachment to familiar people, places and comforts. He'd just hoped to procrastinate a bit longer.

"Okay, let's just say to hell with it, Mike. I'm ready for a new Space Monk adventure too." Jim smiled, reluctantly conceding that the time had indeed arrived, giving Mike a hug, a tender kiss, and a teasing bite of prune walnut square.

The thought of leaving thrilled Mike more than he let on. Seven years in San Francisco, with all its beauty and charm, had been like life in a carnival—desolate and lonely amidst all the fanfare. Mike was so ready he could barely hold it in. He knew about the road, about cutting loose. He'd hit the Haight in '67, traveled to Shasta, Eugene, Boulder, Taos, hitchhiked all the way to Marakesh by '71, crisscrossed the country seven times. A migrant miner's son, Mike knew about this road and how deeply it touched his soul.

Jim, it was clear, would make the ideal traveling companion. He had hitchhiked all over America and Europe in his quest for community. Jim knew this road too and loved it to the core. The road would give Jim's wild spirit a chance to soar, the open spaces would give his mind a place to rest.

The Monks gave notice on the Noe Hill monastery and made plans to pack it up and hit the road. The Nurses, though apprehensive, couldn't more than agree, having coughed up one dough ball too many.

On the last day of winter the Monks held "The House Sale: Another Space Monk Production." Mr. McCauley and his crew had thoroughly decimated the porch and split the guardrails in moving Michael's monstrous piano to the street.

Mrs. Klein had made a major nuisance of herself, confronting every potential buyer with the gruesome details of her cat's demise at the hands of Michael Monk's *bloodthirsty Irish mobsters.*

The impossible nightmare of lugging everything down eighty-five slippery stairs to the street was cause for alarm, considering the precedent set by the piano. And then the rain came, but fortunately, so did browsers, who bought and carried off a fair amount of the possessions, including Michael's mannequins and tacky plaster casts, and several sets of wool sweaters (sucked and unsucked).

By the time it was over the Monks were left with a bit more than would fit in the seven-foot U-Haul, including the Wedgewood stove, which gave birth to both The Pie and The Cookie. The few remaining things were given to strangers.

Michael handed the house keys to the landlord, with an apology and a smile. Without fanfare or a crowd of friends, and in the quietness of the night, we, the traveling Monk entourage, drove off in the seven-foot wee-haul heading north. Jim's papers had won the battle and consumed half the weight.

We felt and looked like nouveau Okies leaving the Castro, heading up Market Street. With computer, books, clothes and papers stuffed into the wee-haul, we headed north in search of a new life.

"Good-bye, Hot and Hunky. Good-bye, Twin Peaks. Good-bye, Café Fleurs. Good-bye, Barefoot Boogie. Good-bye, Taste of Honey. Good-bye, Wang Fat flying-fish market. Good-bye, Rainbow Grocery. Good-bye, Mission District. Good-bye, San Francisco, good-bye, city life," Jim sang out merrily.

The big move: another Space Monk production.
(E. Feldman)

Michael had no such merriment in his heart. He was determined to kiss this urban Alcatraz good-bye . . . forever.

By the time we hit Sacramento, Mike and Jim had visions of macrovigilantes blocking the road and tying the Monks down for leaving The Cookie behind. But that soon passed, as Nurse's Aide fell calmly asleep on the dashboard while Nurse discovered and rediscovered that the best way to engage a moving vehicle was with a steady stream of piss down the back of the seat.

At around midnight on the spring equinox the Monks pulled up to John Deming's home in the appropriately named town of Paradise, California.

Mike, Jim, Nurse and Nurse's Aide sat in the wee-haul listening to the sound of crickets, the rustling wind and a posturban delirium, collapsed on the first real lawn they had touched in seven years, falling fast asleep on the perfectly mowed grass . . . free of the city, free of The Cookie . . . *at last!*

At six A.M. the sprinklers started their morning dance, soaking the lawn, flower bed and sleeping Monks on the green of John Deming's one-acre Paradise estate.

The Monks woke from their wet dreams to a very wet reality.

The water was moving fast. The Nurses dashed under the wee-haul, and the Monks bumped heads in their tangled fury to escape the torrential downpour.

But no sooner had it started, it stopped.

John Deming poked his groggy head out the door, saw the madness and rushed to shut down the sprinklers.

"What are you doing out here? I had a space on the floor for you inside! When did you get here?" John scampered to their side with a towel and a broad smile. "God, you guys look like you've been through hell. Must have been a hard trip."

Now it was all coming into focus for the Monks. Mike was wiping the water out of his eyes taking in his surroundings. Jim took one quick look and curled back to sleep.

"John, is that how you wake up all your guests?"

"No. I was saving it for you guys! Welcome to Paradise! Care to play a game of croquet?" said John with a warm laugh, giving Michael a good solid hug.

Greetings from Paradise! (J. Deming)

Michael looked around at the wickets. *So that's what I was wrestling with all night, a damn wicket,* he silently concluded.

"I thought croquet was for little old ladies, John."

"Nah, it's the hottest game going in Paradise. Everyone's doing it. It's either that or badminton."

John Deming's croquet course was the most wicked course in all of Paradise. And he was right. Everyone was doing it. By the crack of dawn multicolored balls were flying left and right through the walnut trees racing for John's paisley-colored wickets. The magic balls were chased by wild gophers who were in turn chased by Nurse's Aide. The game was played for "poison," and if you were *it,* you could whack opponents' balls silly out toward the poppy fields. But the rules demanded keen attention to the pansy patch by the patio, which was strictly off-limits.

After a brisk initiatory game, in which he quickly and efficiently decimated Michael, John pulled up a chair on his back porch, a cup of fresh brew in hand, and silently admired his one-acre estate. His perfectly manicured lawn glistened like an emerald in the clean morning sun, a testament to his mighty green thumb.

"So, this is all your *stuff.*" John motioned toward the wee-haul. "We're always dragging our *stuff* around, aren't we? Can't tell you how many times I've hauled the same set of dishes, chairs, appliances, clothes. Half the time I don't even need it. So what are you going to do with your *stuff?*" John laughed.

"Well, John, I thought I could store my *stuff* with you."

John let out a belly laugh. "You'll have to wait in line. Everyone's got boxes here. I feel like I'm running a mini-storage. Any idea what you're going to do? You have some money saved?" John was another bottom-line sort of guy and would be the first to tell you if your pants were on fire.

"Six hundred." Mike produced a wad of bills out of his pocket. "I sold everything I could, including the piano. There goes the music career. What a bitch that was getting it down the stairs. Got two hundred for my water bed. Thought we'd buy a car or something to get around. We've not really thought it out, but I guess we're going to travel, see what there is to see."

"When's the last time you bought a car?" John smirked.

"Oh, I imagine it was ten, maybe fifteen years ago. Just never needed a car in the city. In fact, I can't *imagine* owning a car in the city."

"Six hundred, huh? Hate to break it to you, but the only thing you're going to find for six hundred is a lemon. Then where's your money for gas? You'll be lucky if you make it a mile down this road on that." John motioned down the dirt road with a laugh.

Mike and John were happy to see each other. It had been eight years since they'd met in San Diego's North Park. John was an altruistic pharmacist who'd taken an immediate liking to the tall, thin monk and struck up a friendship that took them on at least one cross-country adventure, eventually landing John in the bedroom community of Paradise.

Later that morning, after John gave a tour of his magnificent *estate*, including the crowning glory—the hot tub—the Monks pitched a $20 two-man pup tent by the barn in the open field near the barbed wire fence. The Macintosh computer was safely stored inside. A wall of boxes were unloaded from the wee-haul, along with the lone sewing machine, piles of clothes and the Wedgewood stove, the last piece of The Cookie. We draped the whole mess in plastic.

"You sure you two are going to fit in that tent? Seems awfully small." John surveyed the tent and compared its

John Deming, the king of croquet.

dimensions to Mike's and Jim's six-foot frames. "Looks long enough, but you'll be sleeping in pretty close quarters!"

"Why, is there another bedroom inside?" Jim asked hopefully.

Michael's feathers were ruffled at the thought. *Maybe the tent is a bit small, but the two of us have gotten used to sleeping together in the house. It makes sense to continue as such in the country.* At least it did to Michael.

Just brotherly love. That's all it is.

"Sorry, no extra bedroom."

Mike breathed a sigh of relief. Jim looked a bit disappointed.

John was soon busy at work expanding and refurbishing his precious estate. Busy with the seeder, fertilizer and a garageful of lawn gadgets, John strove hard to outdo *Better Homes and Gardens.*

Jim donned a flannel shirt, a worn pair of socks, his oldest pair of jeans and those macho country boots he'd been wanting to wear since he'd left the city.

After a morning walk and the obligatory eleven o'clock game of croquet, Jim climbed the only hill, which was really only a clump of dirt, and surveyed the bare acre like a sharecropper planning his fields. Jim was just as full of ideas as before and soon had his nose glued to John's gardening books, voraciously reading everything he could get his hands on.

"I can't believe it, John. You've got all this land and it's just sitting here waiting to be farmed. We gotta plant something, man."

John took a look at his one acre and shrugged. "Well, I sort of like it this way. The gophers keep to their half, I keep to mine." John was from the laissez-faire school of lawn management.

And, as usual, he was right. The gophers had dug such an extensive network of tunnels that it was a walking booby trap to cross the field adjacent to the manicured lawn.

But ambitious Jim wouldn't give up. When Jim learned in one of John's books that all you needed was "dirt and a few seeds," his vision expanded from a mere garden to a field of cash crops to feed the world's starving children.

But it was Mike who did the shoveling. Born a country boy, this was home to Arkansas Slim. Picking up a shovel or a hoe was as familiar as taking a whiz in the woods. Mike could no sooner get his hands on some tools then he'd be working up a storm in a field of weeds. Forget raised beds,

French-intensive or square-foot gardening, or Jim's "one-monk revolution," Mike did it the old-fashioned way.

"Mike, it says here you have to balance the soil through companion crops. And the right blend of sea kelp, eggshells and compost will be the first step in correcting the clay soil. But first we have to send out a sample of dirt for a lab test. Says right here for three hundred dollars you can . . ." Jim followed the written word like gospel.

Mike just scratched a hole, planted a few seeds, gave it some water and waited for it to grow. Jim could pull the weeds and read about it. Within a week the Monks had planted two huge patches of Hokkaido pumpkins, a smaller patch of corn, a bed of turnips and some beets.

John watched in amazement as his gopher field turned into a sharecropper's dream. The Monks would've planted all the way to the road had John not reminded the Monks that after we left "who is going to take care of all of this anyhow?"

"Oh, right. Forgot about that, John."

"If you guys like gardening so much, why don't you plant other people's and make some money at it," John said with a wry smile. John was a master at naming the obvious when no one else could see. The Monks weren't sure if they liked gardening *that much,* but were willing to give it a try.

Soon Paradise was awash in colorful pink flyers announcing *Gardens 'R' Go: Yet Another Space Monk Production, Starring Two Able-bodied Men With Big Strong Hands* who were willing to do anything for the right price.

Much to the Monks' surprise, and especially to John's, the offers came rolling in. It was an avalanche of work with no time to learn.

"Whatever you do, Jim, just let me do the talking. At least I've worked in a nursery." Michael was the experienced hand in this game.

The Monks acted as if there were years of experience behind this humble attempt at rural performance art.

"Do you guys know how to install a drip system?"

"Sure, you bet."

That sent the Monks off to the nearest garden store for a crash course on drip systems.

"Will you feed my azaleas? You know what they are, don't you?"

"Yep . . ."

Jim actually didn't know an azalea from a daisy.

"The chrysanthemums need to be pinched back. Can you do it?"

"Why not?"

The chrysanthemums were promptly cut to the ground.

"Could you transplant these flowers?"

"No problem." So Jim dutifully pulled them up by the roots and asked, "Is this what you wanted?"

Fortunately, the main client, Jane Doyle, was quite compassionate. Taurus Jane was an inveterate gardener who, while laid up from an auto accident, was supporting our newly acquired sourdough bread addiction from money she received from the settlement. We used to say we were "on the Doyle," which, in fact, we were.

The Monks grabbed on to these new rural roles like drowning men to a raft, anxious to leave their urban shticks behind. But invariably the conversations centered on how many hours were worked rather than the merits of companion planting. After eight weeks of rigorous weeding, landscaping and hoeing, it finally dawned on the Monks: this is hard work!

Econoline 100, the first Monkmobile.

It was *Green Acres Part II*, with Mike as Eddie Albert and Jim as Eva Gabor. Naturally, Mike was often left with the rough end of the deal, while Jim took breaks to write an inspirational poem about the experience.

But all the sweat, labor and sore backs finally paid off. By late spring enough coin had been saved from the gardening gigs to start shopping around for something a bit more roomy than the Dodge Dart John Deming had graciously loaned us.

John Pillsbury had his cream-colored van parked invitingly in front of his Chico home with a big FOR SALE sign in the window. On a late Friday afternoon, coming back from the Chico Food Co-Op, Jim spied the van and knew instantly that this little gem was going to be our baby.

"Mike, Mike, stop."

As we pulled into Mr. Pillsbury's driveway, we instantly surmised that the twelve-foot Econoline was patiently waiting for some new owners after being jilted for a larger RV.

"Got two gas tanks, holds up to thirty gallons. This is a stove that pops up from the door."

"A stove?" Jim's eyes widened. "What about an oven? Can you bake in there?"

"You mean like bread?" Mr. Pillsbury looked puzzled.

"He means like cookies and pies." Mike cast a cautionary glance toward Jim.

"Nope. No oven. The water tank's underneath. Get about twenty-five gallons in that." Mr. Pillsbury was giving the complete guided tour to the enraptured Monks, who were awed by his real-man handiwork.

"New transmission, new tires. Just checked the brakes. What you boys have in mind? Going on a big trip?"

"Well, no, I mean, yeah, maybe. We just need something to drive around in."

"Not that great for commuting. Where you boys live?"

"In Paradise . . . sort of. Well, we're just visiting, see. Actually, we don't live anywhere!" The words felt foreign.

We don't live anywhere. What's that supposed to mean? I've always lived somewhere. He's going to think we're a couple of bums. Michael attempted to backtrack.

"We're planning a trip across the country and need something to travel in."

"Just for the two of you?"

"We have two cats!" Jim interjected with childlike glee.

Mr. Pillsbury was trying to figure out the Monks. "Well, I don't know if there'd be enough room for two big fellas like you. That bed in the back is just barely big enough for one, let alone two, unless of course you were *together.*" The word *together* hung in the air like an accusation. *Together* as in . . . as in what?

"Can't you make the seat into a bed?" Jim asked, saving Michael from an awkward bind.

"Well, yeah, I guess you could rig up another bed up front, but it'd be awfully short. Me and the wife we just scrunched up in the back, nice and cozy. Like I said, if you're *together,* it's no problem."

Mike was swimming upstream, but wasn't sure which stream he was in. *You thought you could seduce him if he were under the same roof. I know how your mind works, Michael.* Uncle Jack's words were discomforting. Michael could see Jack arching his brows. From an eight-room house to a twelve-foot van. That's one way to test a relationship. Especially one that had no ground.

"How much you want for this?" Jim finally popped the question.

"I'll take twenty-five hundred dollars. Cash!"

"Twenty-five hundred dollars?" Jim feigned outrage. "How many miles on this?"

"One hundred forty-five thousand."

"That's too much. Two thousand dollars and that's our final offer."

"Well, I've got another offer . . ."

"We'll let you think about it and call you tomorrow," said Jim as Michael led him away.

"Jim, are you sure this is what you want to do. I mean, a van?"

Jim was reluctant to talk about it as he was in a hurry to drive across town to Ponce's Bakery before Mimi closed shop.

On the way over not a word was spoken. Jim was fidgeting with a pen, as he was wont to do in moments of hyperactive brain activity, avoiding a look in Mike's direction. As Michael turned a corner, suddenly Jim flung open the door and bolted down the street.

"What the hell! Jim, where are you going?" Michael screeched to a halt watching Jim disappear around the corner.

I don't get it. He's out of his mind. Where's he going, the bakery?

Michael raced around the corner and caught sight of Jim up the street. Pushing the gas pedal to the floor, Mike was at his side in a second, but Jim, seeing the car, hooked a right through a yard and went running through a garden, hopping a fence and turning down an alley.

Michael left the car idling in the middle of the street, running and screaming in hot pursuit of Jim. Three young girls dodged the chase as its course wound through the suburban neighborhood, setting off a chorus of barking dogs.

A car slammed on its brakes, narrowly missing Jim. A game of street baseball scattered when Jim charged across home plate. As Mike closed in, Jim cast a sideways glance, his face consumed by terror, and doubled his speed.

"What the hell is wrong with you!" Michael was screaming himself hoarse, worried about John's Dodge Dart several blocks behind.

Jim came to an intersection. Dodging traffic, he spotted a Greyhound bus. He affronted the bus, made it stop in the street and pounded on the door like a madman until the driver opened the door and let him in. The bus sped off.

Michael reached the intersection as the exhaust was settling on the tarmac. He was totally confused. *What brought this on? One minute we're looking at a van. The next, he's fleeing for his life. I don't get it.*

Michael weighed the possibilities.

It's got to be a joke. He's just pulling a gag. No, he had terror on his face. Something's off. It was the van. Or maybe we're working too hard. No, he's nervous about the van.

Is there an extra bedroom inside? Michael remembered Jim's disappointment at John Deming's. And *Can't you make the seat into a bed?* at John Pillsbury's.

Mike turned and caught sight of the bus slowing to a stop at the corner bus station. The passengers were discharging from the bus onto the sidewalk.

Oh, thank God, it was an arriving bus. He's there at the station!

Mike was off and running again. By the time he entered the bus station most of the other passengers had already found their rides. Jim was standing at the counter trying to buy a ticket with no money.

"Just give me the ticket and they'll pay for it on that end."

"I'm sorry, sir, we can only do that if they have a credit card."

Jim silently walked past Michael to the phone. Michael followed Jim to the phone at a safe distance and watched him call collect to Olympia, Washington, home of his men's-movement buddy Mark Sherman.

"Shit. An answering machine!" Jim was furious with the operator. "Are you sure there's no one there?"

A long silence prevailed. Finally, Jim turned toward Michael and let out a long sigh.

"Guess I'm stuck with you."

The drive back to Paradise that night was like riding through a field of land mines. Jim shrunk in the seat, flipping the dial on the radio with the sound turned up full blast. Michael finally flipped it off.

"What's up, Jim?"

"You know what's up."

"Reading minds has never been my forte. Reading hearts, now that's different. If I read your heart correctly, you're scared shitless that you and me are getting a little too close? Something to do with having to share the same bed?"

Jim remained silent.

"Well, I guess it's better these things come out now before we find ourselves trapped in a twelve-foot van. That'd be one hell of a way to get to know how things stand."

"You got that right!" said Jim.

"So it's the sleeping together, right?"

"Right!"

"No one said we have to do this, you know."

"I want to do it. That's the bitch of it. I want to go on the road. This is a once-in-a-lifetime opportunity. I'm crazy if I just let it go. I've always yearned to travel around. You know, see old friends, see relatives I haven't seen since I was a kid, see the world I've been dreaming of. And here I am. I've got somebody to do it with. We think alike, we believe in the same things, we like the same food, shit, we even wear the same size clothes. It's just that . . . well, it's just you're not . . . !"

"A woman!" Mike knew it was there all along. Jack had been right in the beginning. Mike and Jim . . . worlds apart. *But there's something incredible about us together. I just can't let it go. This trip is the only thing that's going to hold us together.* Michael was digging deep into the wound. *Why drag Jim on the road if he has a totally different agenda. I should have stopped it before The Cookie. Damn prune squares.*

"Jim. We don't have to do this. It's been a year since we met. This is not just a friendship and both of us know that. Neither of us planned it that way. But you've not exactly backed down. I don't know what you really want, but I just keep assuming that if you were that bothered, you'd put a halt to our friendship! Most people just assume that we're . . ."

"Lovers! That's what people think. And that's not how I necessarily feel." Jim paused as a tear came to his eye. "It's all that fucking conditioning. I mean, consciously I'm okay with it. But, just when it feels alright, you know, just when I feel like relaxing and letting down the guard, all that fucking judgment comes up. It's deep. This stuff is deep." Jim paused again and now started to really cry. "Mike, what would you do if I abandon ship now and just go my own way?"

Mike could feel the heat rising through his throat, into his head, clouding his vision. *Always going for those fringe types! Why don't you just settle for a nice clone.* "Well, I'd probably turn right around and head back to San Francisco."

"You would?" Jim was surprised.

"No, that's not true. This is it for me. If the only reason I met you was to coerce me out of my repetitive, overwrought, overworked life in the city, if the only reason I met you was to break the spell of that illusion and get out and see the world, then so be it. I'd probably go ahead and go through with it. Get a van and hit the road. Why do you ask? What would *you* do if *I* jumped ship and you were on your own?"

Jim gave a long pensive glance. "Well, I'd probably do the same thing. I came this far. It'd be crazy to flee right back to a stupid polluted life in the city. I mean, what's the point of doing that? I'm young. I want to stretch my boundaries. Get a feel for other places. I had a quest before I met you. A quest to visit communities all over the world. And to link people together. You know that already. But I was lonely out there, Michael. I needed a partner. Someone to share the dream with. Someone to give it meaning." Jim's eyes were welling up again.

"Maybe I should just look at it like an astronaut." Jim was trying desperately to appease his addled Gemini brain. "That's it. We're going on a voyage into space. The van is going to be our space capsule," Jim conjectured. "We're going to be astronauts in training for future space missions. They, whoever 'they' are, put us together to test our limits, our metaphysical mettle, our attachments. It's sort of unchartered territory, just you and me in the universe."

"Well, I think that's taking it a little too far. We'll still be on earth. There *will* be other people!" Mike added.

"I know. It'll just seem like space travel. It will be our monastery on wheels. We'll be mobile Monks with a mission to go where no other Monks have gone before." Jim was lightening up, already shifting from fear to acceptance. He wanted it to work *so bad.* "Except we'll be different sort of Monks. We won't wear robes, we won't be so damn serious, we'll be in the world, we'll eat fish and there'll be lots of . . . Laurie Anderson!" Jim put his arm around Michael.

"But we're definitely going to have to do something about that bed," Jim continued tenderly. "Knock out a wall or something. It's too small even if we *were* lovers. Know what I mean?" Jim was smiling through the tears now.

Mike always admired Jim's courage, that spiritual toughness Jim possessed to look his deepest fears right in the face and challenge them head on.

"You mean . . ."

"Just don't make any assumptions!" Jim half-joked.

The Monks reached an understanding prior to takeoff: there would be nothing predictable about this journey. It would be defiantly indefinable: no rules, no labels, no agenda, and no holding back the truth.

"Jim, there's one thing that still doesn't make sense. How are we going to support ourselves if we leave Paradise? What are we going to do? Garden everywhere we go?"

"Mike, I've had this idea."

"What is it?"

"How about a newsletter?"

"A newsletter?"

"Yeah, think about it. We could write a little newsletter using that Pagemaker program Noel bought us and send it to all our friends. We'd be like roving reporters filling them in on where we've been, whom we've met."

"You mean like an update on what's happening in Paradise?"

"Well, maybe more like an update on our lives wherever we happen to be. Instead of writing each person an individual hand-stamped letter, why not just write one big letter and send it to everyone we know or meet. I really think people will get a kind of vicarious thrill from our adventures. And they'd get to know each other through the newsletter. Like an extended media family. A party in print."

"It'd be our letter home. That should keep Mom happy!"

"Yeah, a traveling news service."

"A public diary . . ."

"Of a pilgrim's journey!"

"Another Space Monk production!"

"Don't you love it!"

"I'm doing it!"

"Simple, mobile and true. That's what it's about, Mike.

In search of America! In search of ourselves! Can you dig it?" Once again Jim had pushed the limits and come back around.

For the next week Mike was obliged to let Jim do comparative van-shopping to satisfy his Gemini mind, but in the end "the first was best." John Pillsbury signed over his beloved 1972 Ford Econoline complete with two gas tanks, platform bed, water pump, propane stove and those precious little flower-print curtains to keep intruders from peeking into the eight-by-twelve-foot wonder van.

The mobile Monks had themselves some wheels.

It was a dream come true—a roaming intelligence unit, a mobile monastery, a home. The Monks were the happiest, healthiest, most suntanned vagabonds ever to hit the highway.

Later that week the Monks began to yearn for the "big break." Giving John Deming one last chance to beat us in a game of croquet, we spent two days trying to make all the junk fit and two more days throwing most of it away. That is, everything but Jim's debate papers. Mike placed the key to their future, the prized Macintosh, in the center of the van, but relinquished the ruffled fishnet prom dress. Jim finally agreed to sell the Wedgewood stove, admitting once and for all The Cookie was cooked.

As we blasted off down Skyway Road, like a wagon train lightening our load, it felt as if the long-awaited "great adventure" had at last begun. Nurse claimed a spot buried far beneath the bed while Nurse's Aide commandeered the view from on top the dash. Mike drove and Jim rode shotgun. These became the respective stations for traveling.

Barreling up Highway 99 toward Redding, everything seemed brand-new. A burden had been lifted. Our world had opened wide. Nobody had our number. We had no appointments, no deadlines, no meetings to attend. The road was our agenda now. We felt as if we could finally take a big deep breath after years of holding it in.

"Ahhhh, the freedom, Jim, the freedom," Michael mused. Mike was so happy he could have wet his pants. Tickled to the core that he'd actually pulled this off, he thought of his seven years in San Francisco, the long dark night of his soul, and the baby-boomer friends he had left behind, how they'd have to struggle with routine while he cruised the great open freeway.

Top: Proud new owners inside the mobile monastery.

Bottom: Nurse's Aide commandeered the view from on top the dash.

**Trying to make it all fit, John Deming's
backyard, Paradise, California.**

Meanwhile, Jim, the latter-day Thoreau, sat writing in his diary. A diary now overflowing with heartfelt ruminations:

Heading north into the orange-brown haze of the horizon. Cars transporting souls along a plane through time. Past and present merging in one stream of mind. . . . Always moving, always straight with the stream.

For Michael the horizon wasn't far or big enough for his vision. A vision extending far beyond the confines of Butte County, far beyond the state of California, far beyond the United States, far beyond planet Earth. Mike could have driven clear to Mars. He was in that fantastic nomadic space-time trance where there are no limits, no boundaries and no end in sight. Mike in his reverie, Jim in his diary. . . .

Cars shift lanes with grace and ease, never stopping, always onward. I lose myself in this auto-dream.

A dream so grand Jim didn't notice the little green plastic holder lovingly attached by John Pillsbury to the middle door, the little green plastic holder slowly tilting in one downward direction, quietly spilling chopstick after chopstick onto the brown shag carpet. A dream so expansive, Jim neglected to notice the door to the particleboard cupboard Mike built now slightly ajar, allowing a newly bought tub of fresh organic corn oil to slide little by little to the edge of the shelf, allowing the bag of fresh roasted peanuts to tilt on its side with its mouth facing the door, allowing our prized Cost Plus ceramic plates and Michael's old handmade ceramic jars that held the organic grains to follow the same inexorable course.

Images pass of the movies we will make, songs we shall sing . . .

The Macintosh computer, safely secure in its baseboard holder, and the collection of rare books in our newly constructed bookshelf, all started to edge little by little out of their encasements; the peanuts, the plates and the jars all becoming fluid as the tub of corn oil began to slowly spill its slimy contents down step after step of the cupboard.

Mike put on the turn signal and moved Econoline to the far right lane, as Jim put the final touches to his blissful reverie. . . .

I see all my wounds and let them pass.

Thuuuuuuump!

The Macintosh bounced off the bed and hit the hard metallic floor.

I forgive all my transgressors . . .

Thuuuump, thuuump!

The rare books spilled and toppled one by one onto the Macintosh and then around it.

I forgive myself and move on . . .

Blurp, blurp, blurp . . .

The corn oil created a network of levees that led in two directions—-over a first-edition copy of H. L. Mencken's *Newspaper Days* and into the air vent of the Macintosh now leaning painfully on its side, and then downward over several chopstick logs to the feet of the oblivious diarist.

I am connected. I am aglow . . .

"Jiiiiiim! There is fucking corn oil all over the goddamned floor!"

"Campground! It says right here on the map. See the little green tent. That's the icon for a campground!" Jim was holding the map and a pen-size flashlight.

"But what town is it in? It's just floating between highways. How the hell are you supposed to find it! Why can't we just pull off the road and sleep?"

"Pull off the road! Are you crazy? We'll get hassled by the cops. I'm going to go ask someone." Jim bolted out of the van in search of a house.

Jim stomped off in the direction of a farm light, wearing his white jumpsuit, which had been donned for today's departure, carrying half a loaf of unleavened bread just in case he got hungry.

Michael settled in for a long wait, as most exploratory fact-finding missions by Jim usually took half an hour at least.

The Econoline purred in the quiet air as Michael began cleaning up the mess. A week of painstaking work shattered in less than a day's drive. All the carefully arranged shelves he'd built, the cupboard, the tidy little places for jars, cups and containers . . . everything had spilled. Shards of glass were everywhere from chipped containers that had rattled and broken on the bumpy drive. *I can't believe I packed all of our food in glass. Of course, glass is going to break. And what possessed me to think the computer would just sit up on this shelf of its own accord. I'm surprised it stayed put this long.* Despite Jim's endless recitation of Louise Hay affirmations, Mike was giving himself a good thrashing.

Nurse and Nurse's Aide were furiously pacing the floor of the van when suddenly Michael had a terrifying thought. *Oh, my God. A cat box. I forgot about a cat box.*

Cautiously looking out the door, he surmised Econoline must be parked next to a creek, so Mike gambled and let the cats out the door, but instantly had his regrets as Nurse bolted far away, while Nurse's Aide crouched under Econoline.

Oh, shit. What have I done?

Mike spent the next hour tracking Nurse through a wild forest in the diminishing light, down an abandoned country road, into a drainage pipe, up and down a tree and through a vacant farmhouse. Finally he cornered Nurse in a bush and triumphantly returned to find Aide calmly chowing down on a loaf of bread back in the van, having relieved himself under the driver's seat.

"Aide. Bad cat. Bad cat. That's why I let you out. You're supposed to tinkle out there." It suddenly occurred to Michael that Aide and Nurse had never known the joys of outdoor potty training. For that matter, neither had he. What were the big people supposed to do? Go scratch in the sand? *My God. Jim and I need a kitty box. Hmmmm, maybe that's why John Pillsbury wanted us to buy the port-a-potty.*

Jim finally came back with the good news is bad news is sad news that the campground was six miles away and didn't open till July Fourth due to reconstruction.

"We're going to have to stay in a hotel." he swore.

"A hotel? What the hell do you think we bought this van for?" asked Mike.

"Well, where are we going to park?"

"*Right here.* There's a nice riverbed less than a hundred feet away, and there are plenty of places to park down there. We'll just stay here. I don't want to drive in the dark anyhow."

"How do you know we can camp there? We might be arrested or told to leave."

"Get in!" Michael yelled as he started the engine. "And watch the corn oil."

Michael pulled back onto the road and then circled to the right, off the other side under a bridge and onto river rocks. They drove adjacent to the river searching for the *right* place far enough from the road to have some quiet.

"No, over here, it's flatter," said Jim.

"This is fine, it's not going to get flatter than this, Princess."

"But it feels better over there. Just turn the van a little to the right so the end is facing the trees."

"What does that matter?"

"They'll protect us."

"Protect us from what!"

"It'll be a better vibration. Come on, just do it."

Vibration. Michael obliged, heading toward the trees, then coming to a stop.

"No, we're not flat. Let me go out and see. Doesn't it look tilted on your side?"

"The level says we're straight." John Pillsbury had installed small bubble levels by the dashboard for the important ritual of leveling the van for a good night's sleep.

"No, look, if you just pull up six inches—no, make that ten and a half . . ."

"Ten and a half." Mikes eyes bugged out. "Come on, it's flat."

"It's not. I can tell from out here. Just do it!"

The van inched forward another ten inches. On the half inch the van suddenly began a forward motion. Ever so slight but definitely forward and then down.

"No, this isn't right, back up a tiny bit."

Mike put it in reverse. The wheels spun. The van tilted forward even more. The wheels spun harder. Michael rocked the van. *Whrrrrrrrrr. Whrrrrrrrrr.* Sand flew out from under as the van, its occupants, its half ton of papers, clothes and broken jars of food slowly sank into the quagmire.

"Jim, we're stuck!"

"Well, it's not my fault. Let's call a tow truck."

"Jim! We're in nature. It's just us and the sand and we're stuck for the night!"

"Stuck?! I can't sleep like this."

That night the Monks slept like that. On a good twenty-degree tilt.

By morning they were two cranky Monks. The bed, as promised, was definitely too small for two people, even if they had been *together.* Sleeping across the back, both Monks kept rolling like logs toward the edge of the bed. Michael, being the one closest to the edge, held on for life as Jim performed his nightly sleeptalking, sleepwalking rituals that had so cleverly entertained the Nurses for the past year.

The morning sun brought chirping birds and the sound of distant church bells, which nicely accentuated the placid river scene.

Jim rose from his sleep. "Where are we?"

"We're by a river, and it sounds like a church nearby."

After an exasperating time waking to our first morning on the road, Mike set about cleaning the van of its mess and prepared the first Monk meal on a decidedly crooked slant. The ice in the bucket had long since melted, leaving the vegetables and fish in a slush of lukewarm water. *No wonder John Pillsbury suggested we buy a propane fridge.*

While Mike scrambled souring tofu and put Jim's two pressure cookers to work, Jim went out in search of the bells.

"Ask about a tow truck while you're at it!"

An hour later Jim returned noticeably transformed.

"You're not going to believe this, Michael, but we're right next to a Trappist monastery. *Gloria in Excelsis Deo!* It's absolutely unbelievable. You should see the place. Fruit orchards everywhere. And the monks! *Real* monks. We should have a big jamboree out here for them. Think of it. The Space Monks meet the Trappist monks."

"Did you ask them about a tow truck?" Michael had his eye on the rapidly sinking van. This was soft sand and the longer the Econoline sat, the deeper it sank.

"Yeah, there's a garage in Vina, but it won't be open till Monday. We'll just have to wait."

By now Nurse and Nurse's Aide had set up camp under the shade of an oleander bush and were watching the Monks from a safe distance.

Next to a cool river and under the blazing sun, the Monks' first base camp was established and a small cardboard Celtic cross erected to mark the spot for future explorers in the Monk lineage.

Out of the van came all of Jim's papers. Jim was determined to work on his papers to lighten the load, which essentially meant rereading every item, deliberating on its world importance, and ultimately, storing it back inside for future consideration.

The emotionally charged bed problem was adroitly handled by using boards and boxes to extend the bed lengthwise down the van, allowing room for both Monks to sleep. The issue was put to rest, though the line was still drawn down the middle.

Late in the day on a sandy beach more than half a mile

down the river, the Monks were having another heated discussion about what to cook for dinner.

Suddenly the Monks were startled when out of the bushes traipsed a tan, well-built, dark-haired, thirtysomething man, wearing a cap, an Izod shirt, shorts and sunglasses. Since he was carrying binoculars, we took him for a camper.

"Oh, excuse me!" His face turned red as he stepped over the disrobed Monks, who, besides arguing, were sunbathing in the buff. He was in the forward-motion mode, but found himself frozen in his tracks, staring at the sight of two tall, gangly, *naked* bodies.

Jim turned toward the man and stuck out his hand introducing himself and Michael as if the sight of two naked men were commonplace.

"Hi, I'm Jim the Mad Monk and this is Michael Monk."

"I'm Phillip." He seemed unable to say more. There was a pregnant pause. Then it hit us—no robe, no hood, no beads, yet our "camper" was a card-carrying Catholic hermit!

A blushing Phillip was about to continue forward again until Jim interrogated him about his life as a monk— whether the vegetarian Trappists were strictly macrobiotic, were they allowed to watch TV, did they play basketball? After Jim's intense cross-examination Phillip finally sat his binoculars down and took a seat on the hot sand facing the nude Monks, nervously glancing from Mike to Jim.

"I'm studying at the Trappist monastery," he said in a deep, calm, restrained voice. Looking at him, one could tell Phillip had developed a rich interior life, his face was so soft, clean and kind. And his teeth—his teeth!—were perfectly white.

"Are you a monk?"

"I am a hermit. I am on sabbatical here for a year. You are the first outsiders I have met in eight months," he said kindly. There was such a sensitive, gentle quality to his speech. It seemed as if he were just getting used to conversation again after a long dry spell, as each word was carefully examined before being spoken.

Phillip's eyes kept drifting away from the Monks toward an empty blue sky, then back again, coming to rest on Jim's belly.

Hmmm. He sure seems a bit preoccupied with Jimmy now.

"I was on my way to watch birds. They come out midday near the bridge where the train passes. I like to do some spotting before evening hours. If I'm interrupting, I'll be on my way." He was considerate to the point of embarrassment.

"No!" Both Monks spoke at the same time. "You can stay. We were just about to go for a swim and then go back to the van and start dinner."

"Where are you from?" Phillip asked quietly.

Michael knew this was probably going to be the most frequently asked question of the Monk journey. "From San Francis—"

"From the road!" Jim interjected. "We live on the road."

"The road. Oh, you're itinerants!" Phillip said brightly, aware of that long Catholic tradition of wandering monks.

"Yeah, we're wandering monks off to conquer windmills. We're writing a little newsletter to send back to our parishioners," said Jim.

And we all laughed, breaking the ice.

Having studied as a stationary hermit for the past five years, Phillip was excited about the prospect of endless travel without preconceived destinations.

"This is our first day on the road!" Jim said excitedly.

Phillip wouldn't believe it. He wanted to know everything about it. "But this *is* our first day. There's nothing to tell. Except we've met you. You're our first friend!"

Phillip paused.

"Then you two are my first road monks. Welcome to Vina!" he said with a gleaming smile, his brilliantly clear eyes filled with desire.

"Do you and the Monks talk?" Jim asked.

"No. We don't really talk. Unless it's of necessity."

"How long since you talked to someone?" Jim asked.

"You mean like this? Maybe a few years." Phillip was beginning to relax into the Monks and had removed a sandal, digging the dirt with his toe.

"How long since you touched someone?" Mike asked out of the blue, shocking both himself and everyone else with his bluntness.

Phillip suddenly looked like a man caught with his thoughts down. His forehead looked cool and damp, and a surge of adrenaline pressed behind his eyes.

"Touched?"

"Yeah. You know, held. Human contact. Do you have human contact with the brothers?"

"Oh, you mean, do we give each other hugs?" A momentary relief.

"What did you think I meant?"

"Nothing. It's just that touch . . . it seems like you meant something intimate."

"Maybe I did!" Mike smiled.

Phillip was nervously flipping pebbles toward the water. "So what happens now?"

"What do you mean?"

"I mean, should we do something?" Phillip said, motioning toward the river.

"Yeah, let's go on an adventure," said Jim.

"Come on," said Phillip, rising to walk off as the Monks followed him several hundred yards down the river. The wind was beginning to blow, but it felt clean. Mike saw a flock of birds by an old stand of oaks. Phillip adjusted his binoculars to take a look as the sun spread its long afternoon rays across the beach causing shadows to dance upstream. The shadows fell across the Monks, merging with the shadow of the hermit.

"I think the Indians lived off the top of that hill," said Phillip.

Mike looked at Phillip and for a second thought he saw something dark and not completely pleasant in the hermit's loving eyes. Then a passing shadow and the look was gone.

The three of them stood there in the sand facing the rapids.

"Do you ever doubt yourselves?" Phillip asked.

"Yes," Jim said, thinking that Phillip must have been reading his mind. "I'm always weighing the options thinking about what I might be missing, instead of being at peace with where I'm at."

"Or the one you're with," Phillip spoke softly.

"Yeah, you nailed it."

Phillip was quite perceptive.

There was a pause.

"I'm sorry I've asked you so much, but will you answer one last question?" inquired Jim.

"Well, let's hear what it is." Phillip turned from the sun.

"Are you doing what you want to be doing with your life?"

"Why, what's wrong?" Phillip looked alarmed, as if Jim had just probed his carefully guarded secret.

"Nothing, it's just that you seem . . . sad."

"Maybe." Phillip smiled, then walked ahead down toward the river skimming a handful of rocks across the rapids to the other shore.

We all began to walk again, stepping from stone to stone in the water. Some of the stones were so hot they burnt the bottom of the Monks' feet. But Phillip seemed not to feel them.

The Monks hit the water, screaming from the shock of the cold, while Phillip carefully shed his clothes, savoring every moment. He seemed so modest that the Monks turned away, but Phillip also seemed intent on being seen and dove in, surfacing in front of the Monks. "I guess I'm a nudist!" he said in a way a newcomer to the English language might say it.

"You're human. That's all." Mike felt fortunate that Phillip couldn't read *his* mind. He could just hear Uncle Jack: *And it was just brotherly love, hey?*

The water baptism led to a mud baptism on the riverbanks, which led to a burial in the sand, which led to three cave monks grunting in the open air chasing dragonflies across the beach and diving headlong into the river. We splashed in that cool river, stood naked doing t'ai chi on the beach and balanced on the railroad beams singing silly songs. There was a lot of silent uncertainty, but an undercurrent of love, laughter and excitement.

That day by the monastery was a welcome retreat for all of us. The Monks hungered for their first big break from the chaotic energy of the city. So when the bells would ring for "hours," we stopped our play and honored that time with our own style of meditation. In turn, Phillip enjoyed a break from the tight Trappist regimen.

Late that afternoon sitting under the clear blue sky, Phillip's life began to piece together.

"I was born thirty-nine years ago in Denver. I guess you could say my upbringing groomed me for the high-tech life of Los Angeles where I worked as a computer programmer. It was all about image: the right car, clothes, friends. . . . But my life in L.A. bred discontent, jealousy and greed. . . . I worked my way into a comfortable lifestyle, I had a beautiful girlfriend and all, but I found it to be spiritually empty. It was that search for spirit, I guess, that spurred me to embrace the monastic life."

Phillip tightened his lips and, after a long pause, volunteered, "I have taken a vow of celibacy. That is the practice." It was clear there was a passion boiling within this humble hermit begging for release.

A few minutes later we walked Phillip back to the monastery arm in arm. We left with a promise that "we three shall meet again."

The Monks returned to find Econoline at a nosedive in the sand and the Nurses chowing down on a wild duck they'd caught near the river.

"Aeiiiiiieee! Christ, what the hell are you eating Aide! Oh, my God, they killed the poor duckie. Jim get this thing out of here!" Mike screeched in his Joan Crawford best.

Michael Monk stood in terror of the totally gutted duck and the sight of two Nurses, mouths caked in blood and feathers.

"How could you do this! Bad cats. Bad cats."

"But, Mike, that's nature."

"I don't care. There's nothing natural about killing a poor innocent duck who was probably out waddling in the river." Mike glared at Nurse. "I just know Nurse did it. Didn't you, you murderer! I'll never eat duck again as long as I live."

Jim snatched the duck from the Nurses and was about to bury it deep in the sand, but then decided it was a sign from the universe and set about cleaning the duck for dinner.

"Look at this, Mike, it's free meat!"

"You're out of your mind. We could get rabies!"

"We could also have a gourmet feast. Come on, honey, the kids went out and caught dinner."

"Forget it."

"Duck increases your sex drive," Jim teased, knowing Mike's Achilles' obsession.

"Oh, really?" Mike stopped. "Wellllll, I have a fabulous recipe for duck. Save the feathers, maybe we can use them for pillows."

As the sun set on the Monk encampment, the Monks pulled the bed out of the van and onto the river rocks next to a fire pit to prevent another sleepless night.

A vanside dinner was in the making. The menu included onion butter, pickled daikon, millet, the patented rice-syrup-sweetened, "never mind the chocolate" Space Monk fudge brownies and a recipe Mike was trying out called Apricot Duck Gravy.

The double doors of the van swung open. A stove propped up on one door while a cutting table swung up from the other. Mike was busy at the stove, Jim at the chopping board.

"Think of all the meals we'll be cooking outdoors from now on, Mike."

Mike was thinking alright. *And think of all the dishes I'll be washing outdoors without the benefit of a sink and hot water, not to mention the sand and bugs in the food.*

Finished with the vegetables, Jim ran off to the river. Ten minutes later . . . "God, Michael, this is paradise! We have everything we need, and we're right by a fast-moving river," said Jim, returning refreshed from some upstream swimming, our new form of aerobics.

"So what are you making?" Jim was hungry from the smell of duck.

"Well, this recipe is a slight departure from the gravy my grandma used to make. Actually, it's a fundamental departure."

"What's the trick?"

"Well, I've pan-fried the remains of the duck, drained all the fat into another skillet, strained out the feathers and then tossed the duck back to those murderers to eat."

"You did what!" said Jim, shivering by the stove.

"Inconsequential. Wait and see. Then I mixed in three cups of brown-rice flour with the fat, stirred it over a low flame until crumbly, then dumped in these apricots, mustard, lemon, miso, sea salt and water. It'll be the best gravy you've ever eaten."

"What do you . . . put it over?" Jim chattered under a blanket.

"Oh, nothing. It's fine just by itself. You'll just *loooove* that duck fat." Mike was determined to become the best itinerant chef to ever hit the pink highways.

Long after the sunset, the Monks were recovering from the apricot duck gravy, collapsing on the bed by a slow fire.

"Where's that sex drive supposed to come from?" Michael moaned.

"Mike, didn't you tell me that was the first time you'd ever made the recipe?" Jim groaned.

Monday morning, Bob's Wreck and Tow Service found the distress note from the Monks tacked on the garage door in town. By ten o'clock Bob was driving his tow truck by the riverbed pulling a twenty-foot wench. The van had become impossibly stuck in the sand, so Bob had to wedge himself a good distance away. "Another day and you would have been buried at ninety degrees!"

After half an hour of grinding gears our Ford Econoline 100 was finally resting on solid ground with the engine raring to go. We packed in the remainders of our campground, finding a note from Phillip under a pillow.

Dear Monks, back on God's duty. The hermit thanks you for letting Phillip out to play. Please remember to be kind to each other and to all you meet on your journey. My love shall endure for you until the sun and the moon no longer shine. Love, Phillip the Hermit.

It all started in a Toys "Я"Us outside Sacramento, California. Mike was hung up on the tinkertoy building blocks, Jim was into the fairy tales and Nurse

was on his new leash out in the parking lot.

Mike spotted the peppermint Hula Hoop first. While Mike was sniffing the peppermint and Jim was giving the hoop a few twirls, *she* appeared. Without delay she took the hoop out of Jim's hands, slid it around her neck and had that thing spinning circles in no time.

This girl knew her Hula Hoop and she wasn't going to let us make a bad name for the sport. After about a dozen twirls, she thrust the hoop back into Jim's hand and walked off into the assembled crowd.

"Now that's some heavy hoop karma, Mike."

Out in the parking lot it was business as usual: where to park, what to wear and whose turn to cook. One week into the journey and we at least had some of our priorities straight. The Monks had come through Sacramento to print up a stack of newsletters to send home. Mike's Mom had sent $100 for a lifetime-after-lifetime subscription. At least she'd never lose touch with her son. She joined twenty-five other friends who'd opted for the Feed the Monk Fund or the Wool Sweaters Fund, guaranteeing them a dependable word from Mike and Jim.

After a flip of the coin to see who was driving and then disobeying the verdict of the flip, we hightailed it west and south. We couldn't just slip past San Francisco without at least a passing hello to our tribe of rainbow worriers, who, we were certain, after a long spring without their monks, would just be dying to see us. After all, we were the fabulous fagabonds who said, "Good-bye, city life," in search of *Greener Acres*.

With the expectation we'd be swamped by party or at least workshop invitations, the Monks decided to preserve their newly acquired rural serenity by making a nice discreet entry, stay seven days, visit a few friends and then politely move on.

San Francisco had other plans.

Crossing the Bay Bridge as a Monk on wheels was vastly different from crossing the bridge as a wage slave commuting to work. Only a short absence from *the City* and we were now strangers.

Mike battled the commuter traffic realizing that the funky Econoline was a far cry from his former life on Noe Hill, as Jim gazed in awe at the towering skyline, frantically scribbling in his diary:

Scaled down for simple living, we're bushmen in the big city, eating our ancestral grain. We've reduced our lives to the bare essentials so we can see with wonder all that comes our way. Homeless nomads, riding the edge, residing nowhere, belonging everywhere.

San Francisco sat on a cloud. The Bay Bridge seemed more metaphor than fact, like the connecting link between one stage of awareness and the next.

Like a teasing young goddess, she led the Monks down into the fog, swallowing us up in the mist. It seemed the most ethereal city in North America—a place to drift and dream and lose one's self in the stream of the fantastic subconscious.

Michael suddenly panicked at the thought of seeing old friends.

A prophet is never welcome in his own hometown. They'll think for sure we've lost our minds once they see the van.

We exited onto Van Ness and found ourselves right in SOMA, Jim's old chewing grounds.

The Monks had stopped at the intersection with traffic backed up the off ramp, horns blaring as they debated the all-important first destination. Michael put the van in gear and headed through the intersection when suddenly . . . *puuut puuut, puttt puttt, puttt, pssssss, plunk.*

The van stalled in the middle of the street.

"What's going on? You better get us out of here before the cars come!" Jim said looking at the approaching traffic roaring up the street.

We were stuck in the middle of the intersection with traffic blaring both ways.

Michael attempted to start the van. *Wheeeeeen. Wheeeeeen. Eeen . . . eeen een. Wheeeeen. Wheeeeeen. Pu pu pu poot.*

"It's not getting any gas. Maybe it's the gas pump!"

"Are we out of gas?"

Michael looked down at the gauge. "Oops, I'm on empty. I forgot to switch the tank."

By this point a San Francisco cop had pulled up beside Econoline.

Michael was just about to switch the tank and get the van out of there when the cops were out of the squad car surrounding both sides of the van.

"I'm just stalled, Officer, I'll soon be out of here."

"Can we see your driver's license and registration?"

"Yeah, but I'm just stalled. You see, I forgot to switch—"

"Step out of the van. Keep your hands free."

The vagabond Monks were placed under tight scrutiny by the cops and the hundreds of passing motorists. Most assuredly we were hardened criminals, since passing drivers always assume that he who has been stopped is obviously guilty.

"Where do you live?"

"Over on Nineteenth . . ."

"On the road," the Monks answered at the same time.

"Well, see, we're traveling and . . ."

"Noe Hill . . ." The Monks reversed their answers.

The cops eyed each other as they called in license numbers.

We have a house. Or we did have a house, one of the best in the city. Everyone knows us. We have fabulous dinner parties, or we did. We live right around the corner. Or we used to. Mike was having an identity crisis.

"So where do you live? Your license says Nineteenth Street, you say on the road, the van's registered in Paradise. What are you carrying in there? What's that smell?"

"That's our cats."

"There are cats in there? I hope they're in cages. You

can't travel with loose animals like that! What are you, a cult or something?"

Worse than that officer. We're a renegade tribe of ax murderers with fifty pounds of crack under the hood. Who are we? You're asking us? You think we know? That's why we're traveling, to find out. The Monk mind was spinning.

Jim stepped in with his uncanny ability to make the most pathetic situation seem perfectly normal. "We're journalists, Officer. We are traveling around this great country of ours writing stories about the extraordinary people and places we encounter along the way. Peripatetic publishers. Troubadours. See, that's our Apple Macintosh computer back there. We're known the world over as the pioneers of dashboard publishing. We left the city last spring for an extended expedition, and now we're back in our old hometown to tie up some loose ends."

The officers were incredulous.

"Officers, before embarking on this fabulous journey I was a publicist for KQED and Michael here was a CEO at a major record company. We were living in this gorgeous mansion on Noe Hill until we both got fed up with our jobs, sold everything we owned, including our precious upright piano, and hit the road. I'm sure you've had those feelings at some point in your careers. Perhaps you've seen the movie *Lost in America?*

"With Albert Brooks?"

"Exactly. Or maybe you follow Charles Kuralt. We're kind of in that vein. We were up in Paradise all spring working as landscape designers until we bought this van and . . ."

Jim, I don't think they have to know every . . . Mike stood rolling his eyes, but he couldn't get Jim's attention.

Jim was hyped up and on a roll. ". . . and we decided we would keep our friends and followers informed of our journey through this little newsletter we write on our solar-powered Macintosh. We call it *Monk.*" Jim stood beaming with a broad smile.

"So you are a cult!" The officer stood back. "Have either of you ever been on *Donahue?*"

"No, but soon we'll be starting our own television show, and we're working on a script for a movie . . ."

Jim, enough, enough, Mike thought to himself.

Word finally came in over the radio that the Monks were clean, but not before Jim had hustled the cops for a ten-dollar subscription to the funky newsletter.

"I know somebody who'd get a kick out of this. Alright,

you guys, get out of here and clean up that cat smell." The cops smiled.

They finally waved us on as Mike gassed up the van on the second gas tank and sped on up Van Ness.

"A big mansion on the hill? Friends and followers? Publicist! You were an intern, Jim! CEO? I was keeping the books for a start-up that failed. Where'd you get all that?"

"Years as a master debater back in Omaha. Plus I've got Sagittarius rising. Gotta think big, Mike." Jim blew up his cheeks.

"Anyhow, can you believe that? He was treating us like a couple of vagrants!" Mike was still shaking at the outrage, an insult to his Leonine dignity.

Jim looked at Mike.

Mike looked at Jim.

"But you are, Blanche . . . you are a vagrant!" they chimed as one, howling in Bette Davis reverie.

The cafés were bustling along Haight Street as the Monks drove toward the park in search of a parking spot. Cars were jammed along every available curb. There wasn't even an empty fire zone. For what metered spaces there were, the cars looked as if they hadn't moved in years. And the place you'd normally find hippie buses and vans, along the nearby panhandle of Golden Gate Park, was already taken.

"Funny, I never noticed how few parking places there were in this city."

"That's 'cause we never had a car!"

We circled up and down the Haight, down to the Sunset, back up and around Golden Gate, across Richmond and back to the Haight.

After launching an assault on Pacific Heights, we finally found our coveted parking space. However, once parked, we realized we were situated on one of the busiest intersections in town. And the John Pillsbury's bubble levels revealed a decided downhill slant, not to mention the high probability that the tony neighborhood would have the cops on us in a second.

"Where are we supposed to camp, Mr. Mike?"

Mr. Mike was thinking.

"You know, in situations like this, it'd be easier not to have a van," Jim pontificated. "Why'd we buy this thing anyway? We should be on foot. We should be *walking* across America. We're just burning more fossil fuel, contributing to pollution and the greenhouse effect. I'm embarrassed. Do you think it's possible to have a solar-powered van?"

Given the infant state of solar technology and the high cost of a solar vehicle, not to mention the impracticalities of *walking* Jim's junk across America, both Mike and the Nurses knew that Econoline was the only real option under the circumstances.

The Monks finally resolved to park on Potrero Hill on a dead end next to a shabby apartment complex. Trash and broken glass covered the block, but there were a stand of eucalyptus trees, a fabulous view and it was *flat*.

The Monks had found a home.

But parking only thirty blocks from the old Noe Hill monastery, a certain morbidity set in.

"We're much better off than before." Jim was trying to reassure himself. "I mean, we were trapped in that house paying exorbitant rent. Now we can come and go as we please. So what if we don't have a bathroom. That's nothing. Who needs a shower? This is the life, right?"

Mike was busy inside at the propane burner. Out of the city it had been no problem opening the door and setting up a makeshift kitchen on the side of the road or by a river. But on a city street with broken glass and cars and pedestrians, Mike kept the door closed, swung up the stove and had vegetables, canned fish, grains, beans, pots and pans scattered throughout the interior. He was chopping onions on the road atlas and washing carrots under the small water pump when the water suddenly gave out.

"Oh, shit, we're out of water."

"Water? Well, let's fill up."

Suddenly the hard reality set in. Whose house do you knock on to fill up on water, let alone who has an outdoor faucet, let alone who has a hose long enough to stretch out to a van.

"Listen, we'll get drinking and cooking water at that natural foods store around the corner, and I'll just wait on the dishes," Mike proclaimed as he stacked dirty dishes under the bed.

All in all San Francisco gave us a warm reception. However, the Monks alienated the majority of their old friends by camping out on the streets in the funky Econoline. Most former friends couldn't adjust to the fact that visiting the Monks no longer meant traipsing up to the fabulous tree house at the top of eighty-five stairs, wining and dining with a spectacular view of the city. Now it meant a trip down to the street to a van parked in an alley in either

South of Market or the back side of Potrero Hill, then cramming into the smelly van with two nervous cats and moldy food.

City camping had its decidedly rough edge compared to riverside camping, and the Monks were fast tiring of the constant search for a place to shower, a place to pee and above all, sunshine.

Michael finally gave Uncle Jack a call to arrange a rendezvous before heading south in search of the sun.

Jack was shocked when he saw Mike roll up to his Nob Hill condo in his new home.

"And you went from baking cookies to this?" Jack said, shaking his head. "I think we'd better talk." He motioned Mike upstairs to his penthouse, while Jim went off in search of a Metaphysical Alliance Gathering at nearby Grace Cathedral.

Jack was entertaining a chatty young man, who was gabbing on about hemlines, eyeshades and the latest perfumes to hit the counter at Neiman-Marcus.

"So, Jack, how's your love life?" asked Mike, hoping to switch the topic.

Jack took a long drag from his Camel. "Well, you might say I've retired it to pasture."

"Come on, you don't expect me to believe that!"

"The price has gotten a little too high."

"You mean AIDS? That's a lame excuse to bow out from love. The AIDS crisis isn't the end to having a sex life, Jack."

"Oh, God, that's all anyone talks about. I'm sick of it." Jack seemed tired.

"Maybe so, but you can't believe all the media hype. We've been force-fed this fatalistic crap. The reality is that there are plenty of effective alternative treatments. And people are surviving."

"No. The reality is . . . people are *dying!*" Jack issued a long sigh. "You know, maybe your little road voyage isn't such a bad idea. If I were still a fresh young thing and could still live off of my pretty face, I might hit the highway too. But I'd need my Corvette, my espresso and my typewriter." Jack smiled.

"What would you do with all your properties?" his new friend asked with keen interest.

"You want it? You can have it all. Take it, it's yours. I'll even throw in my hotel in France."

The friend's eyes lit up.

"And if you're good to me, I'll even throw in the debts.

That's what makes the world go around . . . *owing money*,"
he said with a knowing laugh.

"So who's sleeping with whom?" Jack turned toward Michael. It could be guaranteed that Uncle Jack would always return to basics.

"Well, we are sleeping together, like we always have, if that's what you mean."

"In that small van? You must be ready to *kill* each other. I wouldn't last a day!"

"No, we're getting along."

"Are you getting laid?"

"Not exactly."

"C'mon, you're kidding!"

"No, I'm not. But I'm not going into details. There's a lot of brotherly love." Mike smiled.

"Brotherly love, hey? Well, I hope you're happy, that's all that matters. I could use some *brotherly love* around here." Jack cast his friend a glance.

When it was time to leave, Uncle Jack rose from his chair, looked out his penthouse view overlooking the Bay, motioned to Coit Tower, all lit in red lights.

"Remember, Mike, when I took you up there as a kid on the back of my Vespa to show you the lights? Your mom had just sent you up here for me to 'straighten' you out. Was she in for a surprise. I gave you a street map and said, 'If you land in jail, here's my number.' I guess I wasn't the best influence."

"But you taught me freedom. And with that, responsibility," Mike defended.

"Oh, did I? Well, I told you that life was made of dreams, all you had to do was pick one and stick with it. This has been my dream, conquering the world. I've stuck with it, and this is what I've gotten." His hand swept around the room and toward the city. "I'm afraid to say I still have a ways to go.

"If you've got a better dream than owning the world, go follow it . . . just look out for wolves, and don't give up," he said, taking another long drag. "You really are after something, aren't you? Guess you and Jim couldn't find it here, huh? Just what is it you're looking for?"

Michael threw his hands up. "I know, but I don't know. Maybe it's my manhood. Maybe it's the dad I never had. Maybe it's just a man. Maybe Jim and I are just searching for a more humane and loving way to live."

"Well"—Jack paused at the window—"if you land in jail, you know my number."

Jack slipped Michael another hundred-dollar bill, guaranteeing himself a lifetime-after-lifetime subscription to the nomadic newsletter, and wished the Monks a "long, safe journey."

Driven by a search for warmth, the Monks hit Highway 1 for the great California coastal adventure. We rambled

past drab Daly City, past the parade of tidy row houses that marked the green hills of Pacifica, until the road gave way to the immense blue waters of the Pacific Ocean. To the south lay the heralded route of many a Golden State dreamer. Mile after mile of sun-drenched, cliff-hanging roadway wound past the spirited enclaves of Half Moon Bay, Santa Cruz, Monterey, Pebble Beach and beautiful Carmel.

The water beckoned the Monks, as Jim hung from the window screaming into the wind, wildly flapping his arms like a condor, freeing our Monk souls from the grip of time.

We are freewheeling monks, bound to emptiness, liberated from the great indoors, engaged to the road and married to the earth and sky before us.

At Cape San Martin, Jim got burned from an hour of wind-sailing. His face chapped and cold, fresh and reborn, Jim was aching to dive deep into the Pacific to relieve the sting.

"Stop. We gotta swim. It cleans the aura. The salt water and cold together. We've got to do it," Jim insisted.

The Monks drove to Alder Creek, parked against the cliff

and raced down to the water like two fickle feathers in the wind.

"Clean your aura? It freezes your blood!" Mike hollered ten feet from the shore, having foolishly dove in first.

The Monks courageously endured the cold water, waves and wicked wind for the better part of the day until the Monk wee-wees were as small as thimbles and the Monk testes were frozen hard as rocks.

The fierce winds off the Pacific blew the Econoline farther south as we shivered, rattled and rolled down that twisting, turning, narrow route to sunshine.

The first signs of warmth appeared a day later at Hearst Castle above San Simeon when a startling revelation took hold of the Monk brain. Out in the vast Hearst parking lot, beneath the morning sun, were row upon row of cars, vans, campers, buses, motor homes, assorted bicycles, motorbikes and even an old converted schoolbus.

"Oh, my god. Check this out, Michael. It's a veritable tribal gathering of nomads, with license plates from every state but Hawaii."

An astonished Mike took in the popular new forms. Professor Jim took a more intellectual approach.

"It's the archetypical American journey, Mike. From Kerouac and the beats to Kesey and the Merry Pranksters, to Steinbeck and his dog Charlie, and now mom and dad and their two barking schnauzers. We're part of a great American tradition, Mike."

"We're not on a journey. We're just tourists. *Tourists!*" Mike bitterly surmised, watching an elderly couple trot their little mutts off for a dump.

It took a few minutes for the reality to sink in. It was the first time Jim had seriously considered that his Great American Road Myth had been transformed into the Great American Spendfest.

These aren't travelers. These are tourists. One goes with a beginner's mind in search of revelation, the other goes to confirm what one has already read. Jim was seeing the light.

As Mike and now Jim perceived, Americans had dropped the Big Questions and the Big Issues and settled for . . . the Roadside Distraction. Today's dharma bums went at it full time—eating, shopping, spending their way to some sort of fiscal satori.

"Kerouac probably foresaw this day, Mike, and conveniently died before he had to confront it."

The Monks paused to consider the options.

Jim heard the voice of that morning's meditation: *Would you rather be right or would you rather be happy?*

"Well, whaddya think?" Mike interjected.

"I think these are our people. Still unknowingly guided by the divine light of Avalokitesvara by paying homage to the shrines of roadside Americana."

"Well, however you want to rationalize it, I'm dying to see this castle."

"Me too."

And the Monks, now healed of their judgments, ran like kids for the entrance.

Hearst Castle had planted an idea, and we were determined to go with it. Not the desire to build a private zoo. It was the tourist bug that hit us. Why resist? It looked like such a solid stretch of city going south, might as well blend in and follow our family into the tourist schlock scattered along the way.

Unfortunately, the Monks were not yet groomed for innocuous blending. Mike and Jim sported shaven heads, wild organic odors and a rapidly diminishing wardrobe, consisting primarily of tattered work boots, I LOVE ME T-shirts and the now-stained Space Monk jumpsuits that were begging to be trashed. Nurse and Nurse's Aide had grown accustomed to and even grateful for the leash after a few narrow escapes in the Tenderloin District of San Francisco. Nonetheless, the half-mad and half-baked Monks revved up Econoline for the tacky spectacles of southern Cal.

Only five miles outside San Luis Obispo, the Monks found themselves in the caveman room of the Madonna Inn, the citadel of low camp. While the rest of our nomadic family was taking a tour of the gaudy guest rooms, the Monks snuck off to nap on the oversize cave bed. But an hour into midafternoon dreamtime, Jim, a notorious sleeptalker, sat up in a frenzy and exclaimed in the queeniest cavewoman voice he could muster, "Well, how do you like my new tyrannosaurus rex dress? It goes nice with the brontosaurus purse, don't you think?" and then hysterically looking around with wide-open eyes, shouted, "But where's my club? *Get me my club!*"

The Monks were quickly escorted out of the caveman room and back onto the road. Our nomadic family kept a safe distance after that.

Half past ten on a Monday morning, inching down 101 past the Ventura Freeway, Econoline boiled under the orange haze of the Valley, as eight lanes of traffic inched slowly forward.

Nurse sat across the engine hub, draped lifeless in the sweltering smog heat, tongue fully extended and ribs pumping for oxygen.

"He's panting. I think he's going to croak if we don't do something."

"Throw some water on him," Jim advised.

"No, no, *No!* Don't throw water on him. That's the worst thing to do."

"But he won't drink any of his kitty water."

"Just let him pant. That's the only way he'll cool down."

Nurse continued to wheeze. The weatherman reported record ozone alert, temperature inversion and no end to the dry, crisp, brown sunny skies that had been plaguing L.A. for weeks.

"Ninety-two degrees in here and we don't have air. Look at all those bimbos with their air-conditioning blaring. That's half the problem . . . all these cars," Jim Nader complained. "I just can't fucking believe this town. Ten million people and no mass transit. It's absolutely insane!"

"Jim, you should talk. What do you think we're driving?"

"I know—it's a koan I've been trying to resolve since we began this journey. We're part of the problem. We should be walking, not driving." Jim gazed morosely at the white divider bumps on the freeway as they slowly inched by. "This is ridiculous. I could walk to Hollywood faster than you can drive," Jim mumbled angrily.

Just then a light bulb went off. "Look, talk is cheap. Time for action. Hey, Nurse, wanna take a walk?"

Jim bolted out the door leading Nurse by his leash, weaving slightly ahead of Econoline.

"Jim, Jim, what the hell are you doing!" Mike screamed out the van window.

Cars inched along as Jim the Mad Monk greeted drivers with a wave and a *gassho*, steering Nurse clear of the wheels.

"Get the fuck in the van . . . are you fucking out of your mind!" Mike screeched.

Jim paid no mind.

He was now far ahead, alongside a silver-trimmed white Pontiac, when a young woman rolled down her window, allowing a cool blast of air to hit Jim across the arm.

"Whoa. What was that?" Jim turned.

"Air-conditioning. You and your kitty want a ride?"

Jim's eyes bulged open wide. The Valley girl was *stacked*, cleavage literally tumbled out of her tank top. Her wall of dark hair was pulled out of her face. "Come on, get in! He's not going anywhere in a hurry," she said, referring back to Mike.

"Ha ha ha ha ha." Jim laughed at the thought. "I mean really, c'mon, I mean, really, you know I gotta . . . I mean, this is too much."

"Get in. Destiny's calling!"

Jim pulled on the leash and gathered Nurse in his arms, entering the passenger side with a big smile and a bow to the cars as Mike angrily threw up his hands. At four cars behind there was nothing a responsible Monk could do.

"Just be a second!" Jim smiled toward Mike.

Mike was *fuming*.

Inside purred the metaphysical melodies of Ray Lynch. The woman was talking nonstop on her car phone when the Mad Monk first entered her inner sanctum.

"If we took responsibility for the mother and wed our desires to her desires, our lives would find no resistance. We bleed inside for her wound. We *are* her wounds."

She winked at Jim as she continued weaving the listener through her goddess babble.

"Hi!" She turned to Jim, hanging up. "Welcome to my ashram."

Inside, the car had an aroma of three, four, maybe five cultures in collision—carpeted like a low-rider cruise ship, shag covering the floor and dash, purple no less, with bucket seats that were upholstered with a Tibetan rug, and sandalwood incense that burned out of an ashtray, not to mention two dozen crystals of various sizes hanging off the mirror. In the back sat a laptop computer.

The woman looked over and smiled through her pink-glossed lips and fluorescent-pink shades. "You can call me Ariel. I'm going into my male. I'm queen of the subconscious. And for your education and enjoyment I'm also a little girl, playful clown, wise sage, seductress, high priestess and modern woman on the run. All right, Romeo, who you be?"

Jim was mesmerized. But for only a moment.

"I'm the Mad Monk."

"What are you so mad about Mr. Monk?"

"I didn't sleep last night!"

"Oh, well, you can throw yourself in my backseat if you want. But, no, I want you up here." She gave Jim a pat on the leg and a come-hither look.

Ariel was camped out in a big cushy bucket seat with an

amethyst crystal overhead. Now the tape switched to Gregorian chants as rainbow prisms danced across the ceiling.

"Gregorian chant. I like it." Jim settled into his bucket seat, drifting off to grade school basketball fantasyland, enjoying the ozone-depleting conditioned air. Even Nurse drifted off into the Buddha fields, his panting finally coming to a stop.

Ariel was suddenly in a trance of her own . . . but a very different style of trance. It seemed she was either hurting or rejoicing, as tears streamed down her soft face. Or maybe she was allergic to Nurse. Or just emotionally housecleaning. Jim couldn't tell.

"There is a reason for every moment," she said. "And there's a reason we met on the road just now. There's some way we're all going to grow in this."

Is she stoned? Jim was a sensitive creature himself, prone to tears, a "We Are the World" kind of guy, but *wasn't she getting a bit melodramatic?*

"Why are you crying?" Jim asked tenderly.

"Oh, it must be that damn cat of yours. God knows I just adore those creatures, but I can't get within a foot of them without going crazy. Zoran says I'm allergic because I was Cleopatra in a past life. But I love you. I know there must be something we're going to heal in each other because I've been so lonely and there you were, just walking down the street. You came for me!"

Jim noticed Ariel's pendulous breasts hanging loosely out of her tank top. Not in any philandering sort of way, just noticing the blunt forthrightness of her total approach. *Either this woman is a New Age nymphomaniac or this* is *God speaking and I am called to be her slave.*

"Do you know we're going into a full-moon cycle? Three days to prepare and then we're there. Nirvana! Just collect the energy, then three days to shake it all out. Seven days of bliss," Ariel said with a sigh.

"You know, this morning I was eating breakfast and every bite was like a metaphor," she continued. "Washing dishes was like a ceremonial baptism at the sink. It was like I was drifting into a timeless zone in which nothing was held back or refused." Ariel took one of those deep breaths they teach you at rebirthing workshops. "I think every feeling should be explored to its roots, don't you?"

"Oh, totally."

There was a quiet pause as Ariel gently grabbed for Jim's hand.

"Do you mind if I ask you a personal question?" Jim said.

"Please do. All we have is the personal. I believe the more personal the better. The personal is political."

"Tell me, tell me, gosh, this will sound really weird. Okay, okay—no, no, I can't."

Jim had this habit of announcing a question, but after checking with Gemini Control, deciding not to ask it.

"Please, please, get personal. What is it you seek to know Mr. Monk?"

"Are you on Ecstasy?" Jim blurted.

"We should share our ecstatic dreams. Last night I dreamt about violence and a chase through African villages with the squealing noise of a woman. Someone's laundry was still hanging on the line. They'd talked so late into the night they forgot to bring it in, two days in a row. It was growing mold on it." Ariel giggled.

"You're on Ecstasy, aren't you?"

"I'm on life. It's a drug without the side effects." She took another one of those deep, meaningful rebirthing breaths.

Traffic inched along as incense wafted through the car creating an aromatic fog. So dense, Jim began to feel as if the car were on something.

"Your car is loaded. Hey, I'm impressed. How do you do this?"

Ariel didn't hear it.

The mood kept changing. It wasn't just her. It was everyone on the freeway together. Somehow, from inside the Pontiac, everyone looked high on Ecstasy.

"What's with your windows? Everyone looks like they're flying!"

"Look at us. We create amazing synergy, and any second things could totally change. Whatever we think now might soon be out of context. Bigger and bigger pictures will keep taking hold." Her voice droned on in a soft purr, caressing the words, as she took those deep deep breaths, staring ahead with a beaming smile as if she were moving straight toward the Light.

"I'm into crystals and gemstones."

Jim was tempted to phone Stanislav Grof to see if this qualified as a "spiritual emergency."

"If you wear rose quartz beads around your neck, your heart will open up."

Everyone is your teacher. Every situation is your teacher. Jim was remembering the recent affirmation he'd read and was trying desperately to follow its edict. But the Mad Monk was skeptical.

"I'm just getting into crystals," she said, "and there are so many things to learn with each stone. They are the most ancient and solid form. Rose quartz will break down the resistance to love. I want you to wear these." She handed Jim a necklace of stones the size of golf balls.

"Wear these?"

Within minutes Jim was swearing Ariel was right. There *was* less tension. His resistance *was* broken. He felt his heart muscles pulling him toward her. His groin muscles were working overtime.

Michael was sitting in the van two cars back when he saw them kiss. Michael's head hit the ceiling.

"Can you believe that? What a tramp. He jumps in the car and now they're making out. I don't believe this!"

The Pontiac was filled with fragrance. Jim felt as if he were sinking into the seat as shafts of light swept up the rear window rushing off the ceiling. Vangelis blasted "Chariots of Fire." Jim's stomach tightened with unbearable excitement.

Michael felt as if he'd passed out in the heat. Leaning on his horn was of no use, as every other car was doing the same, sending a cacophony of sound toward the ozone.

Ariel's car phone rang and she halted the kiss, going off into another dimension. And she began talking and talking and talking. Then she began praying. It overcame her. Jim sat stunned.

"My soul hungers for seeds of truth that might bear fruit in times of need," she cried into the phone. Then hung up.

The kissing resumed and the traffic continued to inch forward. Michael could see Jim's hand down her blouse. They were talking.

"Nurse's Aide. Nurse's Aide, what are they saying?" Michael strained to read lips.

"Do you have a job? How 'bout a boyfriend?" Jim was asking.

She didn't hold a job, but she was working. Her work was comforting lost souls. And she was on her way to the Whole Life Expo. Jim wanted to go. But then she began crying.

"What's going on with you, Ariel?" Jim asked.

"I feel like I'm burning up. Something is eating me inside. I feel horrible, like I'm going to die."

"My God, pull over! Are you serious? Maybe it's the incense, it's pretty thick in here. Could that be it?"

Ariel started to talk feverishly about commitment. "We run from commitment. But that's because we often cause our commitment with another person to become a limitation. We paint the brighter picture elsewhere and create fear with what we have so that we will eventually run away."

"Why are you telling me this, Ariel?" Jim felt as if he'd found another mind reader.

"So you can get back to your father and mother."

"My father and mother? What do they have to do with it?"

"I mean mother earth and father sky."

Jim turned to look through the back window and could see the Econoline now five cars behind. Michael was slumped on the steering wheel, listless in the traffic, flipping Jim the bird.

Jim was drifting, losing touch with reality, remembering something he'd written in his diary weeks before. . . .

Heading north into the orange-brown haze of the horizon. Cars transporting souls along a plane through time. Past and present merging in one stream of mind. Transporting me through several lifetimes. When I was a sailor, a wandering monk, a . . . a . . . CONCUBINE?!

"*Oh, my God!*"

Jim slowly, carefully opened the door. Ariel smiled. "Leaving so soon? Thanks for dropping by. You really should go see the Expo. Great channeling," she said in a disarmingly sane manner.

Jim stepped out of the Pontiac with Nurse cupped in his arm and walked carefully around the car, still wearing the quartz. He stood motionless in the heat until Econoline inched by his side, and then he stepped in.

Mike didn't say a word.

Jim looked at Michael and handed him the rose quartz. "Here, I think you'd better put these on. I can't explain it, but that was one of the weirdest things that's ever happened to me." Jim's eyes bulged in their sockets . . . "Mike, you know something, this journey is a *trip!*"

"And you're only one hundred miles from home....

Who you with?... Well,

I guess we'll see you when we see

you..." The voice trailed off as Mike guiltily hung up the receiver, regretting his two-year hiatus from the Family.

"Who was that?" Jim was in the van, parked on La Brea in West Hollywood, furiously sweeping loose grains out of the spoiled carpet.

"Mom. She heard from Uncle Jack that I'd left the city and was heading south."

"Word travels fast. Was she mad at you for not staying in touch?"

"No. She wasn't mad, or pleading. But she did make it perfectly clear that all roads, no matter what road we are presently on, do in fact lead to San Diego."

"In other words, she expects us for dinner."

"Well, she was a little hesitant about the *us* part. She said she'd need a few days to prepare."

"Why, what did you tell her?"

"That I was traveling with you. She wanted to know if we were, well . . . sleeping together."

"Boy, your family seems to get right to the point. So what'd you tell her?"

"I said yes, of course. But I left it at that."

"Why, we're not doing anything. You mean you let her assume . . ."

"Well, I just thought maybe it's time for them to open the door a little wider. They always said they weren't bothered by who I am, but every time I've raised the possibility of them meeting someone I love, things get tense. And the fact is, they've never met anyone I've been with. I thought it wouldn't hurt for once to just let them assume. After all, I do feel about as close to you as I feel to anyone, and you know that I'll be the first to tell them . . ."

"It's okay, Michael. Let them assume, it's probably going to be good for you. But it seems pretty twisted. Usually gay men take home a stand-in female to pose as a girlfriend. This will be a first."

Parking in Los Angeles, as in San Francisco, was still a problem, compounded more by the fact that the Monks were sharing the streets with thousands of other transients. In L.A. even the homeless had cars, as that night the Monks parked near Venice on a dead end with twenty other homes on wheels.

"Michael, do you ever get the distinct feeling that people think we're just a couple of bums?"

"Well, what are they supposed to think! It might have something to do with the way we look. I think we should stick more to the open road. This is nuts staying in a city. You have to waste so much time just looking for a place to park for the night. And then you get wrapped into the lives of all these destitute people who—"

A knock came on the door.

"Oh, God, it's the cops again."

But it wasn't. An old man from Louisiana was banging on the door causing Econoline to rock side to side. Jim opened a window and the man poked his scruffy face to the screen.

"Hey, man, I'm sorry to be disturbing your peace, but I'm flat broke, man, and like, I'm run outta gas. I got my wife and kid living around the corner in the old Plymouth, and we really need to get us something to eat. Can you help me out, man? I don't take drugs, and I don't mean nobody no harm."

Jim reached in his pocket and gave two dollars.

There goes tomorrow's budget!

A minute later the same man was knocking on a station wagon to the side of us. The Monks heard him telling the next guy that he was from Oklahoma with a sick mother and three sisters broke down in their van up the street.

A gullible bodhisattva is born every minute?

"God, what makes us any different from all these people around here? We're all just living out of our cars and vans because we can't afford the rent," Jim pondered.

"But we *chose* to leave," Mike differed.

"No, we didn't. You said it yourself. We *had* to leave. We couldn't swing it."

"Well, we could have moved to a cheaper place. But we wanted to leave. We are *not* transients."

A mere fraction of an inch away, that's all. Separated only by definition.

"Yeah, I know, we're monks. I'm the one who coined the term. I know all about being a homeless, poor, sanctimonious monk," said Jim. "The self-effacing, spiritually uplifting beauty of abject poverty."

"Maybe we're not so much monks, but pilgrims." Mike paused.

"But where's Mecca? Where *are* we going?" Jim asked.

Michael felt around for the road atlas.

"Shouldn't we be making a plan?" Jim continued.

"A plan?" After years of spreadsheets and business plans in the big city, Michael loathed plans of any kind.

"Yeah, like a plan of where we're going to go."

Somehow it had never occurred to the Monks to *plan* a journey. The whole point of hitting the road was to leave behind all plans, taking it a day at a time, traveling as far as the gas would last. The only plan was set by a flip of a coin or by pure whimsy. That was the beauty of this freewheeling journey.

"What do you want to do?" Jim asked Michael, hoping that between the two of them, at least one of them might have an agenda.

"Well, I suppose I don't have any particular destination in mind. It's not so much things or places I want to see, but people I want to meet."

"Like which people?"

"I don't know. People we haven't met yet. Well, I want to see family and check out some friends, but I'd just like to leave it open. See who climbs aboard."

"You mean a caravan?"

"Sure. A caravan of souls."

"Yeah, find our family, our *real* family," Jim agreed. "In Japan they deify people who have become masters at some craft or profession. They call them 'living treasures.' I think we should be in search of America's living treasures. Ordinary people who live extraordinary lives."

"Yeah, I'm after ordinary people too. But I don't want to place a value on what a person has or has not achieved. I feel that every person, even the most seemingly insignificant, has a unique story inside."

"Mike, you're sounding more and more like an enlightened master every day. I herefore anoint you abbot of the Mobile Monastery. I say coast to coast with this noble open-ended crusade," said Windmill Jim, coming around once again.

"Yeah. That'll be our goal. We'll take the mobile monastery from shore to shore. Everybody must get monked!"

"So we are on a search?" said Jim Quixote.

"It's a search for ourselves and our family."

"Will we have fun?"

"We *are* having fun."

"Will there be sex?" Jim pressed onward.

"You're asking me? You know where the line is . . . wait a second . . ."

Jim squealed on the floor as the Nurses split for the front.

Since Trickster Jim was constantly on the verge of total buffoonery, Michael was growing less and less certain of when to take him seriously.

Jim kicked his legs in the air, rocking the van. Another Monk conference complete. Begun in ambiguity, ending in ambiguity.

For several days the Monks wandered the streets of L.A., taking refuge in the big, blue Pacific Design Center and its central, frigid, soul-satisfying *air*. We literally set up house in the air-conditioned alcove next to the pay phones.

Jim sat barefoot below the phones with an open loaf of bread in hand, an empty carton of soy milk and his precious papers scattered everywhere. He made himself right at home, oblivious to the foot traffic across the hall. On the second morning a well-heeled lady came rushing in to use the phone and had a hernia on the spot. As the elevator opened, a crowd of people stood and stared.

"Oh, my God, he's barefoot!"

We were soon asked to leave, not just the Big Blue Whale, but the Big Orange.

"Keep out of Los Angeles, get that front blinker fixed and

for Madonna's sake do something about that smell!" were Sergeant Friday's parting words as the Monks sped off toward the San Diego freeway.

"Sounds like a broken record. I don't think we're wanted here."

Five hours later we were still on the freeway, inching south in yet another traffic jam. Jim had cooked two meals, cleaned the van, written the newsletter and was again working on his papers while Mike drove, hoping to make El Cajon by sunset.

By the time we arrived in San Diego it was midnight, and Mike was nervous about driving his new home, sidekick and two Nurses to meet a curious family at such a late hour. Two years was a long time to drop out from visiting Roberta (aka Mom). Jay, her imposingly large Dutch husband, would certainly have something to say about *that*. So Mike decided to park outside his old high school in Chula Vista, below the Trojan sign on a dead end. The only worries would be a few carloads of party-hardy kids.

The canyons adjacent to the school were covered with low brush and weeds, edging up to housing developments. The quiet neighborhood was a welcome relief after L.A., and so Michael decided to loosen the Nurses off their leashes and let them roam.

"We're far enough away. They deserve a break."

Nurse's Aide, as always, stuck fairly close to the kitty food underneath the Econoline. However, as soon as Michael unclipped the leash, Nurse bolted into the canyon, disappearing beneath the shadows.

"He'll come back," Michael assured.

The following morning Jim commenced the two-step ritual of first, finding a kosher place to dump the garbage, and second, debating over how long to meditate. It was quiet, except for the early-morning descent of jets landing at Brown Field.

Meanwhile, Mike was pacing around the block yelling for Nurse. But there was no Nurse to be found. Jim was soon enlisted in the search with both Monks hollering around the school.

"Nurse."

"Come here, Nurse."

"Nurrrrrrrrse!"

"C'mon, Nurse, quit playing games."

"Come to where the flavor is, buddy."

"Come home to the Monksters, Nurse."

Annoyed neighbors peered out their windows at the two madmen disturbing the morning calm with this bizarre call for a nurse.

"What's wrong with you two?!" a lady in curlers and scarlet bathrobe yelled, peering out her door. "The hospital is four miles away."

"It's our cat. We call him Nurse and he's disappeared."

Out came Mrs. Blithe, curlers and all, yelling for Nurse.

"Kitty, kitty, kitty. Come here, kitty, kitty, kitty."

Her neighbor, Mrs. Robert Mitchell, came out after her friend, dressed in a yellow floral smock and pink, fuzzy house shoes. After Mrs. Blithe explained to Mrs. Mitchell the predicament at hand, the other early birds joined forces in assisting the Monks.

That is, until Mr. Lindsay leaned out his door and told everyone to "shut the hell up!" Mrs. Blithe had a quiet word with him. And then, he too was out in his jogging suit whistling for the kitty.

"Come here, kitty, kitty, kitty."

Five callers in various shades of morning attire attracted five more callers. Mr. Swift, Allen Goa, Ms. Martinez, Cindy Duncan and Helen Duvall all peeled out of their suburban shelters, fueled by the neighborhood search.

Ms. Martinez brought a walkie-talkie and Allen produced a bullhorn. Now all ten were cruising the streets and canyons in search of the Monk mascot.

The neighborhood was alive with devoted fans of Nurse.

"Nursie. Come on, Nursie."

"Nurseeeeeeee. Come here, kitty, kitty, kitty."

"Pss, pss, pss, pss. Come on, Nurse. Come to Daddy. Pss, pss, pss."

"Nurse, we know you're here. C'mon, Nurse, c'mon, buddy."

"Come here, kitty, kitty, kitty."

Mike started clanking the kitty bowl, which brought Aide to the window, but no Nurse. Mike opened a new box of Cornucopia cat food and shook it, the Pavlovian signal that had worked in the past, but no Nurse. Both Monks then ran around with a pile of wool sweaters, leaving them at various spots on the ground. All to no avail.

After several hours of searching, pleading, and praying— Mrs. Blithe led the prayer circle—a neighborhood committee was formed and a plan of action developed. There would be fliers with photos, traps set, and a reward announced at the next PTA meeting.

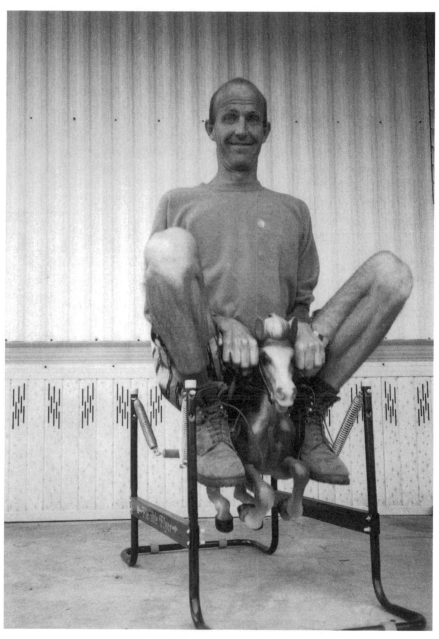

**Our rocking-horse winner, at Singing Hills
Mobile Home Park.**

After the Monks profusely thanked the helpful neighbors of Chula Vista, they returned to the van, where all hopes were dashed when they found a note by an old, urine-stained wool sweater: *"To the Monks . . . I'm not returning until new sweaters are made. See you on the road!"* —*Nurse.*

Despondent, the Monks headed off to the J&R Ranch in El Cajon.

Michael was not feeling prepared to come home. Cruising way too fast over the speed bumps of the Singing Hills Mobile Home Park, Michael searched for space #1. There at the front of a row of seemingly identical mobile homes sat a white double-wide with a concrete slab for a patio. The surrounding hills were parched down to the brown earth while scrub brush and sage dotted the landscape. Nearby

Momma-ka-poo and Bighearted Jay at J&R Nursery, El Cajon, California.

housing developments marched toward the horizon of distant hills, pink from the relentless sun.

El Cajon was at the edge of San Diego. It was so far removed from the beach, it took on the air of a frontier outpost: rowdy dudes, pickups and dust-blown streets, but still retaining the most familiar part of the California landscape —that requisite strip of shopping malls, fast-food joints and quick stops.

Mom stood on her rickety porch under the awning, so glad to see Mike that she'd even broken down and bought a pound of brown rice. Michael leapt out of the van, leaving the engine running, to give Mom a big gangly hug. Mom had her arms around Mike, pinching his skinny sides.

"Well, aren't you going to shut your engine off? Where's your friend?"

"He's inside the van meditating. He'll shut off the engine."

Mom walked on over to Econoline and stuck her head in to meet Jim. She always did take the head-on approach to crossing her barriers.

"Hi, Jim, I'm Michael's mother."

Jim was kneeling on the carpet, flapping his wings like a bird, reciting the Nurse Heart Sutra: ". . . therefore in emptiness, no fur, no feelings, no Meow Mix, no cat consciousness, no eyes, no ears, no dogs, no Aide, no Monks, no catnip, no leash, no newsletter, no space, no van, no escaping with nothing to escape from, no sucking, no wool sweaters, no *Nurse?* . . ."

"He's trying to bring Nurse back. We lost one of our cats, and Jim's very attached to the cats, even though as a Buddhist he doesn't admit to attachments."

Roberta succeeded in hauling Jim out of the van to say that "I'm Roberta, Michael's mother. And I'm very sorry about your cat."

Jim gave Roberta a big hug. "Oh, he'll return, he always does." For once Jim didn't even believe himself.

Roberta gave a big sigh and looked at Michael.

"Well, I spent a few days preparing myself. I mean, I don't think it's ever going to be *that* easy, but you know I just kept telling Jay that it's ridiculous to keep playing this game. If any of my other kids were coming through town with a friend, I'd open my home. I've got to get over this. But, you know, I've got fifty-five years of conditioning to overcome."

"Mom, it's okay. I want you to know that we're not—"

Roberta interrupted and gave Jim a sincere loving look.

"I just want you to feel at home, Jim. I mean it. I'll even confine smoking to the south side of the dining table 'cause I know you guys don't smoke!"

"But Mom, we're not—"

"Just shut the engine off and come on in." Mom didn't want to fiddle with the finer details. It was painful enough to just *think* about it.

Mom directed Jim and Econoline into the narrow carport driveway behind the beat-up Chevie. Everyone came out to meet Jim and marvel at the logistics of *two grown men*, cats, computer and strange foods occupying such a small space. Everyone, including Grandma, Jay, Aunt Babe, cousins, brother, sister and nephews . . . and they all had something to say.

"What are you going to do with all those beans?" Grandma asked covetously, poking her head into the side door of Econoline. "If you don't need them, I can feed them to my goats. And maybe my Mexican friends could use some too." Grandma was the wild and childlike philanthropic forager of trailer park dumpsters, taking her daily loot to the itinerant Mexican laborers hiding out in the nearby hills.

"You both sleep on that bed? There's only one bed in there, and that's not big enough for a small dog," said Aunt Babe, eyeing suspiciously.

"Babe . . . I'll fill you in later!" said Mom with exasperation, using her patented diversionary tactics.

"But Mom, I think I'd better tell you something," Mike whispered toward Roberta.

"Well, Michael Lane, what I want to know is how *are* you making it, that type sort of thing," bellowed the bottom-line, no-nonsense Jay, the consummate Dutch cowboy, with his cowboy boots and obligatory framed photo of the Duke on the wall behind him. Good-natured Jay could not have put it more tactfully.

"You know, Momma and me sent you boys a hundred dollars for this little newsletter thing. But I'm sure, even if Jim's folks did the same type sort of thing, you'd still be scraping pretty darn hard to get yourselves on down the road. Isn't that right Michael Lane?" Jay bellowed good-naturedly.

"Oh, Jay, I'm sure the boys know what they're doing. They've been around the block a few times," scolded Momma-ka-poo, as Jay so affectionately called her. Then on second thought, "Well, how *are* you making it?" asked Mom with a nervous smile and a frown on the forehead.

Michael *started* to open his mouth, but Jim *had* opened his. Everyone stood around the carport with expectant faces, curiously waiting for The Secret. The Secret all of America would love to know.

Mike started to speak, then cleared his throat. Grandma made a funny noise, Mom took a drag on her Salem, Jim turned to Mike, and well, it just hung there for a few minutes as the room turned rather silent.

"Uh, well, we're, uh, well," Mike began. "We're doing a lot of different things like, well . . . I guess, come to think of it, I don't really know. Maybe we're *not* making it. That's it. We're *not* making it."

The room breathed a sigh of relief.

"I thought so," said Jay, shaking his head. "For a minute there I thought you boys knew something we didn't know!" he roared.

"When's the last time you two had a good meal? You can't tell me you're eating well in that van?" interjected Mom in a typical mom's voice.

The kitchen table was spread with food, enough to last a dozen people for a week. A dressed turkey, deviled eggs, Jell-O, yams, corn, string beans, tall glasses of milk and that all-American apple pie. Mom hated to cook, but when she did, she put out quite a spread.

Hmmm. Maybe I have been skipping a bit on food, thought Mike. The prodigal son and his eccentric cohort were soon gorging themselves on the welcome-home feast.

After dinner everyone settled into the front room of the trailer, where sat two big couches, adjacent to which was a bookcase lining one entire wall, overburdened with back issues of *Reader's Digest,* Mom's dusty real estate manuals and photos upon photos of kids, grandkids and adults. Some recorded significant events, others recorded momentary glimpses of years gone by. The couches faced inward toward the television with Jay's La-Z-Boy recliner anchored in the middle.

Mom watched Mike wolf down a plate of food and then was back on her feet walking him back for seconds.

"You're looking so thin!"

"Mom, why is it that my thinness seems to give every stranger I meet the self-assumed responsibility to come and tell me I'm thin? Do people actually think I don't know? I know!"

"I'm just worried. You sure you're taking care of yourself? What are you guys doing anyhow? How do you expect to travel if you barely have enough to eat, and I can tell by looking at you that you don't get much sleep either."

Moms. They always know when things aren't quite right.

"I want you and Jim to promise me that you'll take care of yourselves." Her words cut into Mike like a sword. "I want you to promise me that you'll be careful."

"I'm a good driver!"

"No, I mean, I don't want you to get sick."

"What are you talking about? I've always been healthy. You know that."

"Michael. I'm talking about AIDS."

Michael was shocked. *I didn't know Mom thought about AIDS.*

"Mom, if it's any consolation, I haven't any reason to even be—"

"I don't want to know about what goes on. Just promise me that you'll be careful. You and Jim."

"But that's what I'm trying to tell you, we—"

"It's okay. Just be careful," she admonished.

Michael just let the advice sink in as he took another plate of food to fortify his nervous heart.

Two days later Momma-ka-poo and Jay put the Monks to work down at their plant nursery, pulling weeds and taking clippings from the ground cover.

"It doesn't pay much, but it'll buy you boys a few more miles down the road," said Jay with a big friendly smile. "Money is a funny thing. When you could use it, you don't have it, and when you have it, you're afraid to use it . . . that type sort of thing." He broke into his timber-shaking laugh. "I say, doggone it, just give me a chance to find out!" he bellowed with a boisterous chortle that brought both Monks to full attention. Jay was bursting, and we mean bursting, to the point of redness with total love and enjoyment of life.

He had come to America as a penniless teenager and through hard work had managed to save enough to feed himself and several kids. Though a joyful fellow, he wasn't fooled by pie-in-the-sky fantasies. Taurus Jay had a working man's finger on the bottom line, that was for darn sure.

To balance things out, Momma-ka-poo, the inveterate Gemini, was full of dreams and wild schemes. "Write travel tips, lead tours through the desert, make more newsletters. Why don't you sell it on newsstands? Sell ads even."

Always the entrepreneur, Mom could figure out how to

make a buck off two idle ants if she was pressed for money.She'd built a nursery out of a few neighbors' clippings, taught herself real estate, sold Tupperware and Avon and was now scheming to find the best get-rich-quick scheme in the Get-Rich-Quick Capital of the Universe. Mom was a born-in-the-saddle coyote, yet still a back-to-basics gal who was soon egging the Monks on with their traveling dream.

The Monks spent a hard month in the trailer park, fondling weeds down at the J&R Nursery, wearing their fingers thin, earning a fair wage alongside the other clippers. Mike and Mom clipped side by side. Jim, the consummate Buddha, clipped for a while, then contemplated the clippings, his Great Buddha mind at work.

In all fairness Jim was not just contemplating clippings. Instead, Jim was already planning the coast-to-coast Monking of America.

One night, while everyone was sitting at the dinner table, Jim drew a straight line across the map. A straight line from San Diego to New York.

"This is our plan. Coast to coast. We'll do it, by golly. Just don't hold us to a straight line."

"Well, Gemini, I know you can do anything if you set your mind to it," said Mom to Jim, giving him a good hug. The two air signs had hit it off.

Mike and Jim spent the last day stocking up on enormous amounts of food and supplies, as if they were leaving the last outcrop of civilization behind.

"I do believe you'll find a few 7-Elevens along the way," Mom reassured.

But the great expanse of the easterly lands looked like an endless path through dust and desert. And who knew what might be out there and how easy it would be to find brown rice.

Loaded up with a bushel of dollars, a new crop of ideas and healthy, well-fed bellies, the Monks battened down the hatches and brought Nurse's Aide aboard.

"Well, pilgrims, it's been a pleasure to know your acquaintance," said Jay Wayne to a burst of his own laughter, saluting the Monks in the old military style.

"You guys are gonna make it. I have faith in you," said a teary-eyed Mom, waving with her fist in the air.

Two sets of gutsy entrepreneurs emboldening each other in the quest, Momma-ka-poo and bighearted Jay bid Mike and Jim "Happy Trails" as the blinking taillights of Econoline pulled off into the night toward the great Wild West.

Ahead lay the Ultimate desert experience.

The first day out of California was a major break-through. The Monks never felt so free. Ahead lay the Ultimate desert experience. Behind lay the

past, with the past becoming more and more of a distant memory with each forward turn of the wheels.

Mile after weatherworn mile of road wound through the flat expanse of desert floor. Cactus blossoms carpeted the parched earth.

"Jeez, Louise, this is totally awesome, dude. Flowers in the desert. This is great!" Jim exclaimed.

"Why don't more people live out here?" asked Mike, surveying the unpopulated landscape.

"It's the open space, I guess. Americans are scared shitless of open space. Always gotta fill it up with something, some thought, some activity. All this open space is too much of the unknown. We're just creatures of clutter and comfort, harboring a deep fear of total emptiness."

"Maybe it's the lack of water, Jim!"

The Econoline barreled across the desert on Interstate 17 heading north above Phoenix packing a mean seventy miles per hour. Pretty good for an old metal beast on wheels.

Jim drove while Mike experimented over the propane stove with his latest obsession . . . cooking in transit.

"Jim, slow down to sixty, would you, I'm trying to make chocolate-substitute duck-egg mousse."

Sitting on the bed in the very back, Michael had the stove up high melting carob on the cast-iron skillet, while separating egg whites on the bed. Mike held the cream between his legs, licking his fingers.

"How're you keeping the pan on the stove?"

Kabump. The van hit a pothole.

"Jim, get a load of this. A glob of melted carob on the floor."

"Just rub it into the carpet, it'll never show."

Mike began grinding in the carob. "Good thing this is a brown carpet."

Both flames burned high with a pot of new improved apricot duck gravy boiling on the left burner, the melting carob back on the right, and a bowl of stove-top, slightly burnt, whole-wheat biscuits sitting on the left-door cutting board, made from another recipe his grandma had given him. Mike was tying rope around the pot and pan, securing them to the door.

"Mike, I smell something burning!" Jim yelled.

Kabump. The van hit another pothole.

"Check this out, duck fat all over the floor."

Nurse's Aide was lapping it up like a delirious dog.

"Mike, something's burning!"

"Check this out, the rope's on fire!" The rope was blazing across the stove, inching its way toward the tank. A towel caught on fire. Mike dumped the cream on the blaze in a big splat. The rope sizzled, steamed, and then the flame extinguished itself.

"Damn, my mousse is ruined."

"Can't you use soy milk, I'm allergic to dairy anyhow!" said Jim, looking over his shoulder to Mike.

"*Jim!* Watch where you're going."

Kabump. Whooosh. The Econoline swerved away from the guardrail. The egg whites dumped on the bed. Now Nurse's Aide was lapping up the duck eggs.

"Shit, now I've got to start over. Keep your eye on the road or neither of us will be alive to eat!"

It never occurred to either Monk to pull over and stop. Onward and forward sped the Econoline, resuming its seventy-mile-per-hour clip.

A new batch of duck eggs, more carob and a fresh carton of soy milk were pulled from the pantry, which lined the wall opposite the door stove. Mike resorted to taping everything in its place with electrical tape. Tricky business. The van was moving and shaking as Michael rode the bumps.

"Hi ho, it's the Monk diner on wheels."

"Mike, I smell something burning."

The tape was melting, sending acrid fumes into the van.

"No biggy, just electrical tape. I'll crack a window."

Mike reached to the back of the bed and slid open the two side windows, affording him a view of the passing landscape. Small shelves in the back held the vast array of macroneurotic cookbooks.

Michael stared dreamily out the window, watching the desert go by, longing for mousse. A lone hawk circled the van, a pink cloud hugged the horizon, a clump of biscuit flew by the window, a whole biscuit flew by the window, biscuits were flying by the window.

"Jiiiiiiim! We're loosing my biscuits! Jiiiiiiim!"

Mike turned as Jim turned and watched in horror as the first side door was ajar, trailing in the wind. The plate of biscuits sat at the edge of the cutting board, launching a biscuit at every bump like a ship losing its charges.

"Stop the van!"

Screeeeeeeeeech. Plump. Plump. Plump.

When Jim finally came to a rest off the side of the freeway, Mike had biscuits, gravy, carob and egg whites from floor to ceiling. Still covered with cream, his hair matted with yolk, Mike emerged from the van pulling the smoldering electrical tape off the stove. "*Aiiiieeeeegggg!*" he screamed at passing traffic. "Jesus! What kind of crap is this? Can't even make a decent mousse."

By the time Mike got the egg out of his hair, Jim had cooked a pot of millet, as Nurse's Aide maniacally licked at the carpet. Mike swept what he could out of the van, ground the rest of the mess into the all-purpose brown carpet and settled down to a simple meal, salvaging apricot duck gravy off the floor.

It had been a two-hour rise from the desert heat of Phoenix, over the Mingus Mountains, and now the Monks were at the foot of Verde Valley.

"Where are we?"

"We should be near Sedona," Jim replied, pulling cat hair out of the gravy. "It's the New Age mecca everyone's talking about."

After a full meal seasoned by organic truck exhaust, Jim continued the drive up 89A toward Sedona. The town itself

The vaunted Red Rocks of Sedona. (R. Mayer)

was unpretentious. One quick drive heading north and we passed modest shopping malls, fast-food chains and gas stations. Not very metaphysical.

Once uptown we hit the tourist quarter, with dozens of Gray Line tour buses spilling herds of teetering geriatrics out onto the pavement. White-haired, scarved, bag-clutching pairs of ladies, with their leisure-suited men in tow, invaded the small western and Indian shops.

A Hollywood-western backdrop if there ever was one, the sandstone, adobe colors blended perfectly into the surrounding landscape. But it wasn't the pueblo/Wild-West architecture that gave the town its unique character. It was without question *the rocks*.

Oak Creek, which originated high in the mountains toward Flagstaff, wound through town providing an oasis from the dry desert heat. Where it met the canyon floor stood the most astounding, wind-sculpted, eroded monuments on earth.

"Monk, check it out. Totally awesome rock formations," said Jim.

Hundreds of feet high, shadowing the surrounding canyons, taking on shapes and colors that elevated the imagination, the towering Red Rocks of Sedona seemed like a tribe of giant extraterrestrials stationed under the desert sun.

Amidst the swarm of tourists and rock hounds, the Monks sat at the corner of 89A and 179 gawking at the spectacle.

"Listen to this, Mike." Jim sat reading from a flier he'd found blowing down the sidewalk. " 'Western psychics have identified Sedona as home to four major vortexes. It is said that the vortexes of Sedona fall upon electromagnetic grids that circle the earth. Much like the acupuncture points on the human body, the vortexes are said to be focal points for the earth's meridians.' "

"What's that supposed to mean?"

"It's these big rocks. They're vortexes. Each vortex is supposed to have a certain power. If you're attuned to its energy, then you'll experience a change in yourself."

"What? Like a sex change? I think I heard of this place. Transvestites come here for the operation.

"No, no, no! That's Tijuana, girl. The vortexes change things inside, not between your legs. Well, maybe they do that too. I'm not really sure. It says each person is drawn to the vortex most needed by them. And that if you have stuff you need to work on, it will be magnified a hundred times until those issues are dealt with."

At the far end of town we broke for dinner at Food Among the Flowers, the certified-organic watering hole for the town's New Age circus of healers, mystics and channelers. There, out on the patio, in full view of the mountain where Moses rapped with God in Cecil B. deMille's *The Ten Commandments*, we gorged on banana smoothies and magic muffins.

The walls were awash with fliers announcing crystal workshops, healing seminars, vision quests and the Harmonic Convergence.

"Hey, Mike, check it out. This August is the Moronic Convergence. It says thousands of people are expected to converge upon Sedona to 'experience the vortexes.' "

"Hey, maybe we're at the right place at the right time for a change."

"Indeed, this is so."

The Monks were surrounded by the New Age gypsies of

the road. Silk scarves, beads and bangles, crystals, jewels, rings, precious stones, feathers, bells, headdresses, smudge sticks, incense, trinkets and lots of purple poured through the doors, spilling out onto the patio.

The Monks studied the pamphlets on the table, eaves-dropping on neighboring conversations.

"And my guide from the third plane told me to wear blue on Tuesdays if I want to open my crown chakra in time for transmission . . ."

"I know, I heard Ishkara is channeling from the Starship command out at Bell Rock during the Convergence . . ."

". . . and he told me we are a superrace from the Pleiades and on the seventeenth the mother ship would descend . . ."

". . . as long as at least one hundred forty-four thousand resonate at different power points around the planet to cre-ate the appropriate signal . . ."

"They think UFOs are going to land here, Mike." Jim motioned toward the couple at the next table. "Did you hear that? They sold everything they owned and are just waiting until August to leave the planet." Jim stifled a judgment.

"Uh-huh. Sounds like us," Michael said sardonically.

"Weeeeeel, weeeeel, awl-rrrrrright nowww. We aaahrrr pleased to have spent this ty-em toogay-ther," said Jim to the crowd in his faux Lazarus best as Michael yanked him from the clutch of the true believers.

Stumbling into the parking lot, the Monks turned a corner and *whammmmm*, had a head-on collision with a captivating young man.

"Oh, hi!" Jim jumped back.

"No, Pi!" the man responded.

"What's Pi?" Jim asked.

"I am Pi."

"Pi, as in 'pi r-squared'?"

"No, silly, pie are round."

"Then who is Pi?"

"I am Mr. *Apple* Pi, the Multimedia Man. For only a fraction of the cost I can turn your life into a holographic breeze." He beamed with a broad, cheek-to-cheek smile as his jolly eyes danced across his clean, boyish face. He was dressed head to toe in white. White shirt, white vest, white pants, white shoes, white hat and a white briefcase bearing the legend *Apple Pi*.

He brushed aside his bangs and squinted at the Monks.

The Monks squinted back.

He squinted nose to nose. "Are you . . . the Monks?" He squealed, letting out a goofy giggle.

"Yeah, who are you?" The Monks stepped back.

"I told you. I'm Pi, Mr. Apple Pi, Multimedia Man, remember?" he gleefully reprimanded.

"*Pi!*" the Monks shouted. "Oh, my god, Mr. Apple Pi!"

Only a week earlier the Monks had received an elaborate résumé postmarked Hawaii from this mysterious Pi guy, who offered to join the Monks on their sacred journey. He was the multimedia man who had earnestly dedicated his life to the pursuit of Knowledge with a big *K*. And the Monks were masters of knowledge. Masters of Nomadic Knowledge, that is.

"How'd you find us?"

"Heh, heh, heh!" Pi chuckled in that supernice yet somewhat sinister way he had. He smiled and chuckled that goofy chuckle every time he spoke. It was his trademark.

"Easy. I stopped looking." He chuckled. "And that's not all. I'm here to help where help is needed. I'm the Apple Pi man, and I create the link between people to eliminate duplication of effort. I am the Concept of Effortless Effort. I am the All for One and One for All Concept. The Learn How to Learn Concept, and the Anything Is Possible Concept. I am at your service." He bowed at the waist.

The Monks looked at each other with a shrug.

"Alright, so where *are* you staying?" Mike ventured.

"With you, silly!" Pi beamed.

The Monks looked at each other again, thinking of their precious futon growing smaller by the minute.

"Uh, might you have your *own* sleeping bag, Pi?"

"Yeah, and my own tent. White, of course!"

"Great!" the Monks spoke in unison.

"Hop on board, but watch the guest seat, another one of Jim's pens broke," Mike added.

With their new sidekick, Mr. Apple Pi, the Monks commandeered Econoline uptown in search of a new encampment.

"So, like, why are you called the Multimedia Man?"

"Because the future of Earth depends on the ability of humans to adapt to new information and new ways of thinking. I call myself a multimedia man because there are many different ways that information can be presented. I use technology to help everyone participate in the global expression and exchange of ideas."

"You should run for office, Pi."

"That's my True Leader Concept. I'll tell you about it later!"

After several hours wandering around, looking for "the

right spot," we finally heeded the advice of the guy at the Circle K, who said the best place in town to camp was the Hawkeye RV Park.

Safely removed from the ball-busting vortexes yet right in the heart of downtown Sedona, the Monks and Pi found Hawkeye just off the main drag hugging beautiful Oak Creek.

As Econoline drove into the campground, Mike peered over the hill surveying the overwhelming spectacle of recreational-vehicle madness. Not since Hearst Castle had the Monks witnessed such a gathering of full-timers, as they are known in the trade. Not to be confused with slime bags on wheels, the full-timers were the moms and pops who'd retired from Caterpillar tractor and hit the road full-time with their two miniature poodles in tow.

Down in Hawkeye RV Park, campers, fifth-wheelers and pop-tops were stacked ten deep to an aisle, and the TV sets, radios and microwaves competed with the cicadas.

"I bet they charge good money to stay here!" said a disgusted Mike.

Pay to camp? We'd never. What's the point of having a fully outfitted van. Just pull off the road or down a deserted street. The world is our home! That's the Monk way—make do or do without. We're self-sufficient road warriors, right?

Wrongo.

There was something to this place. Something that took hold as Mike went to the front desk and stood at the counter assessing the price of a night. Something that took hold of Jim's mind as he surveyed the facilities. Something that Pi already knew by the smile on his face.

Hawkeye RV Park and Campground had *hot showers!*

"And they have a washer and drier. A game room. Electricity. Phone booths!" Jim went ecstatic as Mike calculated the cost difference of roughing the dusty road versus a squeaky-clean campground with all the fixings.

Having never spent a penny on a place to park for the night, the Monks found it a foreign concept. Falling somewhere between slime bags on wheels and full-timers, the Monks had sworn to the creed of "simple, mobile and true." To pay for a night was a bloody sacrilege, a literal defilement of the sacred Monk creed. It was too easy, too bourgeois, too much like Mom and Dad.

"Hot showers, Mike," a seductive voice was calling.

"Hot showers, Jim." It was hard to resist.

"Hot showers, Mr. Apple Pi." A devilish chuckle.

Mr. Apple Pi, Multimedia Man.

Hot showers! Hot showers! Hot showers! were calling.
The Monks had found a home for the summer.

The Hawkeye campground sat on a bluff overlooking Oak
Creek. The ice-cold, mountain-fresh water came tumbling
down the canyon, over rocks, through the forest and swiftly
flowed into a fifteen-foot-deep swimming hole adjacent to
the campsites. A gigantic seven-foot hawk was carved in the
top of a dead tree giving rise to the name Hawkeye. And
below the Monk campsite, space #7 was a thirty-foot cliff
from where a monk could hurl himself into the icy waters
below.
    Pi fell in place like an old friend as the three monketeers
set up camp with the efficiency of an Austrian drill team.
Side doors opened out, Jim rolled down the canopy. Up
popped the stove. Pi assembled his white tent. The clothes
hung on a tree. The computer sat on the picnic table. Jim's
papers spread across the dashboard. The food and ice chest
rested in the shade, lights were strung off the trees and the
welcome mat was spread before the door.
    The jam-packed rows of campsites all faced down toward
the cliff, leaving the colorful Monk camp totally exposed at

the bottom of the campground. Everyone watched us like hawks.

Here was America's answer to the refugee camp and the nomadic village. The refugees were from the cities. On the uptown side of the RV park were the upscale retirees. They all drove $70,000 motor homes and paid the full $18 for *complete* hookup. Next came the midtown, middle-class section of Hawkeye, with its vacationing families of four, smaller motor homes and over-the-cab campers paying $15 for *partial* hookup.

The Monks ventured down among the riverside campers with their tents, pull-along pop-top units and converted vans, paying the *white trash* rate of $12.

But despite this carefully preserved parking hierarchy, class lines snapped when the Monk wagon train pulled to a stop at site #7. Within a few hours the uptown ladies, the white trash from the riverside and everyone in between was walking over to see what we were doing.

Well, we were not doing what they would have liked us to be doing. Jim was running around in between nude and half-nude, Aide was pissing on everyone's tires, Mike was standing on his head doing the breath of fire and Pi was

Why else would we go to an RV park except to plug in our trusty waffle iron.

demonstrating his astounding Autofellatio Concept to an astonished skunk who'd come by to steal cat food.

A few mornings into our stay we were sitting on the edge of a cliff with Pi leaning dangerously toward the edge discussing his vast array of Beta World concepts, which formed the basis of his extraordinary life.

". . . and the Male Lesbian Concept is for males who enjoy females who appear to be lesbians . . ."

The Monks listened attentively while devouring the last of the morning's waffles. Waffles had become our latest food obsession after we discovered a greasy secondhand waffle iron in the Dumpster. For the entire morning Gemini Jim had experimented with buckwheat waffles, blue-corn waffles, waffles with peanuts, waffles with seaweed, waffles with onions and, of course, waffles with peaches. The Monks were swigging from a carton of soy milk, which, other than waffles, had become another leading obsession, right alongside Jim's addiction to herbal supplements.

"It's my way of saying to the women of the world that there are men who enjoy females for what they are naturally, without all the makeup, perfume, wigs . . ."

The Monks hung on to the proverbial edge as Pi swayed in the summer wind.

"Pi, aren't you a little close to the edge?" asked Michael.

"Noooo. You've never heard of my Anything Is Possible Concept. I have come up with an equation that actually proves *anything* is possible. Some people might refer to this as being theoretical instead of mathematical. The main thing is that it works. $AIP = [(U*2)^d]^r$."

"But one strong wind and you're going to be over the side, Pi!" warned Michael Monk.

"Then I'll use my No Limitations Concept. The only limitations for humanity are the limitations that humanity imposes upon itself."

Jim covetously chewed on his last waffle while Mike stood up to pull a teetering Pi from a sheer death experience.

"No Problems/Only Solutions Concept . . . there are no problems in the world, there are only solutions."

Mike was reaching out for Pi. Pi was spreading his arms, leaning toward the edge.

"Balance Factor Concept . . ."

"Pi, what . . . are . . . you . . . doing!"

Now possessed by the Fear of Death Concept, Mike yelled out, "Pi, you seem to be forgetting the Mangled Limbs Concept, the Grieving Mothers Concept, the Broken

Dreams Concept, not to mention the End of Concepts Concept!"

Pi was arching back as if to throw himself. Jim started to rise as Mike grabbed for Pi's leg. Pi was slipping off the side, pebbles rolling under his feet. Jim grabbed on to Mike, Mike clung to Pi and . . .

"No Such Thing as Luck Concept . . . luck is simply what happens when someone has prepared themselves for a situation and then they notice the op . . . por . . . tu . . . ni . . . tiiiiiiiiiiieee." Pi had pushed face-forward off the cliff, spread-eagle, back curled, eyes wide, on a bloodcurdling plunge down the canyon wall with a screaming Mike tumbling off the side followed by a tugging Jim, who clung tenaciously to his last waffle on the long way down.

Sssssssshhhhhhhhhhhhhh . . . splashhhhhhhh. The three Monks hit Oak Creek and sent tidal waves crashing against the rocks as they plunged to river bottom.

"Do it again. Again!" screamed three kids from the opposite shore.

"Pi! You're a nut!" Jim hollered as he swam to river's edge still clutching his precious waffle.

Mike was floating downstream where he swung up on a rock gasping for breath. "Pi, haven't you heard of the Advance Warning Concept!"

"Heh, heh, heh," Pi giggled. "I told you. *Anything* is possible. Am I right? Am I right?" asked our Sagittarian philosopher, letting out a big broad smile.

After this first attempt at the rite of falling, the Monks spent an hour trying to stop their legs from shaking. Jim sang ten painful renditions of "Thunder Road," while Mike assumed the fetal position. But with more prompting from Pi, the mad trio was soon up and falling again, as Pi performed kamikaze acrobatic somersaults while plunging deep into the icy waters of Oak Creek.

"A definite E-ticket ride!" Mike screeched.

"This is fucking great!" Jim shouted.

Jumping off the cliff was the initiation we'd been waiting for, the ideal preconvergence baptism.

Fellow campers didn't know what to think. It was one thing to jump once or twice, but we were known to jump twenty times while chanting, "I love me!" So they must have thought we were a little strange.

But let's face it. We *were* strange.

As the fateful day of August 16 approached, crystal madness swept through the canyons as carloads of aspirants arrived at Hawkeye. The full-timers were fleeing town in

Aide with Mac, Hawkeye campground, Sedona, Arizona.

droves, packing up their microwaves, barbecues and televisions as their tightly wound poodles yapped away at the hordes of rainbow children advancing with zealous optimism, swept up in the excitement of the New Age dawning.

The Monks and Pi had created a Harmonic Convergence boot camp at Hawkeye, initiating the scores of crystal-wearing campers who'd arrived for immediate ascension. Michael mass-produced waffles to feed the hungry space cadets, Jim dispensed herbal formulas for every imaginable need, while Pi led happy harmonizers through the Hurl off the Cliff Concept, sending many a surprised initiate plunging to the icy depths below.

Pi was full of concepts. So convincing was he with the White Light Concept, he had the Monks ripping out the red thread in the Hanes underwear and trashing everything that was less than a perfect shade of white. *Eat white, think white, wear white* became the new Monk mantra as we prepared for the biggest nonevent of the decade.

The town fathers were in a panic regarding the approaching convergence prophesied by University of Chicago art historian Jose Arguelles. It was to be the birth of a new cycle in human consciousness. Rumors circulated that half of L.A. would descend on Sedona that summer as planners wildly speculated that as many as one hundred thousand people would converge on the weekend of the sixteenth alone. Community plans were drawn up on how best to accommodate the swell of New Agers, while local businesses rubbed their palms at the thought of one hundred thousand politically correct charge cards loose on the unincorporated streets of Sedona.

The Monks and Pi knew, however, that the greatest need of every seeker would be a certified organic channeler. A great prophet who could become the spokesperson for the ascended masters and starfleet command. A true messenger who could integrate the increased energies from the resonant core and keep up with the flood of entities who'd be demanding equal time on the astral airwaves.

Challenged, the Monks and Pi drew straws, and Jim the Mad Monk was selected to be the authorized Monk challenger for the coveted title: Channeling Overlord of Sedona.

On the eve of August 15 a light green van sped through Hawkeye like a fox on fire as a crystal-decked goddess dropped off a flier at the Monk campsite. It was an invitation to a party where only the elite channelers of Sedona would be in attendance. The Monks and Pi flew into a frenzy knowing this was Jim's big chance to take a commanding lead in the channeling play-offs. Pi was down on his knees obsessively picking gray lint off his otherwise spotless white jumpsuit, Mike was busy bleaching out the cat stains from the Space Monk jumpsuits, while Jim psyched himself up for front-runner status among the highly competitive intergalactic channeling crowd. Tonight was the big moment he'd been waiting for. If he could conjure up the best in entities, then he'd get a stab at evoking fire from the mountain on Convergence Day.

"Which crystal should I wear, the double point or the smoky gray? They say the smoky quartz is excellent for clairvoyance, but I plan to be talking to Starseed command. I think they go for large single points, don't they?" Jim was lost in his new box of crystals.

"What about amethyst?" asked Michael, dripping bleach, with waffle batter in his hair. "Or turquoise?"

"Nah, too Navaho. I'm going for my six-inch single-point quartz with the split facet on its northern lobe. It keeps the challengers on lower astral while I go grab the high-end entities for serious multiplexing." Jim knew his crystals.

. . .

After three hits of ginseng, a splurge on sauerkraut waffles and one last leap off the cliff, the Monks and Mr. Pi arrived fashionably late at the summer's peak experience for the astral-climbing New Age crowd.

"Look at the ring on that one!" said a jealous Michael, pointing out the unabashedly self-possessed channeling hostess. Her finger bore a trademark quartz the size of a baseball, and her neck was strung with so much quartz she bore grooves on her collarbone from the impressions.

"Blessed be, blessed be. Welcome to our gathering. Ishtar is on the roof. Monique is in the kitchen. Lasasha has taken over the lawn, and I think Mishkora has made contact with X2 R3 Command. Make yourselves comfortable."

Sage incense chased the air as the Monks and Pi resonated through the room looking for the punch. Over the sounds of Kitaro could be heard the telltale signs of starship contact, as dozens of high-pitched Elizabethan accents filled the air.

The house was a maze of velvet and satin. Throngs of gold-dusted, star-studded, crystal-clutching metaphysical types drifted around the room making meaningful eye contact. A jungle of sounds assaulted the ears. Deep, penetrating sighs echoed throughout the halls. People edged through the montage, shifting gears from one channeler to the next. Pi found a young pretty willing to hear a dissertation on the No Protein Diet Concept, Jim pulled out his kickass single-point crystal and held it to his forehead, while Mike slithered his way through the crowd to the bar.

"Give me the stiffest thing you got." Michael motioned to the bartender. Mike was handed a celery, carrot, ginkgo-leaf concoction.

The bartender turned and channeled a fourteenth-century Peruvian princess with an obsession for young boys.

". . . and light bears its soul upon the god of thunder where boys pure of heart, of the inner circle, consecrate my flesh . . ."

Jim pushed through a swirl of Sufi dancers into a bedroom filled with crystal clusters draped on magenta carpet. Two white lighters were sounding into the ears of a turbaned man, who was channeling Tibetan masters while sitting on a meditation cushion beneath a copper pyramid.

"These are the featherweights," Jim mouthed toward Mike. "Let's find the heavies!"

Out on the patio, surrounding a kiddie pool filled with lavender water, were the meat and potatoes of the channeling industry. Clad in basic K Mart duds, with no purple, no crystals, no rings or headpieces, sat a circle of overweight, sweaty-palmed, short-haired, frumpy, middle-aged men and women.

"Jackpot!" Jim declared. "It's the Holy Rollers. The Sirius superstars. These folks know how to channel."

And Holy Albion, were they at it. No glamor trade for this bunch. Forget past-life royalty, holy men and wise old sages. These folks were going for the unknown, untouchable hardcore criminal set of the Middle Ages.

The old man by the pool was tapping into a purse snatcher turned grave robber. Heavy competition was coming from his ringside mate, who'd found herself a pair of teenage prostitutes from Geneva.

"I like it!" said Jim, vigorously rubbing his face. "I can get into this shit!"

The sun was setting, and as the first sign of starlight appeared, a surge of bodies pressed onto the patio to gaze heavenward at the night sky.

"Look, a ship!" a lady shouted.

Everyone's eyes shot skyward toward her pointing finger. "There, see it? Those lights, they're moving."

"I see it. I see it," joined a younger man.

"Over there, two more. You can see them circling the center light."

The Monks and Pi were straining to find the lights . . . to no avail. Mike locked his eyes upward, while Jim sussed out the competition, knowing Starseed command would be shooting down the tubes any nanosecond now.

"They're trying to say something," exclaimed our hostess with authority. "They want to make contact."

"God, it's the mothership." A woman collapsed.

The crowd rushed the fence. Forty pairs of eyes faced the westward sky at forty-five degrees, locked onto a brilliant light that made irregular jaunts toward the smaller lights.

Everyone saw it but the Monks.

"Yes, I'm getting something. I'm getting a contact . . . yes, yes." The old man was on his feet, eyes turned in his head, hands fluttering. "We are to bring the news to all resonate core." His voice shifted into a low, guttural, cracking spacespeak. "Third fleet coordinates have been set, the Starseed mothership welcomes you into our circle. We bring you the unified resolution from the outer ring. In the transcendent schools of time the fragmented systems of your stellar command have given . . ."

It was like a bad episode of *Star Trek*.

"It's coming closer, I see it." Lasasha began channeling

from command central. "Greetings my love children. We surrender our presumptions and are linked by the interstellar thread of conscious reckoning—"

"Wait. Wait. It's coming through . . . I . . . am . . . the . . . commander . . . of . . . Starseed," spoke Monique in a heavy French accent.

"No, I'm getting it too. It's . . ." A fourth contender now made contact as the lights began swarming through the skies. "Starseed command has witnessed the emerging from the seventh plane of . . ."

Jim stepped forward through the highly imaginative crowd of channelers, each channeling from their direct contact with the apparent Starseed spacecraft now hovering directly overhead. No one questioned the possibility it might be something other than spacecraft.

Jim held his single-point crystal in hand, clasped his smoky quartz and turned his eyes downward. Staring into the kiddie pool filled with lavender water, he spotted a floating Barbie doll. Jim made contact with Barbie. Her eyes, bright and ethereal, locked position with Jim.

The Starseed Mothership Space Command beamed from overhead through the lounging Barbie. Jim stood with his single-point crystal pointed at the Mattel mother lode. And then it happened. Jim's voice rose above the din of excited channel babble, short-circuiting all the contenders.

"This is Starseed Barbie. I am coming in for a landing. Prepare the way."

The crowd surged around Jim.

"What's he doing?"

"He's channeling Barbie. Starseed command has Barbie on the line and he's picked her up."

"The centralized command presence unifies and divides, adjusts and dispels, purifies and clarifies, the resonate core issue for all light workers. Listen closely. Take . . . I say . . . take a giant step back."

"What did she say?" Everyone was listening carefully.

"Barbie says . . . take a giant step back . . . on the double, kiddies!"

The crowd surged back.

"Up on your toes, hands in the air, turn in your hip, and shout . . . '*I'm square!*' " Jim was on a roll.

"*I'm square!*" they shouted in unison.

"Say, '*I'm square!*' "

"*I'm square!*" everyone repeated.

The party went crazy. Circling spacecraft, channeling

mbotherships, space fleets . . . the channelers were on crystal-powered overload as Jim the Mad Monk launched into a two-hour session with Barbstradamus.

"And I said if you can't walk a mile on six-inch stilettos, then you'll never make it on my ship. Up on those toes . . . up on those toes!" Barbie had them in her palms.

"I want to see more eye shadow. More nail extensions. And for Ken's sake, get rid of all that purple . . . we hate purple on mothership . . . *dig?*"

One by one, Barbie ran her magic as revelers dropped to the floor like flies. Jim stood over the lavender kiddie pool, with Barbie hovering overhead, channeling to his soul's delight. Channeling with the best of them.

And he outdid them all.

Jim, the Mad Monk . . . Channeling Overlord of Sedona.

At the break of dawn, August 17, the Monks and Pi loaded up Econoline and drove to Bell Rock for what promised to be the largest gathering of resonate core workers of the light.

Dressed in stock and trade white, not a lint to be found, the Monks parked on the road and trudged up the trail to join the assembling masses, there to witness the dawning of a New Era in the hopelessly complex sacred Mayan calendar.

"What if Jose was a bit off in his math, and the New Age was really in the midseventies, with the release of Lynyrd Skynyrd's 'Free Bird,' " Jim whispered.

"*Shut up!*" whispered an earnest devotee.

All along the trail were dozens of stone circles surrounded by groups of earnest seekers sitting in silence or chanting. Heading farther up, we broke from the trail and raced for the base of Bell Rock. Gaining our way through thick underbrush and cactus, the Monks finally fell into an opening where sat one humongous crystal.

"My Goddess, that must of taken an army to haul that thing up here. Well, this must be the spot," Mike surmised.

As we heard the thousands of voices echoing up the canyons and watched the ruby red cliffs come alive from the first rays of the morning sun, we put our hands on the crystal.

We closed our eyes and imagined 144,000 persons throughout the world, laying down their heads, their hearts and their little wills to a purpose greater than us all.

We felt the earth turning, we felt the sun warming, we saw the sky lighting the way. And as we looked into the heart of this crystal, we knew that here in Sedona, as throughout the world, there was but one sensible thing to do at such a moment, and that was to get down on our hands and knees, kiss our mother earth and solemnly pray that even naughty little trickster Monks had a place in God's vast carnival.

"Blessed be," said Mike.

"Blessed be," said Jim.

"Ten-four," said Pi.

Following sunrise the Monk entourage climbed Bell Rock and asked our inner guides for our higher purpose. After hours of chanting under the blazing sun, it finally came through in such crystal clarity that even Pi nodded his head in agreement. The Monks had found their Life Purpose Concept.

Mike would be the waffle king. Nurse's Aide would chase the UFOs. Nurse, as far as we knew, would remain in San Diego collecting sweaters. And Jim, bless his heart, would channel Barbie.

Yes, indeed, the New Age had arrived.

Ninety-eight waffles stood side by side as the residents of Sedona came to bid us farewell. The waffles were as hard as rocks, so most people chose to wear

them instead of eating them. Our campsite was strewn with boxes, a collapsed tent, bags of fallen apples, an assortment of gifts, and a suspicious Nurse's Aide, who had grown fond of his riverside home.

Despite our instincts, given the approaching fall and cooler weather ahead, we were headed north. Pi had persuaded us with his Take Pi to Windstar Concept. And we obliged. After all, it was part of *the plan*. Coast to coast, you know, with Snowmass, Colorado, on the way. We gazed at those red rocks as if we might never see heat again.

After a final swing through West Sedona, loading up on herbal supplements at Beverly's Market, consuming a final muffin at Food Among the Flies, we bid the sacred sandstone formations of Sedona a final teary-eyed farewell, as Jim and then Mike broke into spontaneous song.

Bye-bye, Sedona, we love your red rocks, your beautiful rivers, your mountains that talk.

Despite all the gaudy and shallow trappings of New Age hucksterism, the Monks had gotten a bit mushy over this gorgeous metaphysical mecca. As we drove into old town, past the tacky gift shops, past a cluster of bright pink Jeeps, past the illustrious Hawkeye, our hearts ached at the departure. As wacky as it was, the Harmonic Convergence had brought a large community of friends into our hearts. Now the party was over, and we mourned its passing.

Bye-bye, Sedona, we love your red rocks, your beautiful rivers, your mountains that talk.

The Monks sang with all their hearts and all their soul, shedding oceans of emotion as the Monk wagon train slowly made its way up the long steep incline of Oak Creek Canyon.

Old Econoline was definitely beyond its load limit on this trip. We had a burgeoning food supply, including the sacks of apples, a backup stash of apricots for the duck gravy and a few cartons of precious soy. Not forgetting our extra Monk, Pi, at 155 pounds with his 40 pounds of white clothes, Mike and Jim weighing in at a collective 285 pounds, the boxes of brain machines we picked up in Sedona, a new batch of herbal supplements, and Jim's high school debate papers, the van was dragging its tail pipe on the pavement as we slowly inched our way to the top of the mountain and headed for Flagstaff.

Miraculously, a wobbly Econoline made it toward the Rockies in record time, and before we knew it, Pi, who'd taken over the wheel at around three A.M., had landed us in the quiet parking spot of Lathrop State Park, near Walsenburg, Colorado.

Our first night in subfreezing temperatures wasn't too bad. We stashed Pi underneath the bed between the brain machines and his forty pounds of white clothes. Aide slept on his face, and the Monks squeezed between bags of soybeans and sacks of apples.

Early morning, still thinking it was summer, we ran down to the adjacent, high-altitude lake to go swimming. As a truckload of park maintenance men stood and stared, we dove into the icy autumn lake, blindly ignoring the crust of ice along the shore.

It was *cold.* So cold it froze the screams right out of Jim's throat. But determined not to have our fragile Monk egos defiled, especially with a truckload of macho maintenance men watching, we stayed in the cold water and swam for half an hour. As Jim stepped out of the water, he sucked in the goose bumps, tucked in his tummy and stood proudly on the beach. They looked at Jim. Jim looked at them. They looked at Jim. And then Jim fell into a shivering fit that took two hours of break dancing to thaw out.

Summer was now over. The cramped reality of traveling

**The residents of Sedona came to bid us farewell.
The waffles were as hard as rocks, so most people
chose to *wear* them instead.**

with three Monks, a cat and a vast array of worldly possessions when it's cold outside slowly sank into the Monk brain.
Months of camping with the van doors open wide and the
great outdoors as our living room had distracted us from the
fact that home was a six-by-twelve-foot metal box, with no
place to stand. Econoline seemed mighty small. By the time
we hit Pueblo, there was mutiny on the monkmobile.

As the van filled with travel clutter, it became more difficult to find things. It finally got to the point where, upon
arriving in Denver, we misplaced our dear friend Pi.

It was around midnight on our first night in the mile-high
city when we realized our fearless Sagittarian optimist was
missing from beneath the bed.

"Mike, where'd Pi go? I thought he was asleep."

The Monks were slowly cruising upper Colfax Avenue
looking for a place to park.

"What! What do you mean? He's not there?!"

Jim stuck his hand as far under the bed as he could and
came up with an apple . . . but no Pi.

"Pi, Pi, are you in there? I swear to God, Mike, he's not
here!"

"You're kidding, where could he have gotten off?"

The Monks retraced their steps and spent the next six hours driving the streets of Denver in search of Pi.

Meanwhile, Pi wandered the alleys looking for Econoline. He'd woke from a midafternoon nap in the van while the Monks were inside Federal Distress picking up twenty-five cases of Creamy Original Vitasoy, sent by our soy-milk connection in Burlingame, California. Pi decided to indulge in the local computer store around the corner and check out the hot new software. When he returned, Econoline was gone. Pi stood in the parking lot for hours while the Monks went about their business, oblivious to Pi's absence.

As soon as the sun fell beneath the Rockies, the temperature dipped below freezing. Pi, clad only in a light, white jacket, prowled Colfax down toward the State Capitol in hope of finding the Monks. Without wallet or briefcase he was formulating his new It's Not As Cold As You Think Concept beneath the Greyhound bus terminal when he first noticed Econoline turning the corner at Broadway.

"Stop!" he screamed. "Stop!" Pi sprinted after the fading taillights, but the Monks stepped on the gas on their way back to Federal Distress to resume their search all over again. Pi finally gave up and spent the night over the heating grates.

Half-starved, wild-eyed and twenty-four hours later, Pi miraculously found the van in the parking lot of the Regency Hotel. Inside the hotel the Monks were on the pay phones

A wobbly Econoline made it toward the Rockies in record time.

assembling a posse to track down Pi. Going out to a locked Econoline, Jim spotted the open window first.

"Mike, someone broke in. Look, the window. Damn it!"

"Oh, my God, the Mac!" The Monks ran toward the van filled with apprehension. "First Pi, now a break-in? This is not a good sign," said Mike.

"Bad Signs Are Good Signs Concept!" sang out a weary voice.

"Pi?"

Doors opened and there lay Pi in a white heap on the Monk futon, nursing his frostbitten fingers, but, as always, with an optimistic grin.

"Pi. Oh, my God, we thought we lost you!"

"I was not lost. Nor misplaced. Our paths simply took a different turn," he reassured us with his characteristic chuckle.

"Just don't do it again, Monks, or I'll have your balls hanging from the roof of this van!" Pi said disarmingly, but with a smile and, yes, a goofy chuckle.

"Hey, most sorry, dude," said Jim, giving Pi a hug.

"Pi, Pi, I'm so glad we found you," said Mike, giving Pi an even warmer hug.

As compensation, Pi spent the next few nights *on* the bed while the two Monks squeezed underneath. But the monastery was becoming unbearably cramped. Pi was a continuous loop of concepts and ideologies, the Monks were a continuous loop of burnt pancakes and arguments, and the friction was peeling the walls. The small nuances of three men in a small van, all clinging to their worthy causes, all consumed by their special needs, was overwhelming. Pi and his endless crusade for white, Jim and his unrelenting addiction to herbs, Mike and his long, thin arms reaching in the night toward unavailable men . . .

On the third day in Denver, for want of nothing better than a good night's sleep, the Monks asked Pi to leave. Waving Pi good-bye as he boarded the bus to Windstar, the Monks promised to join him the following week, finances permitting.

"Alright, who's going to go in, you or me?" Jim asked Mike as they sat parked outside First Interstate Bank, nine o'clock, Monday morning. "I think it's your turn for a change. I'm tired of being the fall guy."

"No way! Look at me. I look like a street person. At least you have a sweet baby face and trusting blue eyes."

"You have blue eyes!"

"But I'm bald. That cancels out the blue eyes," Mike reasoned, rubbing his shiny dome.

"But you know they'll want two pieces of ID to cash the check. I've used the lost-my-license-in-the-wash routine one too many times."

"But that's the truth!" stated Mike.

"No one believes the truth. Are you crazy?!" yelled Jim.

Mike nodded in agreement.

The Monks' checking account already had a history of mishaps, beginning with the day Mike and Jim decided to merge all their assets into one spanking new, totally balanced joint-checking system.

Considering the shape of the individual accounts, it was a wise move. During the first few months on the road the checkbook, with its slightly more than sparse deposits, was meticulously kept. The entries were dutifully entered in bold, monastic lettering. Careful records were kept of each expense.

As the months wore on, the meticulous ledger became more and more lax. Scribbles started to appear here and there. Notes to Mom, phone numbers of acupuncturists and NBA scores started showing up in the margin.

Soon the well-balanced checking account began taking on the look of the work of a mad diarist on a binge. The occasional reconciliation came more as an afterthought. Hectic life on the road left money management a low priority. The ledger was heavily marked. Bent arrows crossed to previous entries. Rearranged checks and canceled deposits became the norm. The checking account and the checkbook were a mess.

"Why do we have to keep changing banks, Mike? What ever happened to Bank of America?"

"God, Jim. Why do I have to go over this every time we hit a new state. There's no interstate banking. Get it? If we're going to stay in any one state for any length of time, and neither of us has two pieces of ID, we have to start with a local bank."

"But I have my Northwestern alumni card and my social security card."

"They just don't count."

"Why?"

Mike shrugged with a blank look on his face. "Jesus, Jim, I don't know."

With only a driver's license and a social security card

between them, the Monks had left a trail of banks from Paradise to Denver. Six bank accounts to be exact.

Each new region presented a new set of obstacles, especially when the Monks tried to cash an out-of-state check from the previous state's bank account.

"So what are we going to say?"

"We're going to go in together this time. You tell them we just had an accident. Our car was demolished and we lost everything except this one out-of-state check. We have to cash it because . . . uh, because . . . help me out here."

"Because our cat's in the hospital and needs surgery."

"No, idiot. I mean they'll naturally wonder why we don't have a bank card or credit card."

"Well, why don't we?" Jim was back to square one.

"Because the machine keeps eating our cards."

"Is that the truth or is that our story?"

"No. I mean, yes. Now you have *me* confused. Yes, that's the truth, but they eat the cards when we forget the PIN numbers."

"Well, it's not my fault we have so many PIN numbers we can't remember which card goes with which PIN number!" stated an indignant Jim.

"Oh, forget it. We'll just say we lost all our bank cards in the crash."

"What crash?" Jim was getting lost in Mike's maze.

"The crash we just had. Jeez! Now shut up till I figure this out." Mike was scheming in his head. "So, we need to cash a check to get to the airport, our bank cards are destroyed and our bank can't wire the money because we need an account here."

"Then why don't we just get an account here?" asked Jim, now totally confused.

"Oh, my god. Whose side are you on? That's exactly what we're trying *not* to do. We've had to do that the last five times this happened. I'm sick and tired of opening a bank account just so I can cash a goddamn check from another town."

"Okay. Okay. Got it. So, do you want me to go in with a limp? Should there be blood?"

"No, of course not! Shut up a minute and let me think."

"But you're going to tell them we just had an accident!"

"Yeah, but they'll call an ambulance if we're bleeding. We'll just downplay the accident. The main point is to gain their sympathy so they go ahead and cash the check."

"Okay, so I do the talking."

"Yes, Jim. You're more believable. I look like a crook."

Jim stepped back and assessed Mike's four-day beard,

crusty salt-of-the-earth disposition, skin and bone demeanor. "Yeah, you do look like a crook. You could be packing a Magnum under that jacket."

"Bug off! Let's just do it."

At ten o'clock the bank doors opened and the Monks walked in feeling like the mob en route to a heist.

The Monks herded through the ropes toward the front of the line, Jim using a slight limp to go along with the accident story.

"We just had a bad accident and our cards were eaten by your cat . . . I mean, the machine and our check, this one he's got with the old bank in Arizona, or is it the California bank?"

"What he means"—Mike took over as the incredulous teller held her finger over the red button waiting for the first sign of a gun—"is that we need to cash a check and have lost all our cards in an unfortunate accident up the street. Nothing serious, but the car caught on fire and we need to get some money to make our getaway . . . um, hmmm, I mean to make our plane that leaves in an hour for . . ."

Mike stood caught in midsentence forgetting where, if anywhere, the Monks might be flying should such a situation as the one he'd just described ever arise.

The teller smiled curtly, waiting a moment to see if a holdup note was about to be presented.

The Monks stood expectantly. Jim's mind was already on the oatmeal and raisins he'd left burning in the van. Mike was thinking his way out of this, planning to visit the bank across the street loaded with a more convincing story.

"Do you have an account with this bank?"

The dreaded question that sent terror up the Monk spine.

"Of course I don't have an account. I'm from out of state. I just want to cash this check for fifty dollars." Mike was losing his cool, a big no-no when asking favors from banks.

The teller surveyed the check and its Arizona imprint. "Do you have a driver's license?"

Oh, my God, we're in luck. She's just asking for a driver's license. She's going to do it.

Mike produced his driver's license and watched impassively as she locked her cash drawer and moved across the room to a phone. The Monks crossed their fingers as she spent over ten minutes on the phone, casting steely glances toward Mike.

"I'm sorry, sir, there aren't enough funds in this account to cash your check."

"Oh, well, why don't we just write it for thirty dollars."

"Sir, there still wouldn't be enough to cover this check. Unless you want to write it for seventy-two cents. That's all you have in your account, and that wouldn't even cover our service charge. Better take this up with your bank in Arizona," and she slapped her CLOSED sign on the counter, handing Mike his license and worthless check.

Outside the Monks raged.

"What happened to our money?" Jim demanded.

"I can't remember which bank I deposited our money into. Maybe it's all been eaten up from service charges. I can't believe it. We're flat broke," said Mike glumly.

The Monks were down to five dollars and some change. The road was looking mighty bleak for the first time since the journey began, as the mile-high winds of Denver chilled the morning air.

"What the hell are we going to do? We've got enough food and propane for one day. Maybe enough gas to get us twenty miles. But that's it. We're going to fucking starve here if we don't do something quick." Michael was on panic overload.

But Jim was calm and cool. "We'll figure something out. We always do."

Denver, being the big, polluted city that it is, posed a serious problem to survival, until Jim remembered his rare first-edition copy of H. L. Mencken's *Newspaper Days*.

An hour later Jim emerged from Isis Bookstore on Colfax still clutching his rare book but with a fistful of dollars and a wild, excited smile on his face.

"Mike, it was totally awesome. I walked in there with the book to sell and he just started shaking his head when he saw me coming. They weren't about to buy any more used books today. Didn't matter what I had on me. So I was totally mad. I just laid it on the line and told him what was up, everything we'd been doin', you know, the whole cosmic land-rover spiel, and how we're just sort of stuck here in Denver. He was like listening to me, but not listening . . . all at the same time. And then all of a sudden he bought an ad!"

"An ad? What do you mean an ad?"

"In our newsletter. He bought a fucking ad in our newsletter, Mike. Look, a hundred beanos. Can you believe it!"

Mike held the money in his hands, letting it sink in. "I don't get it. What's going on?"

"It's the No Limitations Concept, Mike. Let's stock up on food!"

. . .

The Monks were on a financial roll. After Jim returned from schmoozing half the businesses on Colfax into buying ads, Mike went shopping for our newest food obsession, Coleman's organic beef.

Strangely, just as Jim was performing t'ai chi outside Econoline, who should appear but . . .

Nurse!

Eleven hundred miles and six months after losing our neurotic mascot in the canyons of San Diego, Nurse jumped Jim in the parking lot of Denver's Rainbow Grocery. At first Jim thought he was being robbed, but when Nurse leaped into the van and began looking for wool sweaters, Jim nearly collapsed. Nurse had followed the scent, but didn't like what he smelled.

"Jeez Louise, Nurse, is that you?" No sooner had Jim bent down to talk, Nurse bolted into the great unknown, vanishing as quickly as he'd appeared.

The Monks stood dazed in the parking lot. After spending another two hours down on hands and knees looking for the great Monk mascot, the Monks resolved that if it was Nurse, and he'd traveled this far, he'd find them again.

Anything Is Possible. Anything Is Possible. Pi's concepts now burned in the Monk brain.

"Mike, you know, ever since we met Pi, life has become one incredible concept. Something's changed since we put him on that bus today. It's almost like a part of us went with him."

"Yeah, I know what you mean. I felt like a real tyrant making him leave. So what if his feet were smelly. It was all just a concept."

"Mike, what if we're overlooking the obvious. Here we are, searching for our spiritual family. But our family's right under our nose. Why'd we tell him to leave?"

"Space?"

"Who needs space? Especially from Pi. He's the third member of our tribe. Another Space Monk in training, out braving the perils of the path. In search of family. In search of community. We should *never* have told him to leave!"

How could we reconcile leaving Pi behind when he'd so willingly sought us out in Sedona? How could we forget why we traveled? Family. We're looking for family.

That night Econoline hightailed it to Snowmass to the Windstar Foundation, where we hoped to find our beloved Pi. The Monks cried and prayed that Pi, Nurse's Aide and

Nurse, their most obvious family of the moment, would forgive Mike and Jim for being such self-centered hinayanas, thinking only of their own pseudo-enlightenment.

Driving through the night, the Monks arrived early Tuesday morning. On the drive through frozen Aspen meadows, the Monks were clearing a space for our beloved Pi. Jim sorted through the books, clothes and papers, making permanent room for a third Monk. The crisp mountain air filled Econoline with the scent of pine and juniper. Up the long dirt road to Snowmass the Monks excitedly anticipated the look on Pi's face when we broke the news that he now had a permanent place in the mobile monastery.

Sure it's a bit small, but it's all yours, Pi.

Turning up the driveway, the futuristic domes of Windstar glistened in the morning frost. Pi was surely waiting at the door. Waiting for our arrival. Surely he knew we would return.

Mike stepped out of the van first. The cold air slapped his face blue. A white cloud obliterated the sunlight. Jim looked up toward the door to Windstar, leaving Nurse's Aide to warm Pi's place in the Econoline. As Jim was lifting his voice to call for Pi, the door opened.

"Good morning. Are you here to register?" A matronly face peered around the door.

"No, we're here to collect a wayward Monk." Mike came walking toward the door.

"Oh, you're at the wrong place. The monastery is up the road."

"What he means is we're looking for Pi."

"Pie?"

"Apple Pi." The Monks chimed in unison.

She stood there perplexed, considering what to offer two transients begging for food at such an early hour. Mike produced a photo of Pi.

"He's a bundle of concepts. Always wears white. Have you seen him?"

A look of recognition spread across her face. But our hearts were soon broken. Disillusioned, Pi had spent only a night. Frustrated in his attempt at converting Windstar to his All One Macintosh Concept, Pi emptied his last pocket money on airfare back to Hawaii. We'd missed him by an hour. The only trace of his presence was the white lint scattered everywhere.

Thump, thump, thump, thump, thump. The hour was still early in Roaring Fork Valley. Ten miles from Aspen, on Highway 82, the Monks were busy

lamenting Pi's departure when they were forced to make an emergency pit stop on the side of the road. While Jim meditated on the frozen tundra, Mike crawled under Econoline exploring a flat tire.

"Who put this nail in this tire?" Mike hollered.

"Wasn't me! Honest," said Jim, returning briefly from the Buddha fields.

"But look at it." Mike pointed at a three-inch nail protruding from the side of the Goodyear.

"Must've come off the fence we sideswiped back in Woody Creek. Either that or maybe when we backed into the greenhouse at Windstar. We'll have to change it. Where's the spare?"

Nearly six thousand miles since John Pillsbury sold us Econoline 100, and neither Monk had even *noticed* a spare, let alone checked to see if there was air in the existing tires.

Both Monks lay underneath on their backs looking for the spare tire, marveling at the complexity of the traveling monastery. Mike ran his finger across the smooth-as-glass rubber on the back rear flat, noticing its other three mates.

"I don't believe it, these tires are as bald as my head. And we've been driving over mountain passes!" Mike stood up, shaking his head at the realization. "We could have died!"

Jim was up on his feet searching for the spare. By now the sun was well on its way to a new day, but the ice still remained on the ground. After a thorough search of the entire underside, inside and top side of Econoline, the Monks finally stumbled across the spare tire hanging on the back door.

But finding the spare was only the first challenge. Now came the problem of removing the spare from an obstacle course of bolts, brackets, clips and fasteners. Mike produced a handy manual for the Econoline. As he read, Jim attempted to dislodge the spare. Each step seemed to further complicate the removal, requiring more elaborate tools, muscle power and dexterous moves more appropriate for a four-hundred-pound gorilla with a master's in structural engineering. Lacking the proper-size wrench, Mike finally produced a can opener and freed the final bolt with his patented limp wrist movement.

"So how do you jack this up?" Jim asked Mike.

"What jack?"

Now came the search for the elusive jack. Trying to think like engineers, the Monks used deductive reasoning in locating the jack. When that didn't work, Jim tried the Four-Hundred-Pound Gorilla Concept. The jack was quickly found.

Jim was soon down on his freezing hands and knees, icicles protruding from each nostril, furiously turning the screw of the pint-size jack . . . to no avail.

"Jim. Do you know how to jack up a car?"

Jim grunted.

"You don't know how to jack up a car, do you?"

Mike bent down and forced the jack beneath the axle and started cranking.

"Mike, I think the jack is upside down!"

Econoline was finally rising off the tundra, precariously balanced on the tip of the reversed jack, teetering from side to side. Not wanting to fool with minor success, Mike attempted to loosen the hopelessly frozen bolts. Then Jim stepped in once again with the Four-Hundred-Pound Gorilla Concept and jumped up and down on the crescent wrench until the bolts came flying off and the tire popped off into a ditch.

The Monks felt manly satisfaction creeping into their bloodstreams. The fucker was off.

After four tries at positioning the spare, Mike was finally tightening the bolts.

"Jim, I think we put it on backwards. Look at the other tires."

Jim made a careful inspection. "Ahhh, who's going to notice?"

"We will if the tire comes flying off when we're barreling seventy miles an hour down the road."

Icicles now covered Mike's face as he begrudgingly reversed the tire, tightened the bolts and cursed the day he'd decided to take home economics instead of auto shop at Castle Park High.

Two hours and twenty minutes to change a flat. Though it didn't resolve the other three totally bald treads, at least Econoline had four fully inflated tires.

The Monks stepped in raring to go.

Wha, wha, wha, wha, wha.

Wha, wha, wha, wha, wha.

"Shit, the engine won't start."

"What do you mean the engine won't start? We just put a new tire on."

"Jesus, Jim, that has nothing to do with the tire. Don't you know anything about cars?"

"Yeah!" Jim paused a second. "I know about cars. Especially older models like this. When they stop running, you sweet-talk 'em."

"Sweet-talk 'em?"

"Heh, heh. Isn't that right, Econoline?" Jim caressed the engine. "Come on hot rod, let's get those pistons pumpin'. Whaddya say, sweetheart. Jimmy's gonna give you some high octane. Just put her in gear and let's glide outta here. How 'bout it, babe?"

Econoline sat motionless in the cold morning air. It's oil pan was so dry it had canker sores. The last time either Monk had put oil in the gal was the day Mike spilled olive oil on the radiator while attempting to fry eggs on the manifold.

Econoline had long since adjusted to the lack of loving care shown by her new owners. *Yes, they pamper and polish me, scrub my walls and keep my windshield clean. Yes, they brag about me and take everyone on a tour. But check the oil? The radiator? Transmission fluid?*

Econoline silently sat in the subfreezing air, her radiator stiff from the lack of antifreeze. Her plugs cold and her battery dead.

"Mike, the lights are on. We left the lights on! Why'd we do that?"

"We? Who was driving?"

"You were, dude!"

Econoline waited patiently as the Monks made the long, cold, humiliating walk toward Woody Creek to request a jump start. Long enough to let the Monks think about their responsibilities as car owners. Long enough to let the guilt sink in.

When the Monks returned with jumper cables and a pickup, Econoline stood idling of its own accord.

The Monks jumped back.

"Who started Econoline?"

Econoline wasn't speaking. It stood shivering in the freezing air pumping warm oil through its cold metal body, impatiently waiting for the Monks to hop in.

Econoline had mountains to climb, roads to see and gas to burn. It was four-thirty in the afternoon by the time Econoline reached Denver with a failing engine and four bald tires. What better time to start our ten-hour journey across the Great Plains.

The road into Kansas was long, straight and flat. There wasn't much to it but miles of dreamy brown landscape. They said it gets more colorful in the spring, but during the winter the cemeteries seemed to stand out. They were scattered every twenty miles with huge raised marble and plaster crosses.

By the time we reached North Kansas City the temperature had dropped to two degrees. The heater had broken and the propane tank had finally reached empty.

The Monks checked into the Skyway Motel consumed with more profound quandaries, such as, "Did they or did they not wash the sheets on this bed?" We ushered in Nurse's Aide, our professional odor detector, and sure enough he spent half an hour sniffing out the sordid history of those sheets.

Needless to say we brought in our own.

The Skyway Motel was not known as a *family place*, unless *broken* families count. It had an odd assortment of Buicks, old Cadillacs and semi trucks that pulled in by ten P.M. and left by two in the morning. Drug dealers and pimps worked the laundry room, where Mike traded in two boxes of soy milk for two hits of psilocybin, the first he'd seen in twenty years.

But Jim. It was a bargain. . . . Whaddaya mean you're calling my mom, I'm a grown man.

We settled in for five frozen days, listening to the creaking

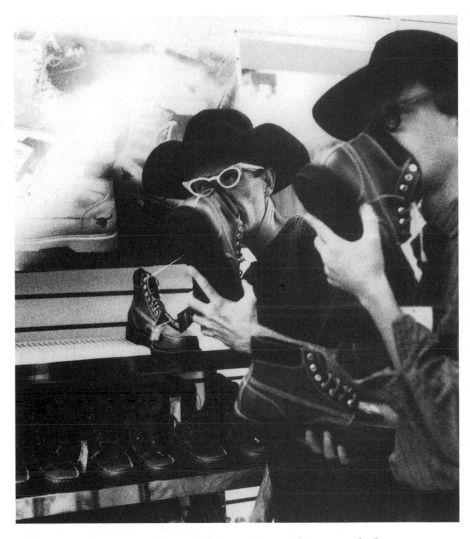

Sniffing out another K Mart blue-lite special.
(J. Deming)

beds and party girls, counting giant cockroaches on the peeling walls. Mike saved the 'shrooms for a rainy day.

The area did have its upside. For it was in North Kansas City that we discovered K Mart, the perfect place to shop. Mike was in a panic over the sad fashion state in the Monk wardrobe department. After all, we were on our way to meet *the family*. So with $90 and four days to kill before Christmas we found excellent buys for the underdressed traveler. But there were a lot more than good buys at K Mart. There was the ambience. High overhead fluorescent lights flooded the pastel pink and green fixtures as we walked across the beige linoleum floor. Convenient parking and pleasant sliding doors gave way to the thrill of knowing that whatever we came to buy would soon be forgotten as we fell under that imperceptible K Mart spell.

The departments and aisles were outfitted in postfifties suburban futurism, which appealed to our 1960s Now Generation mindset. It was all there. From the $9.95 blazing blue-lite specials to the latest designer look-alikes.

Shoes topped our agenda. The convenient self-serve men's shoe department offered an inviting array of plastic leather footwear. Jim was coerced into a $5 pair of black and white preppy loafers, while Mike found a great pair of gray plastic faux-designer walking shoes for just $4.50. But the prize was a pair of *real leather* bright yellow moccasins for only $2.50. Throw in six white tubular socks, and our footwear was handled.

The real savings came from the men's department: two acrylic sweater vests (with matching button-down shirts), a handsome polyester pink sweater that crackled with static, an artificial ikat-weave pullover and four poly/cotton trousers (five inches too big in the waist) with matching padded white jackets all for the low, low price of $76.

It took two trips to carry it all out to our van and months for the polyester fumes to die away, but we were happy with our purchase.

Our destination, Nebraska, held many disputable lures: it was in the middle of nowhere; it grew corn; it had four seasons and broad open countryside; Johnny Carson was raised though not born there; its capital city, Lincoln, was home of Bob Devaney, former coach of the Nebraska Cornhuskers, who once shook hands with Jim when Jim's mom was chairman of the Symphony Guild; its biggest city, Omaha, is the home of Mutual of Omaha Life Insurance (remember *Wild Kingdom?*), and it is the birthplace of Gerald Ford, Marlon Brando, Bob Gibson, Warren Buffett, and most importantly, Jim's family, who were expecting us for dinner.

It wasn't the first time they were expecting us for dinner. On the first occasion we simply didn't know of our dinner date until a month later (due to a slow postal service). But on this occasion as we were cruising up Highway 29 outside Hamburg, Iowa, a funny thing happened. Even though the van was moving, the engine was not turning. Suddenly with a loud bang came that horrible smell of burning wires and hot metal. As the odometer turned past 167,000 miles, we quietly coasted to the side of the road . . . the *freezing* road.

"I smell something burning!" yelled a sleeping Jim from beneath boxes of soy milk.

"Must be another tire!" Mike guessed.

The grumbling Monks donned their caps and ventured outside. Jim kicked at the tires while Mike poked at the engine with a stick.

"Jim, what's this hamburger doing up here?" A month's supply of choice organic Coleman's beef was tied to the radiator.

"Oh, my God, we forgot to bring in the hamburger we hung out in Colorado to keep cold." The neatly tied one-pound packages of beef were shredded from the wind *and* miniature burgerettes littered the engine as the Monks looked in on the feast.

"Looks like Econoline OD'd on beef."

"Well, he's certainly getting into the Nebraska carnivore spirit."

But Econoline didn't look too happy. And despite Jim's sweet-talking, the van wouldn't budge another mile.

A few passing truckers might have taken note of two very tall, lanky, urban, white, nonmechanical, underdressed Monks trudging up the highway toward a small truck-stop café. But what they didn't notice was the five-inch icicles hanging out of our nostrils as the sixty-below windchill and thirty-mile-per-hour wind blew us to the oasis of warmth called the Sunnyside Café.

Our short little twenty-minute stroll off the freeway had turned us into two raving-mad, shivering, hysterical cavemen. As we burst through the door, ice fell from our nostrils. We didn't wait to be seated, but headed straight for the heat.

Our little waitress and the half dozen other folk chowing down in this fine establishment of Iowan dining didn't seem to appreciate the dilemma we were in, or the fact that our toes, fingers, ears and noses were *purple*.

We were curtly instructed to move from behind the cash register where the small Sears Roebuck electric, twenty-four-inch coil space heater blazed its golden orange heat upon our thawing digits. Still frozen, we telephoned the only available tow service in town and waited over by the Indian jewelry and the stuffed animals.

Within thirty minutes good ole Earl the tow truck driver was hauling us twenty miles down the *wrong* side of the freeway (for a mere $50 bucks) into another mounting blizzard, where he kindly deposited us at the Trail's End Motel, right across the street from the only repair shop within twenty miles. After Earl pulled away, we discovered that the garage was closed until Monday. So we dutifully called home to cancel the Christmas dinner date.

Monday morning at the crack of dawn the Monks were up waiting for the mechanics. We soon discovered they only serviced semis.

Eighty miles from Omaha and no mechanic! And the folks were expecting us for another dinner. We had to take drastic action or we might never be invited back again.

Michael hastily finished his two sunny-side factory-farmed eggs he was trying to wolf down in the adjacent Hen House Café. And an hour later Earl the tow truck driver was once again towing old Econoline up Highway 29 to the Big O.

"Think we're going to have to buy another van?" Jim asked Earl as the truck bounced up and down, up and down in the road, heaving its way over the blasting noise of a crackling CB, intermingled with bad pop music and breaks for KFAB news.

"Can't say. Could be a lotta things," Earl shouted over the noise in perfect synch with another bump.

"How much does a tow truck cost?" Mike loudly queried from the back, admiring Earl's eight cylinders, low gears and working heater.

Jim looked at Mike. "God, that'd be perfect! We should just buy a tow truck and tow ourselves around the country. Think of all the wear and tear we'd save on Econoline."

"Kay F Aay Beeee . . . Sports!" the noxiously saccharine radio chorus chimed in.

"We'd never have to worry about the van breaking down. We'll just tow ourselves coast to coast," Mike added loudly.

Earl declined comment, keeping his eyes focused dead ahead, occasionally checking his sideview mirror to see if Econoline was still attached.

"The Kay F Aay Bee Sportstime is . . . one o'clock! . . . Kay F Aay Bee Sports is brought to you by your friends at O'Brien's Furniture. Four locations throughout Huskerland to serve you better."

Earl kept riding the bumps like an old rodeo hand as Mike and Jim rode the surges like a carnival ride, almost hitting the ceiling with every bump.

"Hi, this is Mike Root for O'Brien's Furniture. When I

was in high school here in Omaha, I had a debate partner who never understood the meaning of comfort . . ."

"Kay F Aay Beeee . . . Sports!"

Earl dropped the Monks and Econoline at John Markel Ford during the early afternoon. Sunny weather, but still incredibly cold. It looked like a simple repair job, but since they had to order the part, we loaded everything into a rented white van and drove off to the Holiday Inn.

By now we were becoming quite accustomed to lodging. First the Skyway, then Trail's End and now Holiday Inn.

Though it was not our style, at a temperature of fifty below zero even the best of Monks resort to creature comforts. However, the Holiday Inn imposed a special problem for certain *other* creatures, such as Nurse's Aide, whom we surreptitiously sneaked past the front desk.

For this escapade Michael elected to use the handy nylon duffel bag stuffed with two goose-down pillows and one very recalcitrant cat. Aide not only threw a kitty tantrum, but his litter box, which Mike had forced into a suitcase, left a pungent odor as we wheeled our luggage through the lobby.

Despite these inconveniences, Jim Monk was overjoyed to be in Nebraska. In fact, being back in the land of his birth brought back many old patterns for Jim. For instance, within hours of our arrival he had to show all of his favorite childhood haunts to Mike: Varly Drugs (Jim bought baseball cards here); Christ the Queen grade school, where Jim almost threw in a full-court bucket at the buzzer to defeat arch grade-school rival St. Robert's; his boyhood newspaper route (where Jim loved to deliver but failed to collect); the now defunct Phillips 66 service station (where Jim picked up his weekly bookie sheets before his dermatologist dad abruptly put an end to the hobby); Creighton Prep, the all-male Jesuit high school where people actually remembered that Jim was once a two-time state master debate champion; and last, but certainly not least, his glorious family.

Jim's family were not Michael's in-laws, not by any stretch. We wouldn't subject them to that role, and besides, they were much nicer than one would expect in-laws to be. But since Jim and Michael had lived and traveled together, mutually shared everything from smelly socks to empty bank accounts, then by default that qualified Jim's parents as in-laws.

The dinner that night with the *in-laws* was an informal

affair. Undoubtably the atmosphere might have been a bit tense, what with two missed dinner engagements and the questionable wisdom of inviting two frozen, very hungry road warriors in off the street into one of Omaha's finer homes. But the Monks behaved, showered, shaved, and wore their best K Mart garb to the Dick & Bev estate.

It was an auspicious moment as the Monks drove up Noah Worcester Drive in their rental van. Jim was at the wheel, while Michael practiced, "Hello, so pleased to meet you, what about them Huskers? . . . Hello, so pleased to meet you, what about them Huskers?"

"Shut up, Mike. You sound like a broken Lyle Bremser record," said a noticeably tense Jim, who was rehearsing his new improved politically correct mantras guaranteed to stir fierce emotional debate with his highly opinionated and levelheaded mom, the one debate foe he'd never been able to vanquish.

Two and a half years since the Jimster had rolled through his old stomping grounds, and he wanted to make double sure he left a firm impression that he had become his own man and traveled in reasonably good company.

"Mike, don't wear your shirt like that. You look much better with it open. No one buttons their top button."

"Lay off. It's freezing."

"Why don't you ever listen to me? Why'd you buy those tacky shoes? You look like a fairy in yellow moccasins. It's the middle of winter, maaan. Not even my tackiest friends wear green pants in winter. You belong on a golf course."

"What's wrong with fairies? And anyhow, you said they *lived* on a golf course."

"But it doesn't mean you come dressed for the eighteenth hole. And what did you put on your face?" Jim looked at Mike again, narrowly missing a parked car.

"Jeez, Jim. Watch where you're going. It's just a little rouge and eyeliner. I had to do something with this face. C'mon, I'm just trying to make a good impression."

"A good impression!" The car screeched to a halt a block away on the tree-lined Noah Worcester Drive. "They're going to think you're a total queen. How do you think that's going to make me look?"

"Chill out, man. I'm only a part-time queen. And what's that have to do with you? They don't have anything to worry about."

"They're *totally* worried."

"About what?" Mike furled his brow.

"I told them we were lovers!"

"You what?" Michael fell back against the seat.

"You heard me . . . lovers."

"Lovers?"

"Yes!" Jim drove it home.

"You told your parents we were lovers. Why didn't you tell *me?*"

"Well, I just didn't get around to it. Besides, that's what you told *your family.*"

"But that was different. And to think, sharing the same bed and *I'm* the last to know," Mike cackled.

"What was so different about your family?"

"Well, uh," Michael searched. "It was *totally* different. They already knew *my* story. I just wanted them to confront their fears by seeing me *with* someone for a change."

"Well, that's what I want. My whole adult life has been about challenging my family to go beyond their prejudices and narrow preconceptions. Whether they like it or not, that's my function—to push their buttons so they'll stretch and grow. So, this is their latest hurdle—I told them you're my lover."

"Oh, really? So what am I supposed to be, a guy or a girl? What kind of lover did you tell them I was? If it's a babe, you sure don't give a girl much time. I didn't even bring a dress."

"Don't be absurd. You're supposed to be a boy."

"I wish you'd warned me. I'm not sure if I'm ready to receive their wrath for corrupting their Roman Catholic son!"

"Come on, Mike. I've told them a lot about you. Like you're just a normal, trustworthy, totally sincere, likable, gentle guy, who happens to have saved me from a life of isolated, solipsistic, self-abnegating torment."

"Normal? You're trying to pass me, a homeless monk who lives out of a van, sees angels, believes in ETs, prefers soy milk to good wine and is presently carrying two hits of psilocybin as normal? I think I have a headache." Michael reached into his coat pocket. "I'm feeling about as normal as a pro-choice feminist at a Knights of Columbus convention."

"But you really aren't that much different from—"

"No one's called me normal in years. Let's see, I think it was back in 1965 when I told Ruth Hayes I'd prefer doing my algebra homework to sucking juicy fruit gum out of her you know what."

"Come on, buddy. It's a compliment," Jim pleaded.

"Maybe it is. I'm deeply touched. I just never thought I'd

see the day." Michael took out a small capsule from his pocket, held it up to the window, flashed a smile at Jim and said, "Here's to normalcy," and popped it down his throat.

"Jeez Louise, what are you doing!" Jim lunged for Mike's hand a bit too late.

"I was feeling a bit tense. Just needed a little something to get normal on. Don't worry. You can join me. There's more where that came from."

Jim sat with his mouth open. "Did you just take mushrooms?"

"Oh, stop it. You're late as usual. Dinner is waiting. Let me get myself psychically attuned to this sudden new change in our relationship. I promise everything will be just fine."

The Dick and Bev estate sat up off the street overlooking the wooded acreage leading down to the golf course. Leafless trees cast their long winter shadows across the street. A row of elegant spotlights bordered the winding driveway.

Jim drove up the drive taking long, deep breaths, casting sidelong glances at Mike, who slouched calmly in the seat with a crazy smile across his face. His top button remained buttoned.

As Jim parked the van below the garage, the outdoor lights automatically switched on, flooding the parking area. The house stood like an ominous brown beast in the woods, its multitiered floors sparkling in the evening glow.

"Wow, your parents live here?" Mike gazed at the palatial estate.

Jim opened his door and sat down on the concrete driveway going for one last "Get Psyched to Meet the Parents" meditation. He sat in full lotus, hands clasped on his knees, chanting low Korean chants, stirring the attention of neighborhood alarm systems.

The door to the house opened and a blond head peered out.

"Jim?" a mother's voice sang out. "Jim? Honey, we're about to say grace. Are you coming in?"

Suddenly Jim sprang into action, shutting his door, racing around the van, pulling out Michael and stepping toward the blinding white lights and the voice of Big Mother calling at the large front door.

"Hi, Bev," Jim sang out in rote merriment as he exchanged air kisses with the mom and a hearty handshake with the dad.

"Hi, honey. Oh, my, don't you look nice. You know we were about to sit. Mar couldn't come, do you have anything to bring in, here, you can put your coat here, yes and hello, Michael." Bev extended her hand to an eager Monk.

It was a one-act play, and the stage was set. Inside, the lights swarmed like insects around the Monks as they stood caught in a busy swirl of beaming faces, flashing cameras, loud TV, requests, questions and directives. Dancing prisms from the beveled windows caught the corner of Mike's eye as he stood transfixed on the sky domes leading up to the stars.

Bev led the Monks from the front foyer through the immaculately clean kitchen, where spread a hearty five-course Midwestern meal on the open bar.

"Hope you don't mind, we're doing buffet in here tonight. We've been formal all week. Are you hungry?" Bev looked expectantly toward Mike, with a nervous side glance toward Jim.

The "informal" setting on the "informal" side of the house somehow struck Michael as quite *formal*. Meticulously placed silver and crystal glistened in the bright light. Candles illuminated the recently polished brass. The cloth napkins lay artfully folded over each place setting. Even the chairs matched. Mike was following the floral patterns off the upholstery onto the floor and up the walls. Mike hadn't actually thought about the physicality of eating and had lost his appetite. Jim? Well, Jim might have preferred to wander down to his old basement hideaway and gorge on Cap'n Crunch while sorting through debate cards had it been twelve years previous.

"Sure, sure. Great. What do we have?" Jim's lightning-speed macroneurotic brain had already scoped out the politically incorrect microwave, packaged food, sugar-laden dessert . . . "Mike's really hungry, he'll have something," passing the ball back to Mike, who was suddenly absorbed in a clever ceramic elephant set off the kitchen. In fact, elephants seemed to be everywhere.

"God. Look at these." Mike's mind wandered off. "What a beast!"

The conversation raced for a center as Dr. Crotty approached Michael with a warm, generous smile. "So, Michael, I understand you took 70 from Denver to Kansas City."

"Uh, yes, that's right, Doctor. Then we, uh, took I-29 to Oz."

"He means Omaha!" Jim peeked around Bev, who was showing Jim stacks of photos from the Christmas he had just missed. Bev takes lots of photos—over three thousand per year Jim once calculated—piled into over fifty scrapbooks with names like *1954–1958: The Good Ole Days.* Jim was born in 1959.

"Uh-huh. Well, that's a good way. I guess you could also have gone 76 up to Julesburg and caught 80 all the way in."

"Yeah, but we wanted to score in Kansas City."

"Oh, sure, I see. Now where are you fellas heading next?"

Jim stumbled toward Mike hoping to intercept, but Mike took the conversational ball. "Well, looks like we'll head for something totally different because all roads lead nowhere, yet somewhere, I guess, if you let them take you by surprise . . ."

"Texas, Dad. We'll go to Texas," Jim threw in, rescuing Mike from an early turnover.

"That's smart. Well, I suppose then you'll hook up with 35 in Des Moines and head through KC, then Wichita and on down."

"Texas," Michael muttered as his head began to swirl. *How'd we get to Texas?*

"Actually, Dad," said older brother Christopher, "they could just as easily take 29 down to KC and then hook up with 35 there."

"Yeah, that'll work," affirmed Dad.

Bev was beginning to corral everyone through the buffet and toward our assigned seats at the table. Chris was to sit next to oldest brother Rick, who was upstairs watching the all-important NAIA Division 23 volleyball game, Mike was to sit next to Dad, who was to sit next Jim, who was to sit next to . . .

"So, Jim, I know you don't eat meat, so I cooked chicken. Hope that's alright."

Jim's macroneurotic alarm went off, and he started to grill Bev on the source of the chicken, whether it was fed organic grain, whether it was allowed to roam free, whether the chicken farmers used steroids as a growth stimulant, when he caught himself realizing that even if Shelton's organic chickens were sold in Omaha, chances are Bev wouldn't be baking one here.

"Great, Mom, that's really great. That's nice of you to think of me."

"And I know you like brown rice," said Bev warmly, pulling the Uncle Ben's out of the microwave.

"Yeah, that's true, Michael. I've never traveled Twenty-nine this time of year much. You know if you go through Des Moines, there's a heck of a restaurant just outside town. Shoot, what's the name of that place? I'll remember."

"Mary Lou's Psychedelic Safari?" Michael ventured, settling himself down at the table with an anorexic portion of food, which he'd cleverly arranged in the shape of an elephant.

"Well, no, don't think that's it. What part of Texas you headin' for?" Dad continued.

"Well, Doctor, I guess we'll go where they grow the ten-gallon hats under the noonday sun," Mike spoke over his chicken.

"*Ho, ho, ho!*" The doctor exploded with an earth-shattering guffaw, rattling Bev's carefully laid table settings. "Ten-gallon hats under the noonday sun. *Ho, ho, ho!* Pretty good, Mike, pretty good for you."

Jim got the mental nod from Mom. *Your friend dresses strange, but he's funny. What does his family do?*

"We haven't thought that far ahead," Jim deferentially replied, trying to keep the cutting board from falling.

"Here, honey, before I forget, let's get a shot of you with the chicken." Jim posed with the dead bird. "Oh, isn't that a scream." The camera clicked, but no flash. "It didn't flash? Oh, shoot. I'll fix it later. C'mon."

"Well, I suppose if you catch Thirty-five you'll end up in Dallas. Bev and I have some good friends there. Bev, what's that nice restaurant we liked so much in Dallas?"

"Oh, gad, my memory's so bad, Dick. Oh, what's its name. We liked it so much," Bev yelled from the kitchen.

The rest of the family now joined Dad and Mike at the table. Dad quickly calmed himself and said a short grace as Jim mouthed a silent *Stop it* to Michael, who sat smiling into his napkin.

"Lord, we thank you for this food. We thank you for our health and our beautiful home. We thank you for our loving family. We're so happy to have Jim and his nice friend Michael with us here today. And we hope they have a safe and creative journey together. . . . In the name of the Father, Son and Holy Spirit."

"Amen."

In less than thirty seconds Jim's father had healed twenty-five years of heartache. Jim turned to the doctor and gave his large gentle hand a good loving squeeze.

"So, Michael," the buzz resumed, "tell us about your travels. . . ."

The advantages of having *in-laws* became obvious to Michael Monk through the course of the evening. There was the thrill of having a whole new family without seventeen years of rooming together. Each in-law was obligated to like

Mike whether Mike was likable or not. And they all paid rapt attention to his disjointed stories, however inane, asking about family history, however dull, and complimenting Michael's taste in clothing, however tacky.

Jim knew the family was aiming to please, determined to show they were *not homophobic.*

With this as a backdrop, Michael threw caution to the wind and was soon nose to nose with Bev discussing the nuances of her youngest and most confusing son, Jim.

"And has he been eating?" Bev asked. "He gets so wrapped up in these exotic diets."

Michael's mind stuck on the word *exotic.* "We eat lots of apricot duck gravy, it's totally wild," Michael reminisced.

Bev probed on. "Does he ever eat meat? I just can't believe he doesn't crave red meat."

"You see, you take the duck and cook it in a pan . . ."

"He used to get so mad at me when I used sugar in *anything* . . ."

"Feed the duck to the cats, but save the fat . . ."

"And then I'll never forget the time he would only eat raw foods, he wanted to juice everything . . ."

"And add three cups of brown-rice flour to the fat, stir it over a low flame until crumbly . . ."

"A month later he was telling me to pressure-cook everything . . ."

"Then dump in the apricots, mustard, lemon—it's a duck-fat dream come true."

"And then he said chew every bite fifty times."

The parallel universe of Mike and Bev. The woven tapestries of parallel minds orbiting around Gemini Jim.

A final more dubious advantage of having in-laws was all of the unsolicited advice that was generously proffered. Advice that a now totally amiable Michael took in as sacred truth.

As self-respecting Nebraska in-laws, ample opinions were offered on sound Republican investments, good local mechanics, must-see mainstream films, winning Catholic football teams, travel destinations, how to get to travel destinations, favorite restaurants to sample en route to travel destinations, how to return from travel destinations, and most importantly, health, especially coming from a family full of doctors.

"Oh, Jimmy, your left hand is breaking out. Looks like neurodermatitis of some sort. What do you say Christopher?" said Dad, holding out Jim's hands for inspection.

"Well, Dad, it looks as if there are indeed some neurodermatitislike eruptions, but the pruritic erythematous rash involving the fingers, which also have some eczematous qualities, and the vesicular rash on the palms lead me to believe it might be some form of irritant-contact dermatitis."

"Good point, Christo. Yet the neurodermatitis appearance combined with the eczematous eruptions might indicate impetigo or even fungus tinea manum, don't you think?"

Michael's head bobbed like an Indian pundit agreeing to every word spoken.

"I think I'd rule out impetigo, Dad, in favor of maybe some hand psoriasis, though again I wouldn't exclude entirely the irritant-contact derm."

"I see," said Dad, still holding Jim's hand.

"But Dad—" Jim tried to interrupt.

"So what do you think, Christopher—cool, wet dressings with corticosteroid creams?"

"Sure, I'd go with the soak and corticosteroids, though because the skin is open and broken, we might want to use oral antibiotics."

"Probably an oral corticosteroid like oral Prednisone?"

"But Dad—" Jim tried to butt in again.

"That'd be good. And then maybe a systemic intramuscular corticosteroid like Kenalog."

"And maybe some topical antibiotics," added Dr. Dad.

"Looks hereditary, what do ya think, Dad?" asked Dr. Christopher.

"Oh, yeah, on Bev's side. I see a clear predisposition to getting hand eczema, no question about it."

"But Dad, this all happened only yesterday when I accidentally stuck my hand into some RV waste dissolver," Jim interjected finally.

"Oh, Jimmy, that wouldn't do it," said Dad with a laugh. "Hereditary, right, Chris?"

"Purely hereditary, Jimmy," added Christopher. "Oh, I suppose some overexposure to an irritant like the formaldehyde in the waste dissolver could trigger it, but I'd say it would be very insignificant in the overall etiological assessment."

"It's okay, Jimbo Petro, you just come down to the office and we'll fix you up. You won't notice a thing, buddy."

"Dad, I think I'm going to just go with some salt packs and Aloe Vera, and stay away from the waste dissolver."

"You just come down to the office. My assistant, Col, will set you up."

"Here, Jimmy, let's get a shot of your hand," said Bev. On cue Jim proudly displayed his decomposing fingers and palm. Bev clicked the camera, but no flash. "Oh, what in the Sam Hill, this flash again! Never mind."

"So, Michael, I guess then from Dallas you'll want to hit Houston. So that's Forty-five, if I remember. I think that's right. Here, let's go look at the atlas up in the den." And the Monks followed Dr. Crotty away from the table, Jim saving his food *to go* under the ever-watchful eye of Mom.

The Monks left around ten. Mike had lost himself in the basement, stumbling upon volume after volume of family scrapbooks, films, trophies, and framed photos, learning everything there was to know about Jim's rather illustrious past.

Jim had spent the evening male bonding in the library rooting for the local basketball favorite, while espousing his so-left-he's-right political views to his so-right-they're-left parents.

"You really blew it, Mike. I can't believe you took psilocybin to meet my parents. You were totally screwed up."

"Give me a break. I wasn't on mushrooms."

"I saw you. Right here in the van, you popped a tab."

"That was blue-green algae. Not mushrooms. Are you crazy?"

"What!" Jim didn't believe him.

"I told you I was feeling tense. I just needed a little help."

"Why were you so spaced-out?"

"Like I said . . . I took blue-green algae. Why? What did your parents say?"

"They thought you were good for me. Bev thought you were very normal, but a bit preoccupied."

On Super Bowl Sunday we picked up our van from John Markel Ford. The new distributor cap was only the tip of the iceberg, and we were advised that we might want to explore the possibility of buying a new van.

"Look's like you been hauling an awful lot of weight around for something that old. I'd start looking," spoke the mechanic.

"Get rid of Econoline? Never!" The Monks were far from ready to bury our beloved ton of metal.

"We're a family. You, me, Aide and Econoline. We stick

together. It's coast to coast. Right, Econoline?" Jim used his compassionate car dealer spiel.

Econoline softly purred as her engine hummed after a grateful rest from the road and a fresh case of oil in her bowels.

"Mike, I want to drive down to Lincoln and show you the heart of Cornhusker Country. And while we're there, we'll get Econoline a new set of tires. That should cheer her up." Jim was feeling spend-happy from his Christmas bounty. During the drive to Lincoln, Nebraska, old Econoline sped along with its nose to the road sinking under the ever-increasing load.

It was life with the Monks.

Was it worth it? Before Monks (BM to Econoline) life had been a dull excursion to Mexico once a year with Mr. Pillsbury. Now, here she was, a van of the road. She'd rolled across it all. West Coast beaches, deserts full of bloom, high mountain passes, plains of corn and wheat that stretched to the horizon. She'd seen more in her short life with the Monks than most Ford vans see in a lifetime.

Econoline felt pride.

But then again most vans didn't have the headaches old Econoline endured. Sure, she could overlook the lack of oil and water, bald tires and rusted fenders. And she might even let go of the way the Monks rode the clutch. Sometimes the extra weight did get a bit overwhelming, but better to be weighed down than be sold for scrap.

Econoline chugged on.

Then again. Why did the Monks always insist on driving her on empty? And why did they never change the filters? Let alone chip in on a new cold-weather battery. What was this, spending all the Monk funds on food and nothing on old Econoline? Not even some new blades for the windshield!

Econoline sputtered.

Come to think of it, when was the last time the Monks fed her some high octane? That Jim was always full of sweet talk, but he never delivered. And Mike, he was always bragging what a hotshot driver he was and he couldn't even change a spark plug.

Econoline wheezed.

In fact, the Monks would just as soon be flying to Mars. Old Econoline is just a stepping-stone. Just another ton of metal, subservient to the whims of irresponsible Monkees.

.   .   .

"I smell something burning." Jim was wrestling in the back with Nurse's Aide. Mike looked to his left and saw black oil squirting out the side. The inside seam below the dashboard was emitting toxic fumes. Five minutes outside Lincoln and Econoline began smoking, rattling and shaking so furiously the Monks were holding on for life. Jim desperately held on to the cupboard. Mike wrestled with the steering wheel as he coaxed Econoline off the freeway, down an exit, and through a stop sign. And with a final bang and a whimper Econoline coasted to a stop outside the Waverly Farms truck-stop café.

This time it looked fatal. Oil oozed out the bottom, and thick black smoke drifted out the tail. As we sat there in yet another fifty-below windchill, Econoline popped a dozen sparks, shimmied in the wind and then burped a puff of green smoke out the front.

The Monks sat there speechless. Aide crawled behind the soy milk.

"What'd you do?" Jim glared at Mike.

"Nothing!"

"Shit, this place smells bad. I'm getting out of here," said Jim the self-preservationist, stepping over oozing oil and grease.

And then, as if in agreement, the driver's door fell off its hinge in one last heroic gesture.

"Econoline?" Jim was down on his knees holding the door in his arms. "My God, my God, Mike, call an ambulance!"

Lincoln Salvage and Towing took an hour to arrive. The driver, dressed in gray overalls and the requisite John Deere cap, pronounced Econoline dead on arrival.

The Monks were devastated. Jim stood sobbing by Econoline as Michael signed the death certificate and formalized plans for a speedy burial.

"Jim, it looks pretty bad. We're going to have to have her put away. The driver says he'll take her down to the salvage yard."

"Salvage yard!" Jim couldn't handle it. "My van is not going down to a salvage yard! I'm burying her in Paradise. That's where she's from."

"Come on. Where are you going to get the money to do that? It'll cost a fortune to ship her back to California. This is where she died. She'd want it this way."

"How much is he going to charge us?" Jim asked, looking suspiciously at the salvage man. Nurse's Aide was sniffling back tears inside the van. The motorized matriarch of our family unit was broken and destroyed.

"He's not going to charge. He'll pay us fifty dollars."

"He'll *pay* us?" Jim wiped his tears.

"Well, of course, he'll be able to sell it for . . ." Michael decided against disclosing the hard reality of dead vans. "She'll have a proper burial there. The man said he'd make sure Econoline would be well taken care of."

The Monks painfully signed the papers and hopped inside their old, dear friend for one last ride, as Lincoln Salvage and Towing hooked up Econoline and headed for town.

The ride toward the Lincoln Salvage burial ground was one of the saddest rides we'd ever taken. The Monks and Nurse's Aide took one last look at their blessed ton of metal. All the nooks and crannies, the miniature book shelves, the pint-size stove, water pump, the cupboards and bed. The familiar front seats that had comforted the Monks for thousands of miles, the old sun-cracked dash, the well-worn and loved radio, the ash paneling, the tacky floral curtains and the slop-house carpet that held in its toxic shag fibers a memory of every meal the Monks had ever cooked.

At the salvage yard the Monks unloaded every box, bowl and carton, piling every worldly possession in a big heap on the side of the road. Nurse's Aide stood dutifully by its side as Jim and Mike accepted the fifty-dollar payment for delivering their baby to the undertakers.

In a ceremonial march to the junkyard, a Monk on either side of the van, we chanted a Tibetan motor mantra for auto-body experiences, as the limping remains of Econoline rolled toward their final resting place beside a thirty-foot yellow school bus and a green Ford station wagon. In the frigid winter air, Preacher Jim performed the last rites.

"Econoline 100. Born January first, 1972. Passed away on Super Bowl Sunday, 1988. One hundred sixty-seven thousand and ninety-nine miles she traveled, leaving behind two Monks, two cats, and a few thousand surviving relatives. She was the first Monkmobile and home of the world's first mobile publishing house. She liked to drive and was not a complainer. Many commented on her endurance and stamina. We are happy now she will return to her rightful place in that great vehicular heaven in the sky. Econoline 100, God bless you. You were gentle, friendly and strong. Your devoted passengers, the Monks."

"Amen," said Mike.

"Amen," said Aide.

Good-bye, Econoline.

"Amen," said the Lincoln Salvage undertaker.

And silently, tearfully, the Monks and Nurse's Aide shuffled away from Lincoln Salvage and Towing.

It took two cabs to haul the Monks and Monk stuff into town. The cabbies weren't too pleased at the prospect, especially when they learned we didn't have a destination.

"Hey, Mike, what if we just finish this trip in a cab. We could cab across America. What do you think?"

Michael was already thinking of all the reasons this *wouldn't* work, starting with his patented "And how are you going to pay for it?" refrain, when the cabby gave the idea a big thumbs-down anyway.

After a hefty debate in the chilling wind, the Monks, realizing they were now homeless, decided they needed another home on wheels. That's when it hit us. Why buy another small, crowded van? Why not go for one of the big guys? Something like a class-A motor home!

Well, it didn't start out that way. As the cabs dropped us off at Leach Camper Sales in downtown Lincoln, it seemed as if the spirit of old Econoline was speaking through us. With due respect to Econoline we looked at a few *new* Econoline Fords, not much bigger than our old one. We conjectured that maybe cute and funky Econoline would simply resurrect in another Ford body.

As the sales staff kept their distance from the desperate carpetbagging Monks and their ton of stuff, Mike and Jim bounced from camper to van and back again. But once we stepped into a class A, our horizon expanded. If the spirit of Econoline had re-in-*car*-nated, she definitely wanted to enter a more luxurious vehicle this time around. . . .

Yes, a class A was just the ticket.

Recreational vehicles seemed very sporty. The idea was simple. Take everything you had at home, miniaturize it, put in four cheap walls, engine and tires and you had an RV. It was a condo on wheels—perfect for the camper who liked to watch other people camping from the comfort of his particleboard home.

The Monks' winner was Fleetwood's goofy Bounder. That's because underneath were yards of basement storage, making the Bounder the tallest and roomiest RV on the road. At eleven feet six inches tall, with cute but tacky kangaroo decals on the front, back and side, it took on more of a frumpy bread-truck appearance, but then again, that's why we liked it.

Hello, Bounder. (*J. Deming*)

At least two Bounder compartments were big enough to store a tall person, as long as they didn't need to turn or breathe. Wall-to-wall carpeting and cute little lights made each compartment clean and accessible.

Once inside, it was just like home (well, some people's homes). The Monks chose the twenty-six-foot model because it was the shortest of them all, which gave greater maneuverability on those kamikaze expeditions to big cities. It came complete with a queen-size bed in back, a full kitchen, bath and ample closet space (for the monk who must take it all with him). It had a furnace, hot-water heater and plenty of mirrors to look at yourself (very important in the Monk monastery).

With a ninety-gallon gas tank and an engine clocking in at a whopping six miles per gallon, it was our sole concession to fossil-fuel waste. We installed solar panels to run everything else.

Though they said it slept three, Mike calculated fifteen if you counted all the floor space, the bathtub, the basement storage and the roof. And in the case of smuggling illegal

Taking Bounder for a drink.

Monks you could probably manage about nine more (if they were really, really thin).

All in all, it was set up for total self-sufficiency (at least three days at a time) before you had to start worrying about refills and dumping.

After two test drives and four stiff hours of debate:

"How are we going to pay for this?"

"We'll just get a loan."

"But how are we going to do that?"

"Get our parents to cosign!"

We drove away with our new Monkmobile onto the freezing highways of Nebraska. Having stashed our piles of boxes, bags, clothes, dishes, books, brain machines, cases of herbal supplements and remaining cases of soy milk underneath, the Monks at last had room to breathe.

And as if by Bounder magic, on our last day of RV boot-camp training on the icy streets of Omaha, Jim hit a windfall as he unloaded three boxes of used rare cookbooks at an Old Market bookstore in exchange for fistfuls of cash. Since the winds of winter were upon us, the Monks were now raring to see America in their new home. We camped on Cutis Lake near the Crotty estate, with plans to leave the next day.

That night Mike had a prophetic dream that Nurse was rustling dolphins off the shores of Houston, with Jim singing that old familiar tune . . . "Deep in the Heart of Texas."

On the last day in Omaha the Monks swung by Jim's parents to load up half a ton of Jim's old scrapbooks... "Jimmy dear, would you mind taking these?

They've been down here for ages and I need the space for Ritchie's train set."

"*Não problema*, Bevie, we'll just store 'em under the sex toys."

... and finally, at long last, headed south toward ... yep, yee-haw, ride 'em cowmonk, you betcha, all right now, whooooeeeeee, you got it, partner, gosh darn it, yep, yep, yep! ... the Texas state line. The Monks felt obliged to see Longhorn Country since Jim's spontaneous announcement at the dinner table that Texas was our next destination.

Coast to coast. That's the plan. Just not in a straight line.

But gosh, it takes a long time to get to Texas.

In Oklahoma we started to pick up a bit of warmth and a semblance of Southern drawl. Jim, being the easily influenced Gemini that he is, immediately switched from the witty and affable self he reacquired back home in Omaha to a slower, more deliberate perversion of Southern twang, though it was painfully obvious to any true-blue Southerner that Jim was just a nice kid from up north.

We passed through Tulsa and Oklahoma City in a flash and parked ourselves in Thackerville near the Texas state

Don't mess with Texas.

line. We didn't dare cross in the dark, as we knew this would be a momentous occasion.

There are at least one hundred highways that cross the Texas state line. And at least one hundred pickup trucks for every square mile. It's that kind of state.

We called it the Howdy State. With a landmass covering 262,000 square miles and a population pushing 15 million, there were an inexhaustible array of highways and howdies to be shared.

Crossing the Texas border required a certain etiquette for the first-time traveler, so the Monks consulted their copy of *Judge Roy Bean's Book of Texas Manners*, specifically the section "Crossing State Lines."

We discovered a fascinating state-line protocol.

First, wearing a cowboy hat across state lines is limited to persons over the age of five who know what a rodeo is.

Secondly, tipping a cowboy hat to the side is forbidden except for one-to-three-year residents of the state.

Thirdly, you can spit either five minutes before crossing state lines or five minutes after, but never right at the line.

Finally, first-time crossers are limited to two state-line photos per vehicle and are gently asked to refrain from shouting "Remember the Alamo!"

It had taken us over seven months to *git* from California to the Lone Star State. And as we prepared ourselves on the Oklahoma side of the Red River, our excitement was overwhelming. We primped, shaved and collected a pile of river rocks as mementos of the occasion. Nurse's Aide put on his favorite Stetson and a pair of chaps. The Monks loaded the water pistols, proudly cleaned our good as new Monkmobile and practiced our howdies.

At ten A.M. with a full tank of gas and a pile of river rocks, we crossed the line and immediately felt the difference. Nurse's Aide started rustling up Alley Cat kitty chow, Jim started to lasso country girls and Michael started craving chili and barbecue.

One of the first greetings upon entering the state was a message from Lady Bird Johnson. It was a sign that said, "Don't mess with Texas." We discovered it was a well-enforced edict; for a state with this many cowpokes the highways were surprisingly free of litter.

After a pit stop at the Texas Tourist Information Booth, where we were officially welcomed by our first genuine Texas gal, with her smart little lone-star kerchief and petite cowgirl hat, we hightailed it sixty miles on down to the queen city of Texas . . . Dallas.

Though the city had gone out of its way to overcome its association with the tragic assassination of John Fitzgerald Kennedy, it still didn't discourage the Monks nor thousands of other jaded tourists from searching out the scene of the crime. In fact, it turned out to be one of our very first stops in this thriving metropolis.

Downtown, among some of the most expensive and stunningly gaudy attempts at postmodern architecture to date, we drove the loop of the fateful presidential motorcade. As if possessed, we found ourselves circling the loop again and again, gripped by a morbid fascination for the events that took place on this street years ago. And then to our horror we started channeling the motorcade and began reliving the entire gruesome episode.

On the first drive through, the conspiracy began to unfold. Mike was JFK and Jim was Jackie O. (we mean Jackie K.), with Mike humped over caught in the fire as Jim crouched beside him protecting his injured head, shouting to the Secret Service men. And then Mike was Jackie, Jim John, then Mike was Governor Connally, Jim the driver, Mike as Kennedy, Jim as Connally, both of them as Jackie, Jim the blood, Mike the bullet, Mike the car, Jim the tail pipe, until finally we were both witnesses shouting, "Look, he's shot, he's shot!" as we dove into the grassy knoll waiting for the next bullet . . . waiting . . . waiting.

"Mike, let's do it again," said Jim after the seventh reenactment.

"Whoa, I'm getting dizzy from circling. This is *sick*."

"C'mon, c'mon, one more time. Just do it. We're on a roll."

One more time the Monkmobile circled the loop, shooting shots, yelling for help, with sirens screaming, cops closing rank, Jackie crawling over the side . . . "Mike, pull over, it's a cop. He's telling us to stop. For *real!*"

Michael snapped out of Conspiracy Mind and looked in the rearview mirror at the spinning lights. "Damn, now what?"

The patrolman dismounted his motorcycle, unsnapped his helmet and began walking toward the Bounder. All the fears began flooding the Monk brain.

"What'd we do? They're going to take us to jail. What do they have against transients? Shit, this happens every time we hit town." Mike was digging through maps for the registration.

"Chill out, Mike. Just act calm."

The cop knocked on the window. "Sorry to bother you, sir. Just wanted to let you know, looks like one of your storage doors is open. I thought you might like to know before you lose something."

"Storage door?"

"He means the compartments underneath, Mike. . . . Thanks, Officer," Jim sang out.

"What size rig you got? Me and my wife been thinking about getting one of these," the cop rambled on.

He's talking to us. My God. He must think we're . . . normal. You mean it's that simple? All we had to do was get a motor home and they'd stop treating us like sleazy fagabonds?

"It's just twenty-six feet," Michael gratefully answered with a paranoid smile.

"It's a beauty. Well, take her easy," said the cop, waving us on.

Michael sat shocked. "He didn't even ask for a license. What's going on here?"

"We're acceptable, Mike. We're RV owners," answered Jim proudly.

"Wow!"

No matter how obsessively clean we'd kept Econoline, a van parked on a neighborly city street invariably brought up images of Charles Manson groupies. But somehow a big clunky motor home conveyed images of retirement, serenity and traditional American values, especially when it had Nebraska license plates.

Now the Monks were as American as a fourteen-ounce T-bone steak . . . well, sort of.

After driving off the loop, parking the Bounder, and locking our storage doors, we went straight to the Hyatt Tower and up the glass elevator onto the observation deck, where we spent the next two hours listening to the deejay play old Beatles tunes as this jewel of a city lit its bright rhinestones for the night.

Later that evening the Monks hit the streets for a grand tour of Dallas, discovering . . . *the shopping malls*. To the north, off a wide thoroughfare, spread over a stadium-size parking lot was the ultimate in discount shopping, Hypermart. Using the buddy system to make sure we didn't overspend, we navigated the world's largest single-roofed department store—with so many cashiers you couldn't even see the farthest one (now those folks were ready to take your money)—and were stunned to ring up at *only* $47.80.

However, Women's Wear had snared Mike when he spotted a rack of square-dancing skirts. "Twenty dollars for a complete cowgirl getup. This is too good to be true," Mike muttered to himself. As Jim walked the quarter mile back out to the Bounder, anxious to escape Hypermart's ecologically incorrect lighting, Mike, carting the bag of goods, excused himself to the Hypermart men's room.

Twenty minutes later Mike ran toward the Bounder with another bag behind his back. Just as Mike was about to quietly store his catch in the side compartment below the door, Jim yelled out the window, "So which did you get, the yellow blouse with the white fringe or the red one?"

"Shucks! How'd you know?"

"You can't fool a Gemini, maaan. I carefully evaluated your spending habits over the past year and realized you were overdue for a binge," Jim philosophized. "And besides, I followed you in," he squealed. "Mr. Mike, there ain't no way to hide nuthin' from me," said Jim confidently.

Wanna bet, thought Mike as he stuffed a dirty novel in his side pocket.

And then, as if by divine kitty magic, at just that moment, it happened again!

Nurse appeared, in yet another parking lot. Yep, there he stood only a few yards away, basking in the ethereal glow of the Dallas sunset. Another visitation from Archangel Nurse.

At first, it didn't seem possible. Almost two thousand miles in less than four months! Over the cold, cold Rockies, through freezing Midwestern storms, through the tempting lures of Dallas all the way to Hypermart? But then we remembered, "This is no ordinary cat."

Knowing divine providence when he saw it, Jim ignored Mike and chased Nurse through the parking lot and across the street. But Nurse escaped under a fence. Jim circled the building, while Michael waited by the iron gate. On the other side, near another busy street, Jim called out for a long-lost feline. Just about ready to give up hope, Jim turned back home, but then out of the corner of his eye he spotted Nurse nervously standing in the shadows by a bush on one of the busiest streets in town. Nurse looked at Jim long and hard. Jim looked back, toying with the thought in the back of his Gemini brain that "maybe this is just another Russian blue, maybe this is just another poor stray cat." And just when Jim was feeding that brief moment of doubt, that split-second cancellation of total faith, Nurse split.

Mike stood guilty as sin in the Hypermart parking lot still holding one gingham skirt with white-laced blouse, one hot red ensemble with white fringe, two scarves, boots, hats and a dozen petticoats.

"Oh, well," Jim maturely reassured. "Nurse knows how to find us. . . . So whatcha waitin' for, Loretta? Let's party!" Jim hollered, relieving Mike of his parental guilt.

Jim cranked up the radio to the best country western on the dial, and in a matter of minutes Mike had both himself and Jim wearing the new square-dancing ensembles.

"Oh, my God, we look like our mothers. You're Roberta and I'm Bev!" Jim shouted as he began hoofing down the runway of the Monkmobile hootin' and hollerin' at the top of his lungs. We were so glad to be in Texas we could have spit all the way to the Rio Grande.

Off we sped back into town, that good ole country music blaring on the radio, the Dallas skyline blazing in the moonlight, cowboys and cowgirls tooting and honking and tossing their winks toward the Monkettes. Roberta pulled over at a corner flea market and snatched up two beehive wigs to complete the look. Little did the residents of Dallas know that the crazy cute cowgirls in the Monkmobile were really bodacious *cowboys.*

After we cruised all over the city, catching a set by the punk polka group Brave Combo and visiting with a newspaper reporter who thought we were delightfully weird, the Monkettes pulled into the Dallas West RV Park off Commerce Street.

Dallas West offered city camping with a spectacular view of the skyline. More importantly, Dallas West offered Roberta and Bev an opportunity to deal with another more messy problem. Having spent a week on the road, both Monks had begun to notice a powerful smell emanating from the holding tanks. As we discovered upon pulling into site #7, Bounder needed to go potty. *Baaaad.*

Dallas West was a white-trash trailer park disguised as a campground, which the Monkettes soon learned was the sorry state of most RV parks in the South.

Row after row of trailers were interspersed with sundry campers, pull behinds and class A motor wrecks. The Monkettes even spotted another Bounder and felt that instant glee, that sense of community, that esprit de corps shared by all those who've gullibly purchased boxy, American-made, fuel-inefficient clunkers like ours.

The cowgirls made a grand entrance. After we stirred up the dust, knocked over the utility pole and backed over a picnic table, our fellow campers were more than a little anxious to see who was behind that wheel.

Totally unfazed, the Monkettes stepped out to meet the public. But the public took two steps back, recoiling at the perplexing sight of two six-foot *young, tall thangs* cavorting about the campground in their country best.

"Full hookup or partial hookup?" asked the campground host with his aim-to-please smile.

It was the first time for the Monkettes and we couldn't decide. If we plugged in and used sewage, it was a full hookup. If we only plugged in, it was a partial. After a hard day's drive, it was a tough choice, but the cowgirls decided to go all the way.

"Full hookup, puleassse," we chanted.

"How do you turn the water on? Do you turn it clockwise or counterclockwise?" Bev queried as Roberta plugged her in. Bev couldn't get her directions straight. Finally with the right twist of the handle out came the water. Bev just stuck it in, giving Bounder a drink.

Stepping out: the Monkettes meet the public.

But there were no smiles as the Monkettes finally got down to the serious business of taking Bounder for a poop.

"Make sure you get that hose in there all the way, Roberta, we wouldn't want any spills!"

The cowgirls inspected the levers beneath the motor home, not sure which to pull first. It seemed awfully confusing. One mistake and the *shit could fly*.

Fortunately, a lucky pull on the right lever had the yukky gray water rushing out into the drain, and then, holding her nose, Bev let the *black* water fly.

"Get a whiff of that, girl! Hmmm, hmmm!"

After a job well done, the cowgirls had something to be proud of. We were fully hooked up and the moon hadn't even set, leaving plenty of time for a game of croquet.

"Cheryl Wagner, you're not going to believe this, but I'm calling from Dallas. Jim and I are on our way to Mexico."

Cheryl was flabbergasted. As one of Mike's closest friends, it had been over three years since she'd last heard a peep from the itinerant Monk, not since his days in San Francisco, pre-Jimster.

"Whaaaat! Mexico! And who's Jim?" she said, cracking her trademark, deep-throated, almost hysterical, boisterous burst of laughter. "And what are you doing in Texas? You mean it really exists?" More unbridled laughter.

Cheryl and Mike had been following each other coast to coast since their own meeting ten years earlier in a seedy bar outside Conway, New Hampshire, where they were essentially chasing the same guy, then ultimately dumped the guy and became the best of friends.

"I'm serious. Mexico. Anyhow, Jim's my soul mate, we've a lot in common. And we're nuts about each other, as long as I, well, as long as I wear a, uh, wig . . ."

"A wig?"

"And a skirt!"

"Skirt?"

"But no makeup. He hates makeup. No earrings either. And rings, forget it. Totally freaks him out."

"Michael. Are you okay?" Cheryl's tone changed.

"Totally. Are you kidding, life's great, Texas is great. They say that Houston is the ugly sister with a good personality and Dallas is the pretty sister with a bad personality. They're both nice purty sisters to us, and it's warm as can be."

"Warm?" Cheryl's tone lifted as she peered out her kitchen window overlooking Otter Creek, now frozen over, with another twelve inches of Maine snow on the way.

"Why don't you join us! There's plenty of room. We've cleared out one of the storage compartments. It's perfect for one person, and you'll just love Jim!"

"How are the men?" Cheryl was considering the options.

"You mean the Texans? Funny you should ask that, Cheryl. We've not really, actually, well, to tell you the truth, we've not met anyone. We decided we aren't going to leave the motor home. In fact, we want to see if we can go through Texas without befriending another Texan. It's a trip, Cheryl, we've not been out of here in over a week now, and it's amazing, sort of like being an astronaut. Totally self-contained. I really dig it. It's soooo Robert Frippe."

Cheryl was gasping on the phone, gripping the receiver as she rolled on the floor laughing. "You're out of your mind. What do you mean you're not leaving the motor home? How do you get food . . . where are you calling from?"

"It's a drive-up phone booth. They have drive-up everything here. But food is getting sort of low. We thought maybe while you're here you could, well, help us get a few things!"

"Oh, so that's it!" Cheryl's tone changed again.

"I'll pay half your fare," Mike teased.

"Yeah?" Cheryl brightened up. A perennial traveler, she had, as a matter of fact, been considering how to swing a vacation despite her dwindling finances. If she stayed in Maine, she could have a relaxing but cold (note *cold!*) Easter in the winter wonderland. But if she wanted adventure, fun, excitement, warmth . . . that did it. Cheryl Wagner was on a plane to Texas faster than two cowpokes crossing the Rio Grande, with a plan to meet in Corpus.

"My God, look at all those Cadillacs." Jim slumped at the wheel inching toward Route 59 South, surrounded by a veritable Cadillac Ranch of Cadillacs of every shape, quality and color. The Monks could taste the salt on their faces from the Gulf water, but so could eighty thousand other Texans, Southerners, Midwesterners and Northerners.

Yes, the Monks had unwittingly joined a nationwide caravan of carousing kindred spirits. No, not another Harmonic Convergence. Nothing that high-minded. A more basic

American happening. An event that played to the lowest common denominator, to the worst and most obnoxious qualities in the otherwise genuinely good American spirit.

This glorious weekend marked the beginning of spring break for tens of thousands of brain-dead frat rats. And outside of Fort Lauderdale, Florida, there was only one *very rad* place to be, Mustang Island State Park near Corpus Christi, Texas.

Twelve hours later, among the throngs of thongs, the Monks arrived in the "Shrimp Capital of America." Here the water rules were decidedly different. Unlike in California, the Monks just drove right up on the sandy beach, where we discovered we weren't the only ones committed to staying in the vehicle. Row after row of campers, station

Cheryl Wagner, a Maine (by way of Brooklyn) dame, and our first official Monk visitor.

wagons, hatchbacks, Cadillacs and vans lined water's edge with their occupants partying hardy inside. No beach blankets or pristine coastline for this state. Texas and all its cars just ran right up to the water and *stopped.*

On the following morning Cheryl arrived in Corpus, Continental Flight 227. And on time to boot. But the Monks, keeping a long-standing tradition, were an hour late to the airport. Certainly this was no way to treat our first official foreign visitor.

Though Cheryl Wagner was flying from Maine, she was actually from Brooklyn, but that's a different story . . . a long story. The Monks just assumed she was born in Maine since she took on all the traits of a Maine dame.

A bundle of raw creativity, outspoken and pleasantly opinionated, a naturalist supporting the right causes, Cheryl wasn't afraid to get her hands in the dirt or sea salt in her hair. She could write a good letter and she knew how to really laugh (both an understatement and more of a Brooklyn thing than a Maineiac thing, but we'll let it stand).

Cheryl was a bit tipsy when we picked her up at the airport. It seems the tension of the day—what with losing the baggage, nothing to eat or drink but a few cocktails—was enough to give her a mild high. And when the flight attendant on the plane announced over the intercom in midflight, "Cheryl Wagner, message for Cheryl Wagner. . . . The Monks will be late in picking you up," that was enough to tip her over the edge.

Those first few moments were a bit awkward. You know how it is when you haven't seen a friend for three to four years. Somehow the person looks a little strange, as if they don't quite match up to the picture you've held for all that time. At first you notice the weight, the wrinkles, the hair loss, the general wear and tear on the face, all the while trying to be openhearted, passing no judgment, seeing beyond the aging.

But in actuality nothing much *had* changed. Mike was as tall, skinny and bald as always, and Cheryl was as voluptuous, strong and determined as always, with the same frizzy, dark hair, olive skin and big wild smile she'd had for her thirty-three years on the planet. After the initial shock over nothing, Cheryl and Mike got reacquainted, while Talk Show Jim began interviewing our first official Monkette: "Tell me, Cheryl, what caused you to break your customary habit of sticking out the cold Maine winter and board a Continental flight for Texas?"

"Oh, I was looking for a break from the snow. . . . Besides, you seemed like nice guys . . . though I suspect the real reason you wanted me to come is to buy you food and do your dishes!" she said with a husky guffaw, pointing at the sink full of filthy Cost Plus dinnerware.

"Cheryl, we've been a bit mixed about your arrival, and since we're all going to be sharing such a small space, I thought it'd be appropriate to get everything out in the open right off," Jim the devil's advocate orated to an unsuspecting Cheryl. "Now, the way I see it, the pros of your visit are generic. It's good to see old friends; a visitor will force us to keep the Monkmobile clean; according to Mike, you're a guaranteed good time, good meals, good laughs; and last but not least, I love you. . . . Now get outta here and I mean it," screamed Jim, letting loose a maniacal laugh.

Cheryl stood inside the door waiting, not sure whether to laugh or take Jim seriously, and certainly not sure whether to make herself at home.

"But the cons on the other hand: you're a third mouth to feed, and a *woman*, an affront you understand to a male lesbian like myself, and from the way things look, you have no more money than the Monks." Jim paused pensively.

Cheryl looked to Mike. Mike looked to Jim. Air traffic circled overhead. We could feel it coming. It was a slow-moving, earth-shattering, backbreaking, "hold on, passengers, 'cause here she comes," bust-the-belts, gut-shaking howl the size of Texas, as Cheryl's laugh split the sound barrier, rolling over the top and landing in left field. "HAH-HAHAHAHHUHHHHHUHIHAAAHUHUH!"

The laugh silenced the Monks, leaving in its wake a moment of prolonged Zen stillness.

"Well, to counter your cons, Jimmy," Cheryl continued calmly, taking a deep breath, "I'm wanting to lose some weight, I have a new boyfriend back home, and most importantly, I have brought all of my credit cards in case of a pinch," she stated with mock formality, opening her marbleized bag, producing four changes of clothes, a few things to read and Texaco, Mobil, MasterCard, Visa, ATM, and American Express cards that we think she held out on us.

"I'm quite good at rounding up those cards, and by the time I leave I'm sure I'll have procured a few more," she said with great insight.

"Cheryl, I want to be the first to welcome you aboard the Monkmobile." Jim let down the act and gave Cheryl a giant bear hug. "Glad to have you."

"I am honored," said Cheryl with a straight face, followed by a monumental guffaw.

Cheryl passed the Monk test and was welcomed aboard with full honors. We showed Cheryl her downstairs basement apartment, a cozy three-foot-by-six-foot storage hole with twelve inches of head room, and gave her a brief tour of the skunkmobile.

Then, as might be predicted—a hungry monk *is* a hungry monk—off we went to shop at H.E.B., which roughly translated means Here Everything's Big, a really, really huge supermarket, Texas style.

"Now, Cheryl, you understand we've decided to not go outside the Monkmobile. It's a Self-discipline Concept. So you're our link with shopping." The Monks held on to the hope that it would be this simple to continue their hard-and-fast commitment to the Bounder.

Cheryl had been in Maine through five or six winters and didn't want to risk being forced to hop right back on a plane, and besides, she was equally excited to do some wintertime shopping in a *real* supermarket, so she happily played along.

As anyone knows who has ever lived in Maine, the pickings get pretty slim up north in winter. To be precise, the veggies are the first to go. Picture Cheryl sadly adapting to her precious choice of potatoes, onions, bagged carrots, cellophane bags of New Zealand spinach and those rare birds of iceberg lettuce for $2.50 or more a head.

And now picture Cheryl entering a monstrous Texan supermarket while winter raged back home.

"Oh, shit, I should have brought my glasses."

Cheryl bypassed aisles two, three, five, six, seven, nine and thirteen. She wasn't interested in frozen foods (plenty of that where she came from), canned food, packaged food, freeze-dried food, deli food, the bakery or housewares . . . she headed straight for *Produce!*

Cheryl was caught fondling Hass avocados for nearly half an hour, going bonkers in the red-leaf lettuce (three for a dollar), wildly fantasizing over vine-ripe Italian tomatoes ("I'll take some back with me"), turning delirious over grapefruit ("And it's in season!") and stalling a faint when she spotted her "first mango in five years." She made it out of there with enough to feed an army, including a strange black root we never knew what to do with.

The Monkmobile parked that night back on Mustang Island State Beach, stall #43, partial hookup. It must have been a little disconcerting for a woman of the woods to be spending her vacation in a parking lot between RVs—to our right was a family with four teenagers reading *Hitchhiker's Guide to the Galaxy* and to our left was a Canadian—but Cheryl adjusted.

The beach was about a quarter of a mile over the dunes from our campsite. And Cheryl delighted in the fact that we were in a wildlife preserve teaming with birds, because birds were precisely what Cheryl had hoped to see. She was quite the Girl Scout, carrying with her not only a pair of working binoculars but a bird book that actually had accurate drawings of every bird with which we came in contact.

For the next few days we played tag with the sun, as heavy coastal clouds kept rolling in. It was a freak weather front. Newspapers proclaimed it the coldest spring break in thirty years. And to our dismay, the wind played havoc at our seaside resort.

Poor Cheryl, all the way from the fresh forests of Maine, crammed inside a stuffy RV with bags of soybeans, boxes of brain machines, cases of herbal supplements, those cartons of soy milk, Jim's half ton of scrapbooks and debate papers, those damn river rocks that kept rolling around the floor and two tall Monks who refused to venture past the door. It was getting cramped. She felt trapped. It was cold and windy outside and there was *that Canadian* next door.

"Cheryl, how'd you sleep?"

"Well, not too great. Those flags kept me up all night. They made this god-awful racket, snapping in the wind."

Yes, our Canadian neighbor proudly displayed both his Canadian and Texas flags for all to see. At first we thought this was quite original, a change of pace from usual RV front-lawn decor. But when this extravagance interfered with our guest's visit, we knew we had to take action. Since we were friendly Monks, we started in a cordial sort of way.

The next morning Jim leaned out the window and engaged the Canadian in a little repartee on the subject of oysters. It seemed this scruffy elder statesman of the Popeye the Sailor Man School of RV Living would daily wade his way out into the cold Gulf water to catch a little seafood for that evening's supper. Jim was very impressed with this manly behavior and said so to our Canadian friend.

We had broken the ice. Soon Cheryl and Michael leaned out to say hello as well. Now that we had developed a rapport, we felt it would be quite easy to ask our Canadian friend if he would please take his flags down during the evening so our dear friend Cheryl could get a decent night's rest.

Jim was the ambassador. At around nine that evening he looked over from the Monkmobile to the headquarters of the Canadian contingent. They had just finished their oyster dinner and were sipping wine from their well-stocked liquor cart when Jim spoke up.

"Hi. I wonder if it would be possible to take your flags down tonight. It's awful windy and our friend is kept up by the noise."

Suddenly our manly Canadian fisherman gruffly interrupted his rather agreeable Canadian wife:

"It's too late to take them down. I'd have to untie the whole darn thing!"

In other words, he wouldn't budge. Avoiding confrontation until he reported back to his elders, Jim said, "I see. Well, have a good night."

Back in the Bounder, we plotted our strategy. In the mind of Michael Monk "this required positive action."

And thus was born the Port Aransas War.

On our first skirmish General Mike took the psychic approach. "First, let's visualize the Canadian's flags coming down." All night long, as the wind was wildly whipping the flags in the air, we took turns imagining the Canadian peacefully lowering his flags. We visualized the beautiful Canadian countryside and the loving inner child of our Canadian neighbor wanting only peace with his neighbors. But the Canadian still wouldn't budge. He was probably fast asleep.

The next day, cranky from lack of sleep, we once again had Jim speak as our ambassador. This time the Canadian again scowled at the thought of lowering his beloved flags, which brought us back in a huddle, ready for another skirmish. As the third night neared, we took the competitive approach. "If you can't beat 'em, join 'em."

After stringing a makeshift clothesline we hung every towel, sheet and pillowcase we owned. And quite predictably in came the winds. All night long the flags battled the towels. That westerly breeze kept flapping, flapping, flapping the fabrics in the air, creating such a noise that no one could possibly sleep. And still . . . *nothing.*

The next morning a well-rested Canadian stepped out with his fresh cup of coffee barely noticing our array of noisemakers. And to our dismay he unfurled yet another flag . . . the flag of Quebec!

Well, that did it. Mike and Cheryl busily laid plans for a final resolution. When the sun had set and the barbecue fires had died down, the Canadian tipped his beer and bid us good night. Trying to look casual, Cheryl yawned while Michael put away the dishes. Then, after the last light went out . . . the fun began.

Sneaking past the picnic table, Cheryl crossed the border and staged a raid on the Canadian contingent. Dressed in black with her head covered in moldy Monk stockings, she gingerly climbed the poles where she dismantled the flags from their holdings. Down the poles and back toward the Bounder Cheryl raced to a waiting Michael.

There on the dinette waited the old sewing machine. With the skill of a master, within two hours Mike and Cheryl turned those flags into custom battle jackets.

Next morning a confused Canadian was making the rounds looking for his flags. "Guess that wind finally blew them to the beach," said Jim as the Canadian laid a suspicious eye toward the Bounder. While the two were engaged, Cheryl made a mad dash out the door toward the beach in the brand-new Canadian-flag jacket.

Looking up, the Canadian was horrified to see his beloved flags now part of a Monk fashion statement. "There's me flags!" And in a wild and frenzied chase toward the beach, the Canadian was about to close in when Cheryl, being the enlightened peacemaker that she is, suddenly woke up from her dream.

And those friggin' flags were still flapping!

The Monks, in their normal state of abject poverty, were trying their best to put on a good show for Cheryl. After all, she was our connection to the world outside. We had to keep her in good humor for the treacherous trip to Mexico.

Alas, little did Miss Wagner know that underneath our pleasant smiles, easygoing demeanor and tasty meals, things were not right in the monastery. It seemed that Cheryl caught us with a dwindling supply of cash. But short of downright hysteria, we kept our cool day after day.

When Cheryl finally got the drift (not enough cash to feed the Monks), she uttered these fatal words, "Let's just use my credit card."

"Credit card?" we replied in unison.

"No, I won't have it," Michael Monk insisted.

"Oh, open up, let a friend help," Jim Monk replied.

And thus began the saga of the credit cards.

At first it began as a modest investment in gas. When faced with a boring day at Mustang Island or an exciting drive down Padre Island, out came the Texaco card.

"Let's just put in enough to get there and back," said Michael Monk cautiously. "We don't want to get carried away."

Oh, the fun and excitement of using someone else's credit card: no money in hand, no money in the bank and we could still carry on. Just charge, charge, charge! It's so American, so Texas.

"Don't worry about it"—Cheryl's second mistake—"just pay it when you can."

Three days later Cheryl was walking out of the bank with a "MasterCard cash advance." The Monks were thinking of ways to charge up the card while charging Texaco for another full tank of gas (let's not forget that the Monkmobile can take up to ninety gallons at a time!).

Frustrated by the continual cold front that was robbing Cheryl of her precious tan, and with only three days left of her vacation, we decided it was high time to head south to the Rio Grande for the big trip across the border.

On our hasty drive down Route 77 from Corpus through yet another thunderstorm, we had high hopes of finding those warm, white and car-free sandy beaches that were advertised in the tourist brochures, so at least Cheryl could claim one day in the warm Southern sun.

Brownsville, Texas, was billed as the southernmost city in Texas and the gateway to the Rio Grande Valley, where the Rio meets the sea. But it was not exactly *on* the sea. The closest beach, Brazos Island State Park, was twenty-two miles from Brownsville, and the winds continued to blow.

Frustrated, Cheryl pleaded for us to cross the border farther inland in hopes it would be warmer. In one last desperate attempt to find a suitable border town, we headed up the valley toward McAllen. The subtropical climate—with its groves of papaya, banana, palms and the countless aloe vera plantations—gave Cheryl that hit of the tropics she'd been hoping for.

The sun was finally shining, bright and warm. Having never been to Mexico, and now less than twenty minutes away on a bright, warm day, here we sat in the McAllen RV Park and Mobile Home Club preparing for the Big Event.

"Come on! Get moving!" said our Taurus friend as Mike steadied himself in his cowgirl boots. Cheryl held a firm grip on her Texaco card as we started up the Bounder and drove across the border. Mexican currency, as Cheryl Wagner knew (and she's from Maine?), was at a favorable rate of exchange for the dollar. We had visions of unlimited spending.

We were already planning an extravagant twenty-thousand peso feast: *guacamole, enchiladas, tacos, margaritas, tostadas . . . señoritas, señors, jalapeños buenos dias.* Just the thought of salsa vastly improved our Spanish. But would they understand us?

Cheryl understood us. The Monks understood Cheryl. But a transported New Yorker from Maine speaking Spanish? And what about Nurse's Aide? Were animals allowed to cross the border? Suddenly we grew paranoid.

The border was quickly upon us. We had barely enough time to stash Nurse's Aide in the closet and quickly devour a grapefruit. We thought fruits were banned, but we were confused with California.

Unfortunately, we were very unprepared for our Mexican border crossing. None of us had thought to look in our handy *Texas Travel Handbook* under "guidelines for crossing the border." Thus began our blunders:

1. Mexican border guards do not need long-winded explanations on why and where you were born.

2. When a strange kid jumps on your car and starts washing your window, he is looking for a tip, not a handshake.

3. It is better to speak no Spanish than poor Spanish. The latter may cost you.

The border was pictorially intact. The pope would be proud. Rosaries were everywhere, and there were at least four to five babies per mother. And we were still in America!

Once over the border we were on a bridge crossing the Rio Grande. And there before us in the late-afternoon Sunday sun were the rising stone and brick buildings of Reynosa, Mexico.

With over 250,000 inhabitants, a good 99 percent Catholic, it was host to your standard fare of gift shops, traditional markets and even a bullring.

"Mexico, Mexico, Mexico." Cheryl was wide-eyed with excitement as we pulled into town and immediately began looking for tacos. "Are you sure you Monks don't want to get out and walk?"

Michael peered at the street, insisting on the security of our coach. "No way, girl, we can't leave our Boundermonk. It's a matter of principle. It's got everything to do with our commitment to being one with our environment. Wherever Bounder goes, we go. We're an inseparable team. A compact unit. Simple, mobile and true. Besides, I'll get my petticoats dirty."

Jim continued driving up a narrow street, paved in cobblestones, lined with crumbling adobes. "Oops. I think I took a wrong turn, this is turning into a dirt road."

"Do you know where you're headed?" Cheryl asked.

"Wherever there's food."

The Monkmobile rolled past an empty stucco church. The farther we drove the narrower the street became until the adobe walls on both sides were nearly touching the eight-foot-wide motor home with only a few inches to spare.

Suddenly at the opposite end of the block charged a truck loaded with tires.

"Hold on!" Jim yelled from the wheel as he slammed on the brakes, sending us flying in a heap toward the dashboard. The truck screeched to a halt. A dozen boys and men shouted from on top the tires, making such a loud racket we couldn't hear what they were saying, notwithstanding the fact we couldn't have understood what they were saying had we been able to hear.

It was a showdown.

The street arched down a steep hill behind the truck, whose driver refused to reverse his direction. The neighborhood turned out to see who would back down first. An old woman holding a cat by the tail leaned out her balcony screeching at the Monks.

"*Questa la mesa terra salsa, le guac enchilada ma problemas es carros!*"

"What are we going to do?" Cheryl was getting nervous.

Jim frantically motioned at the driver. The driver flailed his arms in the air.

"*Salsa, enchilada, tostadas, hablas española*, you motherfucking Yankees!"

"Holy guacamole, there's quite an overlap between Spanish and English," noted Jim.

Men, women, dogs and children started pouring out of their dusty-brown, sun-drenched adobes cackling at the predicament.

"*Tortilla y enchilada, guac y salsa, frijoles mucha madres bonitas y rua loco carro yanqui!*"

Suspense hung in the air as Michael considered the possibility of spending the last days of his life parked on this dusty alley, plugged into a neighboring socket, making leather belts for a living.

But rather than keep them in suspense, Jim backed all

the way up the bumpy street, leaving us with one very flat tire.

"And I suppose you expect me to change the tire now?" asked Cheryl impudently.

"It's okay. It's an inner dual, we can ride on the outer tire," answered Mike.

After the dust cleared we headed toward the center of town in search of an open restaurant. We were soon in the old marketplace, but there were no eateries to be found.

"Are you sure you're not lost?" Cheryl asked, getting impatient for a good chile relleno or a tostada or a taco, or even a Frito-Lay corn chip for cry'n out loud.

"Just keep your eyes peeled, there's bound to be someplace to eat," said Mike.

"How are you going to eat if you can't leave the Monkmobile?" Cheryl had her doubts.

Finally, at the edge of the square, we stumbled upon a traffic jam. Out on the streets were hundreds of young men and women in authentic folk costumes. The girls wore elaborately brocaded embroidered gowns and were carrying flowers by the armful. The boys were well scrubbed, hair greased back, sporting traditionally tailored suits, with richly embossed lapels.

"Stop. Stop. It must be a big feast. Look at all these people. I bet it's a community supper. This is the spot," Mike said, motioning.

The Bounder jerked to a stop outside a school gymnasium where there were gathered hundreds of people waiting to get in.

"Oh, my lord!" Jim rose from his seat.

"I'm starving! Now what am I supposed to do, get your food to go?" Cheryl stood holding her grumbling stomach, her glasses fogging over from the heat inside the motor home.

The Monks cast a pleading smile toward Cheryl.

"No fucking way. If you're so big on eating, you're on your own. I'm getting me an enchilada. Or at least a burrito, with a side of guacamole . . ." Her voice trailed off.

"We can't leave the Monkmobile. It's part of our new weird order. Simple, mobile and true!"

"Here, I'll give you something simple—get moving through that door." She gave the Monks a good shove as they flew out the door. "Now that's simple. You're mobile, and that's the truth."

The Monks desperately clung to the door, their boots dangling a scant two inches from the ground below.

"No, no. There's got to be a better way. We can't touch the ground. It's got cooties. It's forbidden. I'll perish out there," Mike screamed hysterically, ruffling his petticoats.

"I have a better idea." Jim calmly pulled himself back in, walked toward the cabinet and pulled out a ball of twine. "Here, we'll tie the end of this twine to our wrists and we'll tie the other end to the stove. Then we can wander all we want but still be attached to the mothership. See, we don't have to break our vow."

"You have a vow?" Cheryl's eyes began to swim.

"We vowed to not leave the motor home for an entire month. It's part of our Space Monk Astronaut-in-Training Concept."

"Oh, my god!" Cheryl laughed.

Sufficiently tied at the wrists and anchored to the stove, the Monks now felt secure to leave their mobile monastic digs. With Nurse's Aide on Jim's shoulder, the foursome marched toward the gymnasium where the feast was apparently under way, their lifeline to the Monkmobile trailing behind.

Inside, the festive crowd was tightly packed around a basketball court, as rows of couples stood facing the front.

"Good, we made it. Looks like they're lining up for the food," said a famished Cheryl, sending the appropriately dressed Monks off to grab the grub.

The Monks rushed the floor, untangling the twine as they moved forward. They took their place in line, standing a good eight inches taller than the tallest Mexican couple.

Jim was a perfect cowmonk with a ten-gallon black hat and six-inch spurs. Mike's cowgirl ensemble was an overstatement. With his blond wig backbrushed to an outstanding ten inches of beehive supreme, he stood towering above the pack in his square-toed boots, wearing a red, white and blue dress with tiny, six-inch American flags fluttering off his shoulders, and plastic alligator earrings dangling off his hyperextended earlobes.

The crowd gawked.

The Monks were hungry.

The gymnasium vibrated.

The Monks smiled.

And then . . . the music began.

Loud, blaring, brassy, classic Mexican folk music blasted from the sound speakers, ricocheting off the bleachers, as the rows of couples started to dance.

Mike and Jim were instantly caught up in the whirlwind, inextricably bound arm and arm to the nearest Mexican, tromping wildly across the wooden floors, stamping their heels against the hardwood. Their hard-booted patterns cracked the floor in synch with the music.

Trumpets blared through the chorus of guitars and percussion, the crowds surged forward to the edge of the arena. Shimmering gowns and fluttering sleeves swept through the gym as the fifth annual Reynosa Valley Regional Folk Dance competition got under way.

Swirls of satin and lace could be seen throughout the room, as the bright colors of each regional troop dashed across the floor. The Monks were completely disoriented by the excitement and were mindlessly swept off to the center of the gym to the maddening roar of the cheering crowd.

"Aiiieeeeeee!" Mike screamed from beneath his towering wig as his twine twisted and turned in the complexities of movement. Jim was holding his head high, howling to the trumpeters, joining in the fun.

"Yeeeha! Yippppeeee yai ayyy! Ride 'em, cowmonk!"

For a solid hour the competition continued. Each dance troupe took center stage stamping out a routine to the thrill of the mothers and boyfriends in attendance. *"Salsa, guaca, frita olé!"* Each group wore a distinctive costume unique to their area. The spectators swayed with the music —clapping, yelling, encouraging their favorites. The gymnasium was alive with dancers, bursting at the seams with sound.

And no one seemed to notice the Monks as we left dancing onto the moonlit streets of Reynosa.

Outside, under a rising full moon, Cheryl led the way to the Monkmobile, now surrounded by romancing teens in the warm night air.

"Phew! I thought you were goners for sure. Guess you were finally forced away from the Monkmobile."

The Monks looked at each other. And held up the twine, still attached at the wrist.

The Monksters were hysterical with hunger by the time the ravenous entourage found an open restaurant. The classy El Indio was serving what could have been called oriental seafood. But even with our limited Spanish we were quick to assess that this restaurant was a total gringo rip-off and left it for the more revolting—yet cheap and satisfying— pleasures of Pancho's Cantina. Truly a dive to end all dives, we knew we were in the right place. It was near empty, save for a few quiet locals.

Cheryl led the Monks in by their twine across the yellow linoleum tiles under bare light bulbs to the Formica booths.

It was stone silent as we sat opposite statues of Jesus and Mother Mary, which faced off with paintings of sports fishermen on velvet. A display case offered a good selection of rosary beads and ten-week-old pastries. Definitely a find!

Happy at last to be eating a true Mexican meal, we threw caution to the wind and ordered the catch of the day with lard-drenched refried beans, rice and salad . . . *plus* . . . a spare tostada, some chips and those Corona beers Cheryl had been thirsting for. All this for under nine dollars!

Our waiter brought out our fresh catch of the day, which meant a whole fish dipped in batter, including its head, tails, scales and other vitals. It took a lot of lemon to get that one down.

In the postdeparture gloom we wound our way back into the beautiful downtown McAllen Trailer Park and dutifully planned the final six hours of Cheryl's visit.

The night had taken another turn for the cold, and we were cranking on the heat to take off the chill. Outside, the blustery wind heaved clouds under the moon, which was close to full. A six-thirty A.M. departure and an hour's drive to the airport didn't leave much room for sentimental, lingering good-byes. It took a couple of Virgo risings to pull this one off.

Cheryl Wagner was the most efficient, organized, alert, Ready Eddy the Monks had ever encountered. At the crack of dawn she was up, knew who she was, what planet she was on, when the plane left, what clothes to wear, and whose turn it was to do dishes. Most remarkable was that Cheryl Wagner, former resident of Manhattan, caffeine capital of the world, had not consumed one drop of her favorite brew at any time during her week stay!

Six-thirty A.M. and Cheryl was standing bright-eyed, if not bushy-tailed, at the Harlingen, Texas, International Airport on her way back to Maine.

Her mission complete, she was ready to resume her position on the most northerly outpost of civilization . . . in search of the perfect romance.

The Monks, not quite with it at such an early hour, weren't sure if Cheryl was coming or going. Had she just arrived or was she leaving?—always a favorite question about any guest in the Monkmobile and one that we are still asking.

We think she left.

Our brief sojourn into Mexico had us wondering if we should return across the border. But we were too uncertain of how to survive with

little money. Could we plug in? What about mail? What about full hookups? Definitely these were things to consider.

Jim wanted to visit the "zone of silence" near the state of Chihuahua where no radio frequencies can be sent or received. We were anxious to check out the unusual wildlife and the numerous UFO sightings from the region.

But looking at the map, at the gas tank and at the recent flat tire, we resorted to flipping a coin. But just as we flipped the coin, a Federal Distress truck pulled up to the side of the RV with a huge box for the Monks. Our biweekly ritual of having our mail service forward all our mail was guaranteed to flood Bounder with even *more* paper, as the Monks waded through life back in the *real* world. Namely, a life of bills, letters from friends and more of those gruesome Doris Day animal rights fundraising appeals.

"Hey, look at this, it's a letter from Uncle Jack," said Jim, opening the box and handing Mike a letter postmarked San Francisco. Jim madly ripped through the mail and opened a letter from Santa Fe with a carefully inscribed return address: *Yma Sumac, San Ildefonso Pueblo.*

"Mike, listen to this. We are invited to visit 'the Queen of the Quest, the Piscean Prince, the Raunch of El Rancho.' "

"Who are they?"

"No, it's all one person. Chuck Yma Sumac. He says if we're ever in Santa Fe to look him up. Remember? We met him in San Francisco at the Zen Center."

"Does he have a shower?" Mike asked. Despite the creature comforts of the Monkmobile, the periodic state-park shower was not doing the job.

Inside Jack's envelope was a torn page from a bed-and-breakfast guide, advertising an inn for sale with a note on the side: *Have you been to Santa Fe? I'm thinking of sneaking away to look at this property. What do you think of the area? Want to meet me there?*

"Hey, Jim, guess who else is in Santa Fe? Jack's going to be there in two weeks. Maybe we should head up to New Mexico."

"Santa Fe? But that's going west. It doesn't make sense to go backwards! What happened to coast to coast?"

"Maybe we're supposed to drive in concentric circles on our way to the East Coast. Two steps forward, one step back. Like a spinning top across the continent. Anyhow, if we hadn't been in such a hurry to take Pi up to Colorado, we *would* have stopped in Santa Fe."

"But it destroys the rhythm!" Jim threw in a straw man, which Mike had long since learned to ignore.

"But he says he'll treat us to dinner! And here's another hundred-dollar bill." Mike held up the crisp green manna.

"Well, Chuck Yma Sumac did say he'd feed us all the soy milk and brown rice we could eat."

The Monks were sold, once again slave to the call of a free meal. We made the practical decision to head on up the Rio Grande to Santa Fe. Not a bad choice. With such names as Laredo, El Indio, San Ygnacio and Del Rio, we knew we were heading into some "Wild West" country.

In Texas you get used to driving a few hundred miles to get to the next town. In between towns are vast scrubby prairies with no signs of civilization save for an occasional picnic table every thirty miles. Jackrabbits—some the size of dogs—abound everywhere, jumping in and out of the road back into the prairie. It is an unbelievable hypnotic experience to drive two hundred miles at a stretch and still nothing in sight and miles to go.

Eighty miles later, while passing through Laredo, we had

two more flats. From the start, we knew this town was tough. Pickups with mounted rifles in the window outnumbered cars thirty to one. Liquor stores were open on almost every other block, and there were only two guys in town not wearing a cowboy hat.

Trading in our ten-inch television for a set of tires, Jim nearly blew his top when they insisted on charging us ten dollars apiece to take the blown tires off our hands.

"*We* have to pay to get 'em outta here," noted the surly garage mechanic from Michigan, who'd grown suspicious of the Monk rope attachments to the mothership Monkmobile.

After moving a ton of scrapbooks, excess soy milk, soybeans, herbs and the ever-present stash of river rocks, room was made for two blown tires. And off we drove on our new treads.

"Don't you think it's getting kind of crowded in here?" asked Mike.

"Feels like the good ole days!" answered a perversely satisfied Jim.

At five in the afternoon we were on our way out of Laredo loaded with gas and cruising to the tunes of Nanci Griffith ("I'm in a lone-star state of miiiieeeend"). By now we had learned the joys, and necessity, of traveling at night.

Nighttime on the highway between any two cities in western Texas was exactly the same. In between towns are vast, scrubby prairies with no signs of civilization save for an occasional picnic table every thirty miles. Jackrabbits—some the size of elephants (depends on the time of night)—abound everywhere, jumping in and out of the road, frolicking back into the prairie, howling at the moon. Now those are some jackrabbits!

Quicker than five double-sided Nanci Griffith tapes, we were in Del Rio, Texas. A sign near the city limits said, "Welcome to the land of tomorrow," which, roughly translated, meant we were now officially entering "*mañana* time."

Del Rio, sufficiently isolated from the hustle of the Valley and the urbanization of the Gulf, had managed to burrow itself into that fabulous time warp of *mañana*. If it needed to be done today, it could, and most certainly would, *wait* until tomorrow.

The Bounder barreled through town heading out to safe harbor at the Amistad Reservoir Recreation area, twenty miles from city center. At the Rough Canyon Marina the Monks nestled into a rough, primitive campsite (no hookups) and looked out at the teeming wildlife refuge with flocks of wild turkey, javelina, dove, quail, geese and squawky herons in from Canada. We were ecstatic to find we were the only campers in the entire place.

On Saturday morning it was hotter than hell and no one was in the water. It was like a high school dance where everyone waited for the first dancer to go out and make a fool of himself. However, more than likely, it just wasn't considered the manly thing to do. In the South you ride *on* the water, you don't get *in* it.

The Monks took their customary half-hour extended-rope space walk outside the steaming Bounder. Jim madly performed on the roof of the RV, for an assembled flock of wild geese, doing Nanci Griffith with a fabulous air guitar, while Mike played the part of thirty thousand totally out-of-control screaming fans.

Up drove two strangers.

We quickly retreated inside just in case we were playing to the wrong house and watched the newcomers from behind closed curtains. After all, we had managed to travel the entire state of Texas without befriending a single native. We didn't want to press our luck.

From out of a small brown VW Rabbit jumped two young men. We spotted something unusual about them right off. For starters, they were not wearing cowboy hats, boots, nor Falcon Lake fishing caps and did not pop open a Bud on cue. To our amazement, they moved about gracefully and efficiently, as they quickly cleared the grounds and set up camp.

There was something in the way they worked together that was startling. Not the typical macho bantering while pounding in stakes. One of them was tall, somewhat lanky, with a short military haircut. The other was short and muscular, with slightly longer hair and glasses. Each move was precise and effortless. We had the feeling they had performed this ritual many times before.

The shorter fellow might have caught us peeping, for he waved in our direction. Rather than seem unfriendly, Jim the Mad Monk ventured back outside and found them absorbed in their car, foraging through bags.

Jim climbed to the roof of the RV to get a better look at the sunset and the fellow campers. Suddenly they turned and, spotting Jim, walked straight toward the Monkmobile, asking in a distinct German accent, "Would you like to join us in a fire?"

***Jawohl!* It's zee Germans, Berndt and Stephan.**

"Join you in a fire?" Jim smiled to himself. It sounded intriguing if somewhat dangerous.

Ten minutes later we joined them at their campfire, careful not to singe our lifelines to the Bounder.

What better place to rendezvous with two Germans touring the States than Del Rio, Texas. And what fate that the first two humans we should befriend in the entire state of Texas, with its 15 million inhabitants, would be at this near-empty campground.

Berndt and Stephan were two computer-programming students taking the year off from their studies to tour the States and drive to Alaska. Three weeks earlier they had begun their trip in Maine. There in New England they purchased a used VW (could have been one of Wagner's old junkers) and set out on the voyage of a lifetime.

Packed in their car were the bare necessities of travel: an assortment of aluminum cooking pans, a few plastic dishes, a small tent for two, sleeping bags, clothes, camera and maps . . . lots of maps.

Their first week across America had sent them heading south for the same reason we and thousands of other travelers were here . . . warmth! Hot on our trail the Germans had managed to hit almost every town and park in Texas that we had visited.

"So vat is the meaning of these ropes you vear, hmm?" Stephan asked.

Michael politely explained the Monks in Space Concept and their month-long commitment to remaining in or attached to the Monkmobile. The Germans politely nodded, assuming this to be yet another bit of the Americana they were so desperately seeking.

"So what do you feel is the difference between Germany and Texas?" Jim launched into his typical round of interrogations to the jolly Germans, who were building a bonfire in the ninety-degree heat.

"We don't eat as much the fast food," Stephan began as he offered the Monks a Big Mac and a Coke.

"Or use the microwave oven," joined Berndt.

"But what do you think of Texas?" Jim continued as the fire began to rage.

"The white man has made Texas very tame."

"Why, what'd you expect to see? Wild horses and mountain lions?"

Mainlining a hit of soy, the Monk beverage of choice.

"Yes. But the white man has made it very safe."

"Are you disappointed, or is that good?"

"But yes, of course, it is good. Without the white man there would not be the Indian reservation, and how then would the Indian get his mail. Nor would there be the national park to safely view the animals."

"Is that all the white man is good for?"

"But no. There is milk!" Berndt offered the Monks a carton of milk. "And sausage!" These Germans had a perverse sense of irony—certainly not fitting the standard *Hogan's Heroes* stereotype.

Michael refused their offer, offering in return a carton of soy milk, which they vehemently refused.

"Cows are superior to soybean. Take a look at soybean. He can't walk. He can't speak. He doesn't play soccer. Certainly not a very sociable creature. I love the cow's milk. I like it on my musli in the morning. I like the ice cream at night. If I were offered soybean, I'd say, 'No thanks, give me the cow.'" Berndt lectured with an all-knowing smirk.

"But milk is mucus forming. It's totally against nature to take the milk that was intended for another animal. We don't have the stomachs to digest it." *Fit for Life* Jim was getting roused to preach. "Cow's milk was designed for one reason only: to feed young calves. That's it. Humans are the only species on the planet that drink the milk of another species. It's absurd!"

"I'd rather be a cowboy than a soyboy," snipped Stephan. "Soybeans are stupid, bad-tasting beans."

"But dairy takes ten times as much energy to produce as an acre of beans," Jim countered.

"But drink the soy? Have you ever seen a zebra nursing off the giraffe, hmm? No. And so, have you ever seen a dog nursing off the horse, hmm? No. And so, have you ever seen an armadillo nursing off the Chihuahua, hmm? No. And so, have you ever seen the human bean nursing off the soybean, hmm? It is ridiculous, of course. But every time you take the soy milk, you are nursing off the soybean!" Berndt crossed his arms.

"Well, sorry I brought it up." Michael took the soy milk back inside the Bounder, returning with something the Germans had definitely never laid eyes on before, the mighty yam!

"And vat is that, hmm?" The Germans' eyes bulged.

"Yams. Long, sweet, tender and very phallic. Especially when cooked in the hot coals of a blazing campfire," said

Mike invitingly as he wrapped the yams in foil and tossed them into the fire.

The Germans had never tasted a yam in their lives. They nervously watched the yams as the coals singed the foil and began baking the fat, succulent tubers. When Michael finally pulled them out of the fire and opened them, releasing a steamy, delectable smell, the Germans lost all composure. Everything German about them fell to the wayside as yam magic swept around the campfire. Stephan was drooling over the juicy orange sweet meat, lapping it up in big, sloppy bites and, upon finishing his ration, begged the Monks for one more. Both Germans were down on their knees when Jim returned with the last of the Monk yam supply.

"By God, we could make a killing exporting these hams to Germany, hmm, Stephan?"

That night, in an orgy of yam, soy, Coke and sausage, an intercontinental cultural exchange program hit the Texan plains, as the Monks and Germans exhausted themselves in fire-ring banter on the origins of the Texan drawl.

"But it is the heat, is it not?" asked Berndt. "That is what makes the talk of the Texan, *ya?*"

Jim, the master of monologue, the Channeling Overlord of Sedona, had another opinion. Jim once again summoned his guides and delivered his higher wisdom to an unsuspecting German duo, who ate up every word. "It is not the heat alone. And though Southerners all have a similar way of speaking, the Deep South accent is *not* a Texan accent. They are two totally different things, one not to be confused with the other."

"Then from where they come?" asked an earnest Stephan.

"The Deep South, which derives its dialect from a broad mixture of English, Spanish, French, African and Native American tongues, obviously when given its humid summers and iced tea, blends into its more languid upper-Gulf Southern-style accent."

The Germans enthusiastically nodded by the amber coals of the fire, munching on sausage.

"But Texas, gaining its ancestry from a superrace of pure-bred Pleiadians with a little Spanish thrown in, has apparently cultivated a more sophisticated, if not totally distinct, guttural-sounding—as if you've just gargled three pints of Beck's beer—Texas *drawl*."

That put the Germans fast asleep under the big Texan sky, as the Monks quietly roped themselves in for the night.

• • •

The next morning the Germans were so excited they went out and bought a whole bag of yams, as well as a week's worth of groceries for the Monks in gratitude for the evening's yamfest.

Soon every night there was a campfire followed by our yam-roasting ritual. So honored had the yam become that there arose the existential edict: *I Yam What I Yam*, a clear paraphrase from the Buddha dharma of Popeye the Sailor Yam.

On our final night on Amistad Lake we cooked an entire bushel of yams. This final bonfire of the inanities was proclaimed the Holy Yam Jam, as the Monks and Germans became holy yam brothers bound by the great Yam in the Sky Concept.

So fervent were the Germans in their newfound yam faith that they swore to follow the sacred yamological decree for the rest of their travels: *Let there be yams to eat and let it begin with me.*

Our newly expanded international Monk entourage voted to continue the journey up the Rio together by caravan. We had discussed the possibility of towing the Germans' VW Rabbit behind the Bounder so we could all ride the Monk-mobile. But then . . .

"What's that smell?" Berndt got a whiff of Bounder's holding tanks, and the fastidiously clean Germans gracefully declined a ride.

So into the setting sun we played road tag till we arrived at Big Bend National Park, seventy-five miles south of Alpine. Anxious for a taste of *real* camping, the Germans headed for a remote, back-country campsite accessible only to hikers. The Monks headed for the breezy Rio Grande Village RV park for our first full hookup since Cheryl Wagner, with plans to connect with the Germans the next day.

Once down in the RV park it was business as usual. Wall-to-wall RVs, all plugged in with their barbecues and TVs blaring. A strange contrast to the wild frontier that surrounded us.

The Rio Grande Village bordered the Mexican village of Boquillas del Carmen, which was a stone's throw across the Rio Grande and well touted by all the tourist brochures as a *step into the past*, one of the last *authentic* Mexican villages.

The Monks, not wanting to miss another opportunity to witness authenticity, soon devised ways to leave the Monk-mobile on free-floating Monk-in-space missions without the cumbersome rope-around-the-wrist attachment. We ascertained that if a piece of the Monkmobile was firmly attached to each Monk, and the duration of the *free-floating space walk* was not more than two hours, with a five-hour recuperation inside the Bounder, then such a walk would be permitted.

The following morning the Monks dutifully pulled out the old, flat discarded tires from under the bed and strapped them on. Then taking a backup supply of soy milk, Mike and Jim boarded the only means of crossing the river—a leaking wooden rowboat big enough for about ten passengers.

Six hours later, upon our return from our second tour of Mexico, there on the table was a note from the Germans.

"Dear Monks, can't wait. Must move forward. And so, here's some yams. Love, hmm, The Germans."

"Guess that's the last of them." Jim could now comfortably relax into his Colonel Klink and Sergeant Schultz imitations without fear of German retaliation.

As we drove out of Big Bend, it felt as if we were leaving a strange B movie. We blissfully cruised along the dusty, bumpy highway to Alpine.

"And so, Mike, vee only have five more days bound to zee Monkmobile. Vat do you sink you'll do vis all dis freedom, *Herr Kommandant?*"

"God, I could go for something even more intense. Maybe we should try solitary confinement in the basement storage compartment."

Jim happily waved at a highway patrolman parked on the side of the road.

Thirty seconds later we were stopped by a posse of patrolmen, with rifles, guard dogs and some pretty stiff faces. "Put your hands behind your back and step outside the vehicle."

The Monks gingerly stepped out of the Bounder with the lifeline tied around each wrist. The officers surrounded the Monks as they walked as far as the rope would stretch.

"What's with the rope?"

"It's, uh, it's . . ." Mike canceled out the possibility of even trying to explain the truth behind this. But what would an officer expect to hear. Michael was searching.

"It's a leash!" Jim volunteered.

The officers seemed to comprehend and asked no further questions, as they sent a German shepherd inside. Minutes later he emerged. No loot, no pot and above all, no illegal Mexicans. We acted too friendly to be free of suspicion, but they let us go.

As we drove away, it felt as if we were leaving a foreign land, another world most Americans can't conceive of. The Texas of tacos, dust, orange sunsets, huge skies and illegal aliens. The Texas of no-frills shopping, big pride and the Holy Yam.

Texas is a mélange of all that is Mexican, Hispanic, Wild West and Dixie. Texas is not a state. Texas is not even part of the South. Texas is still its own country.

Yes, we had done Texas. And not met a single Texan.

It was eleven when we cruised down the bumpy dirt road leading off Route 4, north of Santa Fe. We could barely read the pink and green road

sign: *Welcome to the San Ildefonso Pueblo, Temporary Hideout of the Raunch of El Rancho.* We knew we were on the right road because we could smell the hairspray a mile away.

Yes, we were paying a visit to the Piscean Prince, the King of the Kaphas, the Queen of the Quest, the Oracle of Orals, the Terror of Twinkie Town. Yes, the *Raunch* of El Rancho, none other than Chuck Yma Sumac.

At around midnight Bounder pulled up to an irrigation ditch outside a railroad-tie fence surrounding a beautiful dusty pink adobe. The Monks quietly walked toward the gate, trailing the rope lifeline behind, hoping to surprise our host.

Being the B-movie actress that he is, Chuck was waiting at the window, barely concealing that a close friend had broken the secret of the Monks' late-night arrival, having spotted the Bounder near Santa Fe.

Chuck didn't like surprises anyway.

"Hello, dahlings. You thought you could sneak up on me?"

Chuck Yma Sumac, the Pojoaque Princess!

"Chuck?" the Monks screamed, startled by his shadow in the window. "How'd you know it was us?"

"Yma has her ways."

"And just who is Yma?" ventured Michael.

Chuck turned his head sideways, tilted up his chin, stretched the back of his palm across his lips and flipped on the stereo as a symphony suddenly blasted over the loud-speakers the vocal acrobatics of Yma Sumac, the *Peruvian Princess*. Chuck Yma Sumac lip-synched an astounding fifteen-minute impersonation for the Monks, who fell to the desert floor, busting at the gut, rolling in the sand laughing. Note after exquisite note shattered the eardrums as Chuck Yma Sumac pranced from the window, across the room, and out to the patio under a blanket of stars.

"Bravo, bravo, bravo! We love you, Yma!"

The Monks were screaming for more, as every coyote under the moon joined in the orchestrated cattle call for Yma. Wearing a white veil and turban, Yma sang a rousing encore, rambling across the parched earth, doing the tango with an imaginary partner, leading to a high-pitched, warbling crescendo, breaking away to applause . . . self-applause, of course.

"Dahlings, I've been to hell and back, and I was ready for some company," confessed a panting Yma after his stunning performance. "You wouldn't believe it if I told you, so I won't. Come on in. But don't make yourselves too comfortable 'cause it's not mine."

Chuck led us inside to a perfectly furnished adobe. "Watch your step, don't sit on that bench, it's just for looks, be careful of the kachinas, don't eat the *ristras* or you'll be sorry and the bathroom is . . . oh, my God, oh, my God, get that fucking lizard out of here!" he screeched, grabbing a broom, whisking the reptile out the door.

"Santa Fe isn't all it's cracked up to be. I thought I'd find healing here. But I tell you, it's just one big refugee center. There are soooo many screwed-up people. It's almost like New York. Everyone wants your money."

"Why'd you leave San Francisco then?" The Monks were looking for a place to sit.

"Twinkie Town? That two-bit excuse for a city!" Chuck's voice threw into mock rage. "I had enough of that angel food cake of a mecca. Believe me, it took its toll. My complexion was the first to go. Then my sense of humor. Can you believe it? *Moi?* Well, believe it! It finally got to the point where not a one of my decalcified macro friends would splurge for a pint of chocolate Häagen-Dazs. Please, spare me. Yma had enough and I couldn't wait to catch the next train out of town. One night I packed all fifteen bags of clothes, my chopsticks, pressure cooker, nail polish remover, and other necessities and headed for New Mexico. This house-sitting job was waiting upon my arrival. At least here I can restore my ravaged body, voice and soul, far removed from my uppity fans. Here, in the quiet and clean seclusion of my Native American pueblo. Isn't it divine?" He dramatically spread his arms a full circumference around the house . . . that is, the estate.

The Monks nodded approval.

"I'm bored stiff, dahlings," he hissed. "I haven't been laid in so long women are starting to look good. Quick. I need a doctor. Help!"

Chuck wandered into the kitchen and put on a pot of tea. The kitchen smelled of herbs and homeopathic remedies.

"My job is to keep things looking nice and *Southwestern* until someone *buys* the joint. But since I've arrived, I decided this is perfect for Yma. I mean, why should someone else live here when Yma needs her peace? I say, 'Buyers beware.' " He winked at the Monks.

The phone rang. It was a new real estate agent looking to show the gorgeous estate tomorrow morning. "Dahling, do you have any idea what time it is?!" he screamed. "Well, look at your watch. You don't want to show this dump anyhow. It's way overpriced." He hung up the phone. "You can call me the *Pojoaque* Princess. And that's a quote."

Chuck Yma Sumac truly *was* a princess. On this picture-perfect hacienda in full view of Black Mesa and only a stone's throw from the home of the late great sculptor Marie "Black on Black" Martinez, Chuck held court.

Though he was merely house-sitting for its equally eccentric but far wealthier owner, Chuck clearly acted as if it were his own palace.

"So." Yma finally settled down by the ornamental fireplace. "What are you boys up to and what the hell is at the end of those ropes you're wearing?"

The Monks looked at each other, then back at Chuck. "We're on an experiment to see how long we can stay connected to our motor home. It's sort of like training to be an astronaut."

"Oh, God, I had a boyfriend like that. What a dog he was. He wanted to be on a leash whenever he was home. He was more trouble than he was worth. He came up to me one day and told me, *Yma*, that I needed a shrink. Well, I took one look at him and said, 'You're absolutely right. I do need a shrink to figure out why I ended up with someone as fucked-up as *you*.' I tell you I was out of there faster than a girl on a shopping spree. Well, I did go see a shrink. And you know what he said? He said, 'I think you have unresolved issues with your mother.' I told him, 'I don't need a shrink to tell me that! You think I need to pay a shrink a hundred dollars to tell me about my motha!' I'm telling you, everything's going to hell around here. Yma needs a face-lift, dawling. Do you want a doughnut?" He went to the cupboard and pulled out a box of chocolate-covered doughnuts and thrust them in Mike's face.

Mike started to reach for one when Yma jerked them away. "What am I doing? I almost corrupted a Monk."

"It's okay. I want to be corrupted," Mike countered.

"Ooooooooh. Did you hear that?" Yma turned to Jim. "That is music to Yma's ears."

The Monks were falling asleep on their feet as Yma went on late into the night. "It's the blue-green algae. You ever taken that stuff? It's like high octane. One little capsule and I'm flying. Too yin if you ask me. Have you ever talked to them? God, what a bitch she is. I told her, 'Honey, you need to cut down your intake.' You can get strung out on the stuff. Are you a dealer yet? No one knows what they're doing anymore. I want to move to Paris. Oh, God. Who's going to pay for all of this? I'm getting stretch marks. Help!"

The next morning the Monks slept in till eleven and weren't the least bit surprised to find Chuck Yma Sumac still slumbering inside the pink adobe. He rose at noon and spent his day tending the organic garden and blissing out to Brother Charles. "Yma loves theta and eating whatever he damn well pleases."

That afternoon the Monks pulled the Monkmobile through the wooden gate, across the river-rock driveway and parked down against the garage.

"Please, can you put it down there, it clashes with the adobe and the neighbors might talk."

As the Monks settled into the Pojoaque Princess RV Park, it dawned on Yma that the estate's owner, now strategically married to a rich New Yorker, might start to wonder why her sumptuous villa on the Indian pueblo, surrounded by mountains, mesas and chirping birds, with its charming Santa Fe–style decor and beautiful Madonna-with-child gazebo, was not as yet sold.

Rather than encourage the other prospective owners, Yma seized the opportunity of a lifetime and decided to place an ad for a wealthy paramour, who would buy the property outright and support him in the luxury that only he/she deserved.

"Jim, you look like you can think. Help me write an ad for the *L.A. Times*. I need someone with money, quick. I have a lifestyle to support after all."

Jim sat down and labored for hours with Chuck until he finally came up with a classified that Yma could live with.

Wanted: Sugar Daddy. *Emotionally unstable, obsessive-compulsive, spoiled-rotten, recovered Macro-ACA seeks asexual Sugar Daddy to enable him in his life of luxury. Send photos and financial statements to Yma, the Pojoaque Princess.*

While waiting for responses to pour in, Chuck decided he needed working capital to tide him over until his rich sugar daddy arrived.

Yma invited the Monks in for afternoon tea and rice cakes in the cool dining room of his adobe with a clear agenda on his mind. "After considerable observation of you two, I think you are in need of someone to manage your lives."

"Manage what lives?" Michael protested.

"Your lives. You're a mess. When's the last time either of you had your cuticles done. And that smell. How can you live with that smell from that motor home. Does your mother know what you're doing . . . running around the country? You're practically homeless. What you need is someone to manage your appointments for you."

"But we don't have appointments."

"No appointments? Well, no wonder your life's a mess. Yma will take care of that. Everyone has appointments. And secondly, you have got to do something about your clothes. My God, you look like you shop at *K Mart*."

"But we do shop at K Mart."

"Ugh!" Yma fell into a seat. "This is going to take a lot of work. We'll have to start off with three thousand a week. No, I'll cut that down to two since you're family."

After lengthy negotiations over resources, duties and logistics we agreed to hire Chuck as our first full-time roadie and settled on a bonus of three dozen chocolate doughnuts each month.

"But I must have a contract. You can send it to my lawyer."

"Who's your lawyer?"

"You'll have to find me one. Just take it out of my doughnuts."

Jim drew up a contract for Yma to sign that evening.

Chuck pulled on his Logo Paris glasses as he carefully read the agreement with a skeptical look on his face.

As fitting for a true princess, Chuck will not perform any actual duties. He won't change tires. He won't grease axles. But he will be required to keep his nails trimmed and to experiment with a new hairdo every three days.

His salary will be one box of chocolate doughnuts and one Milky Way per day . . . if he's good.

It is also stipulated that he search through nearby trash cans for discarded bubblewrap before he resumes his reading of the latest Hollywood trash biography.

That night Chuck threw out the contract after realizing he could never survive in the Monkmobile and escorted the Monks to a night on the town. The Monks wore air filters from the Monkmobile as the only link with the mothership. This would allow two hours away from home, and as far as Yma was concerned, "it's a definite fashion improvement."

We had just finished a good long swim at the local gym and had showered and shaved. We felt healthy, clear and clean. And being the purist Monks that we are, we reasoned it would be the perfect occasion to enjoy a wholesome home-cooked macroneurotic meal. But Chuck would have nothing of it.

He was from the school of thought that reasoned, "I was a good boy and did my exercise. I *deserve* an indulgence." Chuck was not a monk. Or least not a monk in denial. "Let's go find something sweet."

"But Chuck . . ."

"Okay. Well, then let's go find chocolate. Wait. Stop here. Oh, what am I saying, I'm driving. My God, did you see the buns on that one? Oh, baby. Come, let's splurge. Who's buying, you or you?"

Mistakenly assuming that we too must surely embrace the same dharma, Chuck whisked us off in his newly bought Subaru for the Sonic Happy Eating in downtown Espanola. As open-minded monks, we obliged.

"I'll have a double cherry sundae with all the sprinkles and a vanilla shake, with fries. Oh, yes, give me the apple pie as well." Chuck turned to the Monks. "Hurry up, what do you want?"

Jim declined, thinking that would provoke sudden enlightenment. Chuck ordered a foot-long for Mike. "You look like you need something warm in your mouth . . . a wiener. . . . Make that two foot-longs—you want relish?—make that with sauerkraut, and how about a chocolate shake, I'll help you with that." Chuck was heading for insulin shock.

For the Monks, the Sonic Happy Eating was enough. But Chuck had only just begun.

"Are you serious? I swam fifty laps tonight. I deserve more. Yma *must have more*. Of course, nothing that a box of chocolate-covered doughnuts won't cure! Yikes, turn here, Yma." Chuck was talking to himself as he turned into a reputable Espanola convenience store.

On our right was a carload of disreputable drunken lowriders sucking on their beers. "Oh, my God. Can you believe the filth? Yma needs her bodyguard. Quick, Jim, distract them. Flirt with them. I don't want them to hurt the Pojoaque Princessa."

While Jim flirted, Chuck slipped out to purchase his nightly cache of doughnuts and candy, as the carload of drunks mistook Jim for a good-looking señorita.

More than a closet prima donna, an expert guide and a vastly underrated shaman, Chuck was a true friend. However, it was this last attribute that became a little tricky. After our second night Yma could no longer stomach our nonstop Monk abstinence from chocolate and sugar.

"Let's go comb Black Mesa for skulls. I spotted two steers out there last week that looked like they were about to drop. All you have to do is boil the head and then bleach the skull. After we bleach we'll just store them in burlap. Do you know how much I can get for these in L.A.?"

"Chuck, we don't want to go collecting cow skulls now."

But Yma wouldn't hear no, so off the Monks ventured with Chuck on another expedition, returning with our brittle fare, bleaching, cleaning and storing them in burlap bags. After three trips in one afternoon we'd collected a garageful of skulls, and the Monks finally said "enough." This might have been the Monks' fatal mistake. Yma didn't take rebuffing very well!

By the end of the third afternoon we noticed a marked change in Chuck's delicately arranged world. The Pojoaque Princess saw he was not getting the attention and respect he desperately deserved. And the Pojoaque Princess was *finally* coming down off his blue-green.

"I think I'm getting a headache. Yma can be very nasty when she has a headache," Chuck warned. "I think you had better split, darlings, before I smother you in chocolate."

It was the last day of our month-long commitment binding us to the mothership. The Monks decided to spend the final twelve hours locked in the closet for the ultimate closed-space experience. Our month of training had paid off as both Mike and Jim were now totally bonded with the Monk-mobile and prepared for deep-space travel. Unfortunately, both now suffered from slight cases of agoraphobia.

After the brief hiatus at Chuck's, we were ready to invade Santa Fe and find Uncle Jack. Since we knew this would be a momentous occasion, we took Yma's advice and put up a Georgia O'Keeffe print, hung our skulls in the shower, slipped on turquoise earrings and corn necklaces, threw on Indian shawls, read the first three chapters of *Death Comes for the Archbishop* and settled in for a meal of blue-corn tortillas, atole, piñon stew and red chili with egg, potatoes and pinto beans. Well fed and well dressed, we revved up Bounder, warmly left the Raunch of El Rancho, the Chocolate Pojoaque Princess to his own demise, and headed for town.

There are five ways to enter Santa Fe, six if you count landing in spacecraft. Three roads take you through miles of grade-B shopping malls, cheap motels,

sandwich shops, Laundromats, roadside businesses hawking *ristras*, and fast-food emporiums selling tamales, posole, burgers and fries. In other words, your standard American town with a twist. The other two passages circumvent "the strip," winding around narrow, adobe-lined streets, passing countless art galleries and escorting you into the ultimate Hispanic American theme-park town square called the Plaza.

But whichever way you go, the look is Southwest. We were, after all, entering the trend-setting, style-setting, architectural prima donna of the West, the very city that created *Santa Fe style*. Yes, the hometown of Saint Fay herself, and she won't let you forget it.

It was adobe for days and days. Stringent zoning laws ensured that all of the buildings in the Plaza district conformed to the traditional styles that suit the environment: products of earth, trees and sunshine. In short, adobe. And they're the real José too. Santa Feans really did live, work and play in these earth and wood structures (no trailer parks for these kids).

Driving into downtown the Monks wondered what or who

was Saint Fay. Like the saints of California—Santa Barbara, Santa Maria, Santa Santa—she possessed similar qualities: Spanish cathedral, Spanish padres, Spanish oppression. Our minds were reeling with possibilities. We knew there had to be some sordid history beneath this charming mountain mecca.

Mouths agape, the Monks were sizing up those thick-walled adobes as we headed toward the Plaza. Dangling our turquoise bracelets and waving to the natives, we felt like Jesus in Jerusalem: "Home at last." We took the scenic shopping-mall route, so by the time we hit downtown we were so exhausted from the traffic jams we called off the invasion and made a hasty retreat east of Guadalupe, a safe zone relatively free of history, turquoise and tourism.

The Monkmobile chugged to a stop outside Kinko's. As we had just run out of gas, it was dawning on us this might become an arduous, if not embarrassing, afternoon. Afraid of staining his new white cotton squaw dress and fringed leather moccasins, Mike hired an aging hipster on a bike to peddle five gallons of gas from the Kwik Fix on St. Francis. But the gas spilled on Mike while he primed the carburetor, ruining yet another K Mart blue-lite special.

Mike donned his outback look (straw hat, white shorts, faux peasant shirt) and walked around the corner to buy stamps from Pak-Mail, as Jim scoped out the area for phone booths. Ahead of Mike, leaning over the counter, legs spread extra wide as if doing the splits, was a young man. His khaki shorts fit like a glove around a set of perfect, sun-bronzed, marble-smooth legs fit for an athlete.

Oh, to be that young, Michael Monk mused as he noticed his own legs, mere toothpicks by comparison. *And sun-bleached hair to boot. This guy's a surfer, I just know it. . . . But in Santa Fe?*

Michael moved to the adjacent counter ordering "Surf's up!" stamps in a loud voice. Not wanting to stare, he wished he had more courage to talk to total strangers. But then again, why bother: his voice might crack, he ate garlic for breakfast and he thought he had a zit!

Still smelling of gas, Michael stood licking and sealing envelopes, every so often slobbering on the counter (familiar attention-grabbing tactic) while avoiding eye contact with the "surfer," who was writing a note.

Nearly finished, Michael let out a sigh, the stranger lifted his head, their eyes met and . . .

"Holy blue corn . . . Kyle?"

"Leapin' kachinas, Michael?"

"Pueblos and tortilla chips, what're you doing here?" Mike yelled.

"Haciendas and sopaipillas, what are *you* doing here? I was just writing this note for you. I heard you guys were in town!" said Kyle.

Yes, once again, synchronicity in the Life and Times of the Monks. Destiny was at it again, thrusting parallel paths onto the same street corner, proving that you can never escape the wise and watchful eyes of Saint Fay.

Kyle was last seen in Colorado where the Monks met him in a restaurant prior to their departure for Omaha. Kyle was just returning from Australia and ecstatically related his adventures with dolphins, a subject in which he was keenly interested. Michael, proud to be seen with the *bronzed marble legs*, was worried sick about his garlic breath.

Moving outside onto the pavement, they stood talking, only inches apart, and Michael began to experience an ever-so-mild anxiety attack, a common occurrence in Michael, and needed to sit down. There are three reasons why these attacks plague poor Michael. Factor one: the engine won't start. Factor two: it's past his lunchtime. Or factor three: he's about to channel.

Kyle, not noticing, kept right on talking about dolphin research, desert dolphins, dolphin midwives, his planned trip around the world to study dolphins and the book on dolphins he hoped to write.

The more Kyle talked, the more Michael began drifting into . . .

. . . *a blue sea full of cetaceans, swimming downstream to a huge cavern filled with wild-eyed mermaids and dancing squids. Suddenly Kyle and Mike were in a deep-sea carnival, alive with schools of dolphins jumping like deer through curtains of sea kelp. Legions of crabs were ascending from the floor clicking their heels as nubile sea waifs wrapped seaweed around their waists, blowing sound bubbles toward the surface. Swimming counterclockwise they were all suddenly holding the arms of an octopus with a face of a dolphin and the turban of a Sikh with a button that read, "Saint Fay, Queen of the Seven Cities."*

"What?" Michael awakened, not having heard a word since Kyle began talking. "Queen of the Cities?" A question Kyle simply ignored, unaware of what was inside Mike's addled brain. Fortunately, Kyle suddenly remembered he was late for an important interview and excused himself, allowing Michael Monk an opportunity to disengage with a promise to meet later.

What began as a mild anxiety attack had now blown into a full-fledged midday nervous disorder, only this time caused by factor two. It was past Mike's lunchtime and he needed food . . . *pronto*. The Monks made their way to the Marketplace on Alameda. A heavy debate ensued inside the store whether to feed Mike's soy-milk addiction with a quick mainline of Soymonk or wait and cook something unappetizing like seaweed and carrots.

It was Jim who first noticed the bobbing white silos from the other aisle gliding toward cosmetics. They seemed to float of their own accord unattached to the heads below. Out of curiosity Jim peeked around the corner and reported, "The turbans are here!"

And sure enough, around walked two white-clad women sporting foot-tall turbans. "The Sikhs," they quietly nodded.

Mike, a longtime fan of turban fashion, complimented the young Sikhs. "Nice wrap."

This met a somewhat cool response.

Jim chimed in, "Yeah, that's really awesome," and began the breath of fire, which entailed hyperventilation with his eyes fixed upward—another Sikh custom. The turbaned ladies, showing no apparent interest, just breezed on by.

Certainly a harmless incident. However, within half an hour what began as a trickle became a downpour, as the Monks were confronted with turbaned pedestrians everywhere in town. Down on the Plaza amidst the Indian crafts bobbed the turbans. Across the street from the Burrito Factory stood a group of four. Out of La Fonda came three more.

A carload of six in a new Mercedes turned the corner on Palace. Three more white heads drifted by Woolworth's. Two more by the old cathedral. A single turban by the fountain, a pair coming out of a museum, another foursome in a car. It was turbans for days and days. And were it not for the cubist adobes, it might have seemed out of place. But hey, with mud huts stretching for miles and miles, the turbans seemed to fit right in.

Fortunately, there is always someone to hold your hand in moments of culture shock. And who should turn the corner when both Monks were on adobe turban overload but the bronzed marble legs with a dozen strands of chili *ristras* for the Monkmobile.

"What's with all the Sikhs, Kyle?"

"Oh, didn't you know? This area is one of the strongholds for Sikhism in America. There's a whole community of them up toward Espanola. They're intense. Anyhow, I brought you some *ristras* to hang over your sink. It'll help with the smell."

Thank God for old friends in new places.

That evening Mike and Jim met Uncle Jack for dinner. As promised in his letter, Jack offered to treat the Monks in Santa Fe. We arranged by phone to meet at the most popular restaurant in town, the Pink Adobe. The list to get in was a mile long, and Uncle Jack was waiting at the entrance trying to get a table when the Monkmobile rambled up the narrow street sending tourists and cars flying in its wake. One thing we'd learned early on with Bounder was the Whoever Is Bigger *Wins* Concept, as Mike intimidated three other cars out of their parking spaces, so he could park the beast adjacent to the restaurant.

Uncle Jack stood shaking his head as Mike bounded out the door to greet him.

"Where in God's name did you get that?" Jack was amused at the sight of two Space Monks popping out the door. "The last thing I would have ever expected to see prancing out of that motor home is two silly queens. Is it yours?"

"Yep," Jim proudly exclaimed. "Ours and the bank's!"

"But of course. Banks own everything. What happened to the little van?"

Michael took Jack by the arm, noticing how unusually frail he looked, and explained the gradual demise of Econoline and the stroke of luck that had placed them in Lincoln, Nebraska, where the Bounder was discovered.

"Well, a definite improvement. How many beds are there?" Uncle Jack was quick to explore the bottom line, careful not to commit a faux pas in the presence of Jim.

"There is one bed. We both sleep in it, and . . ."

Jack arched his left brow.

"We're *full* of brotherly love," Mike boasted.

Jack smiled a satisfied smile, dropping his eyes in mock modesty. "Well, I'm sure your friend Jim doesn't want you to go into details," even though Jack was quick to surmise the situation.

The Monks walked into the crowded Pink Adobe and, to the astonishment of Jack, were immediately escorted to a table. Jack was unaware that the Monks had bribed the host earlier in the day.

"Well"—Jack took out a Camel—"since I didn't get any phone calls from the road, I assume you managed to stay out of jail. I've been following your newsletter and it's entertaining. But how are you two surviving?"

Michael threw up his hands. "God, Jack. Why is it every time I'm with family the first thing that comes up is how I'm making it?"

"Maybe because it's of relative importance. You have to feed yourself, don't you? I wouldn't ask if I wasn't concerned."

"I know, but it just makes me feel like a little boy. You know what I mean? Anyhow, Jim and I are making do. We live simply, like monks. So it's not as if we need a lot of things."

"How are *you* making it? You're looking a bit haggard." Michael probed, hoping to change the subject.

"It's depressing every time I open my address book and realize half the people are no longer living," said Jack, taking a drag on his cigarette.

"AIDS?"

"Uh-huh."

"Jack, are you doing okay?" Michael was feeling his own concern.

"No, I'm fine. Fine." Jack put down his cigarette. "But now the cost of that thing!" Jack motioned out to the street. "That's not exactly a simple investment. And the gas. And everyday expenses. Are you going to tell me that living on the road like this is actually cheaper than living in one place?"

"Jack, what are you getting at? Of course we're struggling. But this journey is an odyssey to us. It's more than just a mindless joyride around the country. With each mile we discover another part of ourselves that we didn't know ten miles back. With each person we meet we find another reflection of ourselves that had yet to be seen. The whole momentum for our travels is fueled by our quest for self-knowledge."

"But couldn't you do that in one place?"

"Maybe. But the road sort of brings things into sharper focus."

"Beginner's mind I call it," added Jim, who was basically left out of the conversation, which suited him fine since it left time to analyze the restaurant menu for any politically incorrect dishes and food-combining no-no's.

Jack took a long familiar draw on the Camel, extinguished it, put his hands flat on the table and said, "Listen, I wanted to see you in Santa Fe for more than just to say hello. I want to make you a business proposition."

The Monks looked at each other.

"I'm looking at some property here, a nice bed and breakfast up on Canyon Road. Absolutely no one knows I'm here. It's just a little fact-finding mission. But I'm trying to wrap up a lot of loose ends with my other properties. There's a good opportunity here in real estate. And so far, things look pretty good. If I go ahead with this plan, I'm going to want someone to manage this place for me."

"Why don't *you* move here, Jack? Leave San Francisco."

"Well, I am, as a matter of fact, thinking of leaving. But I want to retire to France. You know that. What I'm talking about is someone I can trust, here in Santa Fe. Someone I know won't screw me over. Someone who I know will manage well without supervision. Someone as good as family." Jack looked at Mike.

The Monks leaned back in their chairs, noticing the crowds now waiting at the door. The waiters rushed through the service station carrying steaming plates of chicken and posole from the kitchen, amidst loud clattering and laughing from other tables.

"I'll set you up with a reasonable salary and we can negotiate other amenities. I'm willing to make you active partners." Uncle Jack nodded his head. "I think it's time you settled down somewhere, Michael. Don't you think you've carried this road trip far enough by now? I could understand going for a summer, blowing across the country. But you've been at this for quite a while. Don't you think you've seen enough?"

Michael looked into his napkin. Something was odd. Something was twisted here. How often had he sat before Jack with a scheme in his head, a business proposal, a plan for mutual partnership on some frivolous project, and now Uncle Jack was delivering a proposal back on the doorstep when he least expected it. There was something driving Jack. Something beneath the surface.

But the Monk journey. It is important. There are reasons why we travel that we can't answer. Something compels us forward with each turn of the wheel. Coast to coast. It's all in a plan.

"Jack, I'm sure you have my best interest at heart . . ."

"No, Michael. I have my own interest at heart. It's simply a proposition I am offering. You can certainly think it over."

Michael looked at Jim, who was innocently adrift in menuland, then out the door at the Monkmobile parked against the curb. Nurse's Aide was lazily sunning on the dashboard as passing strollers stopped to stare. There was a long pause.

"Maybe it's my manhood, Jack. Or maybe it's my pride. But I feel I'm for the first time in my life doing what I'm supposed to be doing. I know it sounds like a load of psychobabble, but every day belongs to me, however I want to do it. I'm my own man. I've gone years doing things that rationally seemed like the right thing to do, but just didn't *feel* right. That's exactly why I left the city. I was tired of living out of my head and wanted to start living from impulse and intuition and freedom of choice. I wanted to make every day whatever I wanted it to be. I really like this, Jack. The road. Me and Jim and this crazy spiritual journey we're on. That's what's true for me. Simple. Mobile. And true. Despite the hardship, despite the overbearing uncertainty that exists, I know I'm doing what I'm supposed to be doing. And I can't believe I'm going to say this, but I just have to say no. Because if I didn't say no right now, then I might be tempted. And if I were tempted, then I'd be returning to the false illusions that perpetuated my life in the city. I'm going to have to say no." Mike's answer hung in the air like a spent firework on the Fourth of July. For a few minutes the three sat silent as the bustling Pink Adobe turned its tables and the evening sunset cast its long shadows across the adobe walls.

Jack finally smiled an almost benevolent smile, with just a trace of sarcasm. "To be young, and with a dream!"

"But Jack . . ."

"Oh, no. I mean it sincerely. It's perfectly fine with me. It's so seldom to find someone with a vision anymore. Everyone cashed in on the material game. Whatever you decide is fine with me. I just wanted to explore the option. If you're doing what you want to be doing . . . then that's what counts. Freedom. What more could any of us want? To be free."

For a split second Jack seemed tragically forlorn, still strong, but alone. But he quickly recovered.

"Like I once said"—Jack paused, holding an unlit Camel against the tip of his lip—"if you ever land in jail, you know my number."

They all laughed and shook hands across the table, ordering a bottle of wine, toasting the proposed venture and lavishing on themselves a dinner so fine that the Monks sank into the wooden chairs, fulfilled with an extraordinary satisfaction. Fulfilled with choice. Fulfilled with purpose. Fulfilled with brotherly love for Uncle Jack.

Jim stood at the bank of pay phones inside

Sanbusco's cool, clean oasis.

The Monks were flat broke again,

so Jim the Mad Monk was pursuing another brainstorm after coming down from the mountain like Moses with a sales pitch for the masses.

"I'm going to pull us through! You just watch," Jim confidently announced to Michael as he settled himself by the bank of pay phones.

Wearing his totally faded, tattered and torn, stained and mildewed, old white Space Monk jumpsuit, he pulled a park bench up to the phones and set a stack of papers on one end and a day's supply of food on the other, including a loaf of bread, two liters of soy milk and a pressure cooker of rice.

Passing shoppers in the indoor mall eyed the suspicious Monk and walked the other way.

On top of the phones sat bottles and bottles of herbs, which he had been taking since midmorning to charge himself up for the job at hand.

Jim paced the floor, practicing his skillful breath of fire, chanting a few syllables, and then went down on his knees meditating against the white wall, before jumping back up and loudly clapping his hands as he yelled, "Alright, do it! C'mon now, let's do it!"

Jim stood up to the phone and punched in the magic

numbers like a woodpecker pecking a tree, pecking at the hard surface to grab the bounty inside.

"Martha my dear, this is Jim the Mad Monk of *Monk*, the world's only mobile publishing house. We're the two guys that run around the country with a cat in a twenty-six-foot dented motor home writing about the wild and wacky people we meet along the way. Have you been Monked today? Haven't checked? Well, I thought it'd be a totally awesome way for you to promote your Socially Irresponsible Investment plan. Check this out—our readers are both social *and* irresponsible . . . we have this new incredibly well-designed special section, I mean we're talkin' gorgeous . . . Martha? . . . Martha? . . . Who loves ya, Martha? . . .

"I hate it when they hang up on me."

Jim the Mad Monk was selling his heart and soul to any would-be entrepreneur willing to risk a few pesos to place an ad in the growing nomadic newsletter.

The pay phone rang.

"How's it going, Jim?" It was Mike, calling from around the corner.

"Great, great. Just keep it coming. Keep those carbos comin'. This takes a lot of energy you know."

Mike suspected a pile of uneaten food was still waiting on the bench.

"Yeah, we're cookin', we're cookin', man. We're doin' it. But it's a bitch getting through to these people."

Another pay phone rang.

"*Monk*, Santa Fe Division. Oh, Debstradamus, thanks for getting back. I was callin' about . . . Yeah, we're the two guys . . . Yeah, like Charles Kuralt on acid. . . . Kind of Kerouwacky. . . . Yooouuuu got it."

Another phone rang.

"Vast corporate headquarters of *Monk*, the world's only mobile . . . can you hold . . . just go into deep samadhi for a second, alright?" Jim threw down the phone, leaving it dangling in the air, and picked up another. "Now what size ad did you have? . . . Hold on, let me ask my traffic manager."

Jim reached over to another phone.

"Mike, what size did you say could fit?" Jim whispered.

"Whatever size they got, are you kidding me! We'll make it fit!"

Jim was back on the phone. "Yeah, if you go one size larger, I'm sure we can squeeze it in. In fact, I think you bought the last full-page space."

Another phone rang; it was an operator calling with a collect call. Jim accepted the call and was off on yet another tangent.

Jim had four phones going now. "Yeah, just mail it to . . . *Monk,* please hold. . . . Like I said, we're the two peripatetic publishers with the solar-powered Mac, will you hold . . . yeah, there are solar panels on top the RV. . . . Of course they work! . . . some of the time, can you hold? . . . You've reached *Monk,* and boy are you lucky! . . . Mega apologies, got everything you need? . . . Be sure to enclose that check, we're running low on soy. . . . *Iiieeeeem* waitin' for my *Monk* . . . great, thank you soooo much. . . . *Monk,* hold . . . and I mean it this time, please hold. . . . Helen of Troy, how you doin' babe? . . . Check this out, we're at deadline and a major advertiser couldn't get us their ad on time, so we have a remnantfication happening here and we can give you a ridiculously low rate . . . I mean, I'm embarrassed to say the price . . ."

Mike hung up his end and walked to the store. Just as he passed the deli, a corner phone rang. It was Jim!

"How'd you get this number?" said a shocked Michael.

"I have every pay phone number in town. Now, what if we put the ad for the brain food on the back?"

"We already have the eggless doughnuts on the back."

"Oh, right, got it. I'll sell 'em the inside front."

By five o'clock, Jim the ad sales maniac had launched a new career selling national ad space for the Monks' dashboard publishing empire, not wasting a thought on how any of this would work out.

"Don't bring me down. Don't bring me down!" repeated a hyped-up Jim at Mike's slightest indication of doubt at his master plan.

"I got us some dough, didn't I? Whaddya say! C'mon, *what do you say!* Gimme five, dudette!"

Michael shook his head. "I gotta love you, Jim. You're one crazy fucker."

After days of snake dancing at the Sanbusco phone booths, shamanistic driving through the narrow streets of the Plaza, and vision quests to a now-abundant automated teller machine that accepted *all* our cards, it was time to leave Santa Fe. However, Saint Fay, the patron saint of Santa Fe and our steady guide and teacher, had other things in mind.

She'd let us play campy tourists all we wanted, but at some point we'd have to wake up and embrace our larger purpose. Fay knew we had a unique situation: a cosmic Land Rover, an Esalen on wheels. She knew we were more than we appeared to be. Like a few others who could see beyond the form, Fay grasped why we were here and why we were nomads. She saw us as human antennae picking up the finer vibrations from the cosmos and then spreading them like gravel dust over the demineralized planet, a galactic intelligence team for the new weird order, using humor to deflect the headhunters and woo the initiates.

That's why Saint Fay had predetermined that before the Monks left the area they had to visit an authentic healer. After all, this is the healing mecca of North America, the Lourdes of the West, the New Age General Hospital. To come all this way and not make this effort would be a cardinal sin for which we would never be forgiven.

We had our pick from the finest medicine women, channels, psychics, acupuncturists and plastic surgeons in New Mexico. But instead, we chose an unheralded, unknown avatar living nine thousand feet up in the hill country above Espanola. The Land of Coyote, Wolf and Pickup Truck.

We'd heard that her compassion was boundless. A heart as big as the Rio Grande, intention as pure as Santa Fe Springs. Wisdom beyond wisdom, a teacher beyond all teachers, one look in her eyes and all worries were forgotten. She was young but ageless. Deep and spacious.

And . . . she was a dog.

The drive from Taos to the home of Girl Doggie was one of the most scenic drives in all of New Mexico. Beautiful green valleys, vast expanses of rainbow-colored desert, met a fathomless horizon. It was a little Shangri-la on the western edge of the Santa Fe National Forest. Here in the tiny village of Ojo Sarco was the Carol and Girl Doggie Bed & Din-Din and adjoining Ojo Sarco Car Garden and Trailer Park—one site, partial hookup, but it came with full use of Carol's bathroom.

When the Monkmobile flew in the driveway on a late afternoon, Carol was out pushing a shopping cart through her car garden.

Carol came running for the Monkmobile with her hand out as if to say *Halt!* when the Bounder took a dive into the ditch and sank into a hole.

"God, you guys. Looks like you're going to be staying here a while. Didn't you see my sign?" Carol pointed to a small, artfully painted sign with swirling flowers that said "Big Hole!"

"Oops. I had it turned the wrong way. Dear me.

**Carol "White Horse" Clark, at the Ojo Sarco Bed
and Din-Din and accompanying car garden.**

By now Carol was blushing as the door to her adobe
opened and out raced the highly esteemed Girl Doggie wag-
ging her holy scepter high in the breeze.

"This is Girl Doggie and I am her loyal girl owner. Woof,
woof, woofeee! Girl found me out in the desolate hubbub
of Farmington, a real yukky place, and made me drag her

back here where she could contemplate the meaning of life, death and what's for dinner tonight. And she says, 'Why are you sitting in that stinky motor home?' "

Girl Doggie waited at the door, ready to lavish her girl slobber on the yet-to-be-initiated Monksters.

The Monks stepped out as Girl Doggie planted a big, wet, slobbering, splattering tongue across the face of both Monks, which sent cat-preferring Mike running back into the Monk-mobile for a towel.

"Better bring more towels. Girl gives a very very wet welcome."

The Monks knew Carol from San Francisco where she pioneered her White Horse line of outrageous wearable art, decorated with crazy-quilt hand-painted designs and doo-dads (such as rhinestones, glass jewels, plastic versions of the Golden Gate Bridge and more). In fact, Carol herself was a walking fashion statement, though not the kind you'll find in *Glamour*. Decked out in perfectly coordinated pink or peach threads, Carol was a pioneer of a style of fashion called Clarkism. Pop yet functional, bright yet natural, whimsical yet subtle, Clarkism is Carolyn's colorful and slightly goofy personality in the form of fabric.

"Carol, this is great! But why'd you move way the hell out here?" yelled Michael.

"I couldn't get away from those yucko-blucko germs if I stayed in the brrr-freezing city. And besides, Girl Doggie was here waiting for me. Weren't you, Girlllll." Carol squealed her high-pitched Girl call of the wild. "Woof, woof, woofeeeee!"

"God, Carol, you're such a back-to-basics gal!" said Jim, who was now down in the dirt getting a pounding by Girl Doggie.

Yes, another Taurus (move over Wagner), Carol was always in touch with how much it costs, where to get it and what to use it for. A walking commentator on the bottom line—money, food, sex and salsa—Carol was a professional consumer, searching through the vast treasure chest of life, knowing exactly what she's after.

And, as we learned, she had a fine eye for detail—she can spot polyester one hundred yards away—and she maintains very high standards, especially when it comes to partners. *Male* partners that is. Which makes it so surprising that she should end up with Girl Doggie.

"Come into my palatial doggie-den." Carol motioned the Monks inside.

The long mud adobe hut sat on a hill facing a rolling valley that dropped down toward the desert several miles away. Carol was a virtual hermit in her high desert retreat.

For years she'd been asking Big Universe for a male companion with bulging muscles, long wee-wee and a hot new car. Instead, she received a slobbering female dog who whined when she left, had no wee-wee and no means of transportation outside of four thin legs.

"So what's Girl Doggie thinking, huh? What's Girl Doggie thinking?" asked Carol. Jim was down on the floor wrestling with Girl while Carol whipped out a bowl of guacamole and chips for the Monks to feast on.

But then Carol took a deep breath. "It's a very deep dark secret. But Girl Doggie wants me to tell you if you promise to rub her belly."

Jim was already rubbing.

"Well"—Carol opened up a Dos Equis beer—"Girl Doggie is really an extraterrestrial canine from another planet, and one day Girl's ET owner from space is going to come down from the sky to marry Girl Carol so we all can live in a great big germ-free saucer and grow ET babies." *Hee, hee, hee.* "That's why I moved to this big plot of land. It has a big enough backyard for Girl Doggie to romp around in and the handsome ET to land on."

Indeed, their home in Ojo Sarco *was* the perfect answer. With her cache of Campbell's V-8 juice, Natural Nectar candy bars, Pritikin rice cakes, chewing gum and Super Blue-Green Algae, her subscriptions to *Threads* and cable TV, another white horse to ride on, a good neighbor in Emmy, plus an endless supply of acrylic and plastic-fiber paints, and most importantly, a good supply of blue-corn chips and salsa, Carol knew she could hold out for days before she was forced to raid the happy-hour hors d'oeuvres table at the Santa Fe Hilton.

Here in this tranquil mountain retreat Carol could do her packing, unpacking, decorating and redecorating, fantasizing and planning, plastering, spray-painting, cooking, cleaning, moving, shaping, fixing and fixating (all the things Taureans do), while Girl could meditate and play all day long.

"Girl Doggie is the most popular doggie in Ojo Sarco. Aren't you, Girl?" Carol continued, as she dished out some chicken wings for everyone's consumption. "Girl's made many friends in the area. Everyone likes her because she is so friendly. So warm and animated. Isn't that right, Girl?

She was an angel of goodness in this ancient land—well, that is, until recently. . . .

"You see, I'd just returned from the Santa Fe Germ Clinic when one of my 'friendly neighbors' marched down to the bed and din-din, knocked on my screen door and immediately demanded an explanation.

"Explanation of what? I was like dumbfounded, you know!" Carol chortled.

"It seems that five of this woman's prized hens had been mysteriously eaten for supper the night before. Well, actually the innards had been sucked dry, while the bodies were left untouched. Yuck, you know! Whatever it was also got a prized peacock. Just then, it was really strange, Girl's ears picked up, but she laid low. I just couldn't believe it. My Girl wouldn't step so low as to eat the neighbor's hens. It had to be a case of mistaken identity. But I was confused. Was this another great lesson from my Girl Yogi or was it proof that Girl was just a stupid mutt after all. You know?" Carol was getting emotional.

The Monks were settling in, dragging the futon couch into the kitchen as we continued the virtual food orgy.

"Oh, it was awful. Girl was under suspicion in the greatest crime ever committed in Ojo Sarco. The chickens eaten. No doubt about it. And Girl did have this habit of bringing home these yucky wild rodents. So maybe the suspicion was warranted. But that's all I know."

Of course, the Monks thought all this incidental feasting was simply an expression of Girl's Buddha nature.

"I don't believe it for a second," said Jim. "An enlightened fowl-gazer like Girl would never stoop so low as to eat anything but Shelton's chicken wieners, right, Girl?"

Carol was still noticeably anxious about the whole thing. Her beautiful old adobe, car garden and germ-free kitchen paled by comparison to this frightening reality. Was Girl a fraud? Had Carol been misled like so many other well-intentioned initiates? Was this *not* her true teacher?

"What do you think? That's why I called for you to come meet Girl Doggie. I've got to know the truth about Girl. Did she or didn't she eat the chickens?" Carol was suddenly sobbing into her bowl of salsa. Then a moment later lapping it up with her chips. "That's another thing. I've been having the worst mood swings since this happened," she sniveled.

"It's plaguing me. Night and day. I can't get it off of my mind. Did she or didn't she? Somehow everything pivots around this question: the fate of the planet, the meaning of trust and truth in the world. If she did, what should I make of Girl? If she didn't, then who did? I need your help with this one, Monks," Carol tearfully pleaded. "Will you stay a week and help me solve this crime? You can have anything. My fridge, my phones, my shower. Oh, but you just can't have my rice cakes. That's all for me. Yum, yum."

The Monks agreed.

Being the Quintessential Child of the Information Age that he is, Jim went out on a little espionage. His mission: to find the real killer and save our hallowed leader from further ignominy. Jim had an "in" with one of Girl's best friends, Rex the horse. He'd also made friends with a few disincarnate bean farmers at the cemetery up the street. Through them he learned that no predator until now had dared to eat those chickens.

Jim continued with his search, stringing together the pieces of this puzzle: dead chickens, innards removed but the bodies untouched. No sign of predators. *What did this mean?*

Over the course of the week Jim, the Channeling Overlord of Sedona, was able to get inside Girl Doggie's brain. He could actually hear her thoughts, repeat her conversations verbatim. And he discovered, *Yes, yes! As I thought, Girl has Floating Chicken Memory!*

But Jim needed better evidence.

One day while taking a break from aerobic phoning, Jim stumbled upon a black box buried under tall grass near a Chevy truck in the infamous Carol Car Garden. He opened up the box and began to read. He couldn't believe his baby blue eyes.

Dear Horse Rex,
You missed some great chicken.
Love,
Girl Doggie

Dear Rex,
About that chicken. Nobody really knows I ate it, alright? There's a lot of suspicion, and the owners of the birds threaten to shoot me, but Boss Carol doesn't believe I did it. So keep it cool, alright? I'm trying to make it look like that stupid runt did it.
Miss you bunch,
Girl.

Dear Rex,
   Things are getting tight. Real tight. I need your
help. Tonight at around eight P.M., before Boss Carol
goes to bed, canter on by. I'll explain it all then.
   P.S. Does a dog have Buddha nature?
   Woof!

The revelations about Girl's clandestine correspondence
stunned Jim into an awakening. He remembered how much
he loved free-range chickens, especially when served with
Michael's homemade biscuits. If Girl really did eat the hens
. . . then maybe the Monks could eat Girl! We could blame
the death of Girl on a posse of vengeful chickens. Get the
heat off of poor Carol. Serve up doggie rump roast at the
next church potluck. Oh, it seemed so perfect.

But Jim hesitated. He'd come a long way since his days as
a Chinese barbarian, and he wasn't going to blow it now.
The next day he vowed to hide the truth from Carol and
concoct a fictitious plot that would absolve Carol and Girl
of all blame.

But Jim hesitated again. Though the letters to Rex seemed
authentic, was that really Girl Doggie's paw print? Would
Girl be so careless as to put all this in writing? Maybe there
was another plot!

Late that night up at the cemetery, while out for his evening stroll, Jim gazed back at the secluded town of Ojo
Sarco, glistening in the evening air. From the post office to
the church, the farm lights seemed to form parallel lines.
And all of those alfalfa fields seemed just a little too neat.
All of those barns a bit oversize. All those adobes a bit irregular. And for cryin' out loud, what's with that monstrous
skateboard ramp those folks from the city built! "This whole
darn valley looks like a landing strip for . . . for . . . ETs!"

Jim hesitated.

But the truth came in crystal clear.

It *was* a setup. Ojo Sarco was to be the landing site for a
flock of ET aircraft. This fact had been communicated to
everyone but Carol, the new kid on the block. The death of
the hens was rigged to see if Carol was one of them or truly
an outsider. The owners actually had the chickens for supper, eating only the innards because they're trying to watch
their cholesterol.

And most intriguing, Carol's recalcitrant landowner was
part of the plot. The landlady's refusal to fix the stove, eliminate the stench caused by decaying goat doo-doo beneath the

bedroom floor and refusal to lower the rent even if Carol made much-needed repairs were further attempts to test the metaphysical mettle of our dear friend from Frisco. And finally, the missing link. The letters were forged by Horse Rex, working for the space people.

Jim raced down the hill and spilled it out to Carol.

Carol sat shaking on the porch of her adobe taking it all in as Girl Doggie sat in the shade expectantly. Having at last discovered the truth, Carol breathed a deep sigh of relief. With tears streaming down her face, she turned to Girl. "You didn't do it. You didn't, you didn't, you didn't! Oh, my darling precious, miracle doggie. My tender, innocent, healing doggie! My . . . my . . . my ecstatic, happy, cheezy doggie. Bowwow. Woof woof! It's all over. You're free . . . you're free!"

We celebrated Sunday morning. Barbecued chicken, chicken salad sandwiches and chicken pâté made for excellent feasting while driving toward the Santa Fe National Forest through the town of Penasco. There amidst a steady stream of low-riders, along with hundreds of townsfolk and tourists celebrating the feast day of St. Lorenzo, the patron saint of Chevies, we gave Girl Doggie all the chicken wieners she could possibly eat.

Girl, as it turned out, wasn't a normal dog after all. She's a rooster dog.

"Cock-a-doodle doo . . . any cock'll do! Woof . . . woof!"

Enlightened fowl-gazer, Girl Doggie.

. . .

The next day, with Girl's timely blessing, the Monks jacked the Bounder out of the ditch and hit the great highway. With a renewed vision and trust in the world, we were ready to continue our journey east in search of our extended family.

As we pulled away in the dark night of the New Mexico desert, we tried to remember why we had come to New Mexico. Chocolate? A free dinner from Jack? To find our Higher Purpose? To escape Texas?

We were puzzled. The highway spread out before us. It was dark . . . and silent. Our brains were empty, our souls cleansed. Just cruising down the highway, we stared blankly into space.

Bliss, serenity, rapture . . .

Just then a pair of white lights appeared on the horizon. Then another. Then another!

Suddenly a stream of white Mercedeses came zooming by. Honking, waving, sticking their heads out the windows. White heads, tall heads . . . *turbaned heads?* They were smiling, laughing, making faces, trying to touch the Bounder.

"Oh, my God, Jim . . . it's the Sikhs!"

"Sat Nam, you guys! Sat Naaaaaaaaammmmmmmm!"

Several days and $800 later after a severely shorted electrical system was detected and imperfectly repaired, the Monks were busing toward *Minn-eh?-soh-tah*.

"What's in Minnesota?" Mike had persistently asked Jim.

"Just some old friends of mine," said a distant Jim.

Though the Monks were happy to be back on the road again, it couldn't overcome the angst that was brewing in the monastery.

"Jim, you've been acting like a stranger since Santa Fe. What's going on with you?"

"Nothing that you'd want to hear."

"Of course I want to hear it," said Michael, knowing full well that he did in fact *not* want to hear it.

"I've just been thinking about what I'm missing by choosing the life of a traveling monk over marriage. That is, with a real woman. So many of my old friends are now happily married couples, voting Republican, breeding kids, buying homes, taking vacations, hiding from the poor, eating red meat. I don't know. I just wonder if I'm missing out on something I'm programmed to experience. And besides, how can you be satisfied traveling with someone who wants to be with you only fifty percent of the time?"

Mike remained silent as he rolled the Bounder north, wondering how long *this* would last.

The farms of northwest Iowa stood like checkerboards against the dreamy Midwestern sky. And as the Monkmobile meandered across back roads, for as far as the eye could see was a landscape of corn, soybeans, storage bins, turned fields, tractors, plows and sows. The air smelled of earth and hay, musty and sweet as its fragrant belly jostled Jim's mind with fine visions of the Crotty farm.

Jim reminisced about the journeys of childhood when the Crottys made their monthly pilgrimages out to the old homestead. Mike studied the map, the gas tank and his rumbling stomach. The Monks didn't talk the rest of the way up.

By the time the Twin Cities emerged over the horizon, Minneapolis was glowing in the setting sun, and the Monks were glowing from an overheated radiator. As they pulled into the alley behind Tonya's apartment building, there was barely enough room to park a car, let alone the twenty-six-foot Monster Monk. But bright-spirited Tonya was out rearranging cars, Dumpsters, buildings, trees (your basic Sagittarian mover and shaker), and soon the Monks found their nest just two blocks from Hennepin, a major thoroughfare. Jim bounded out to meet Tonya as Mike watched Jim's disposition immediately change as he walked into the building beaming with excitement.

"What do you think, Aide?" Mike turned to Nurse's Aide. Aide arched his back and split for the back, declining any role in this discussion.

Mike watched as a smiling Jim and Tonya walked back out to the motor home. Taking out the electric cord from the Monkmobile, they ran it through the parking lot, across the lawn, up the steps, over the porch and under the door into Tonya's apartment, plugging it into her kitchen wall. She even extended phone privileges, allowing an extension line to be run from the wall, past the bathroom, through the kitchen, under the door, over the porch, down the steps, across the lawn and through the back Monkmobile window, where it journeyed across the bed, up the runway to the sacred passenger seat.

Mike watched a bubbly Jim thank his Sagittarian hostess.

"It may be funky . . . but there's no dress code. Just make yourself at home," she said in her high-pitched nasal Hubert Humphrey best.

Yes, the folks in Minneapolis were exceptionally accommodating. And Mike was taking it all *the wrong way*.

The Monkmobile was quite the spectacle as it jutted out into the alley, forcing cars to squeeze by, scraping the fence. But no one was complaining. Everyone waved! Everyone smiled!

"Why is everyone smiling?" a skeptical Mike asked Jim.

Never had he seen so many white teeth and so many glad-to-meet-you smiles. It was uncanny to walk around the lakes, dodge in and out of stores, rummage through trash cans, mug little old ladies, lift a radio out of a car and see everyone smiling, ready to shake a hand or plant a compliment on your shoulder.

"Maybe it's the air, or maybe it's the clean water?" Jim conjectured.

There certainly *were* an abundance of lakes to swim in, right in the neighborhood. Lake Calhoun even hosted sailboats and wind surfers, swimmers and canoes.

"All this water must have a calming effect on everyone's nerves. I think if you live next to a lake, all the negative ions do something, or is it waterfalls . . . no, wait, I think it's lightning, that's a negative ion, isn't it? Maybe they've all been struck by lightning?" Mike was falling into his usual quandary regarding the physical sciences.

"Maybe they're just gritting their teeth," said Jim as he grimaced a smile.

Mike wasn't very satisfied with that explanation either.

"Listen, Mike, I need to go see a few friends tomorrow. Alone, if that's alright."

Mike knew he had no choice in the matter.

The next afternoon Jim went to visit his *friends* while Mike spent the day researching the Minneapolis Smile Factor. Straddling Loring Park, across from the Walker Art Center, he was charmed over a little lunch by the Loring Café's erudite ectomorphic restaurateur, Jason, who was going to understated lengths to explain why everyone smiled so much.

"Oh, you bet, I think it has something to do with the weather and the Nordic values. A bit of Scandinavia, a bit of good cognac and that clean white skin. It's a very white thing to do, smile that is. I'd do more of it myself if I had the time."

Mike moved on.

"Oh, you bet, I smile because my mother told me to smile," said Milo, a bona fide, dyed-in-the-wool Minnesotan smiler. Milo had charmed Michael with his smile on the street and had Mike begging for more. As an up-and-coming real estate mogul, Milo had plenty to smile about as he surveyed Loring Park and its condo potential.

"I just love all these white teeth!" confessed Mike from behind his shades. "But it does get a little bright, sort of like fresh snow in the sun."

Meanwhile, Jim had unearthed many old friends. All, of course, married. His grade-school golfing pal, Jackson Quull, was a weight-lifting banker preparing for imminent betrothal. His high school flame, Kay, now had three kids and another on the way. His college thinking buddy, Jim-2, was a successful lawyer at a successful firm, with a successful wife, a successful child, in a successful suburb of St. Paul. Even his former Nebraska debate partner, Anthony Lansdowne, had found a mate willing to tolerate his affected limericks.

What with the majority of his childhood friends now firmly entrenched in family life, why was a good-looking boy like Jim wasting his youth on a road fling with Mike?

Conflict was definitely brewing in the monastery.

Mike spent the evening furiously cleaning the motor home. It was the first time he'd put a serious hand to sweeping up all the dust since Texas. Not a word from Jim. Mike was almost afraid to knock on Tonya's door. He could hear voices, and laughter, but couldn't make out any conversations.

Was Jim in there? Why wouldn't he come out to the Monkmobile? Were they all laughing at Mike?

The more Mike thought about it, the more he scrubbed. He was down on his hands and knees furiously brushing the carpet with a steel-bristled brush, trying to get up months of spilled duck fat. He had already wiped the entire surface inside and out two times over, cleaned the fridge to the point where it reeked of bleach and was even thinking of cleaning the oven when he realized how upset he must be.

My God, I'm cleaning the oven! This is bad. Where the hell is he? Looking at his watch, Mike saw that it was now past midnight. *He said he'd be back for dinner.*

It was only when Mike caught himself cleaning out the electrical sockets with a toothbrush that he realized it was time to call it quits.

At two-thirty in the morning Michael finally went to sleep with no sign of Jim. All the lights were out in Tonya's apartment.

The next morning Mike watched as Tonya danced out the door with a big cheery smile, waved to Mike and hopped in her Toyota, off to work at the day care center.

How could she smile at me? Mike was drowning in a slow-boiling, suspicious stew.

Finally around ten, Jim appeared at the back door, smiled and waved, then went back in the apartment.

Mike followed him in, anger dripping down his pants.

"Hi, Mike, how's it going, buddy?"

Mike didn't feel like a "buddy" this morning and thought about how he might open up this delicate gem of a conversation without resorting to overstated clichés. He took a deep breath and reasoned that even if his worst fears were true, he was not going to let himself be reduced to petty comments and accusations.

Jim stood smiling.

"Where the hell were you last night? I waited till two in the morning! I was worried sick about you, man. Why didn't you let me know!" The words came rushing out like a pre-programmed response as Mike stood amazed at the influence of daytime soap operas.

Jim stood back ready to rebound, knowing that his response would either set the tone for an argument or offer the way for constructive understanding. Jim took a deep breath and thought how he might carefully avoid provoking Mike, using his Buddha wisdom and Libran moon to create a well-balanced, harmonious rapprochement.

But then he lost it. "I don't have to report everything I do back to you. I'm a free man. If you weren't such a fucking control freak, maybe I'd want to be with you. Besides, I was just hanging out with friends."

The Monks both bounced back at the intensity of this one, while Jim, the Channeling Overlord of Sedona, wondered whose life he was channeling now and moved to deflate his outburst.

"I know you were in that house doing it. I saw those lights on all night. You can't lie to me!" Mike started to grab Jim, stopping in midair, wondering if there was a way at this delicate moment he could turn such overpowering animosity into unconditional love and acceptance. But the moment was lost.

"Boy, you're way off. Tonya has a boyfriend, maaan. I wasn't even here last night!"

"Aha! See? See! I knew you weren't here!" Michael's eyes bulged out of their sockets. *Got to get ahold of myself. Come on, girl. We're both responsible adults here.*

Jim stormed back into the house yelling, "Leave me alone, I'm going to the store!"

Mike stared out from the back porch and slowly retreated to the Monkmobile. *Oh, God. I've got to get a handle on my jealousy. I'm blowing this way out of proportion. He probably* did *just spend the night with some friends. And Tonya did mention something about her boyfriend coming over for dinner.*

Mike was letting the guilt seep in for being such an overbearing, raging queen. *What was the word Jim had used? "Control freak." God. How awful.*

Michael was back in the Bounder doing what hysterical homebodies do best when under stress. He was in the kitchen cooking up a big pot of chili.

I should make Jim his favorite pie. I should never have accused him like that.

A knock came on the door. In walked a dark-haired woman, wearing a low-cut blouse and tight jeans holding a notebook in her hand.

"Is Jim here?"

"No, he went to the store. He should be right back."

"Well, could you give him his notebook. I bet he's wondering where it is."

"Why, where was it?" Michael cast a quizzical look toward the intruder, a look in between a glad-to-meet-you smile and uh-oh, I think I'm meeting someone whom I really don't think I want to be meeting.

"Oh, just tell him I found it by the bed." She smiled and bid a speedy good-bye as she dashed for her waiting Mercedes.

By the bed?

By the time Jim walked into the motor home Michael's blood was as hot as ten pounds of cayenne. Hotter than the meanest Texan chili. Hotter than *hell.*

"Hi, Mike. I'm sorry I snapped at you. You're entitled to a reasonable explanation."

Mike faced Jim, with a hot spoon in his hand, chili dripping off his pants, down into his shoes. Jim stopped at the door suddenly knowing something was very wrong and wavered between telling the whole truth or just bits and pieces of the truth.

"Do you think I'm stupid? Do you think I'm stupid!"

"What?" Jim feigned ignorance.

"Who was she?" Mike opened with enough control in his voice that it could be taken as either an accusation or a simple question.

"She?" Jim returned the same neutral tone of voice.

Mike considered his next statement with the concentration of a circus acrobat about to walk the high wire. He could calmly approach the wire and steadily walk out to the middle, or he could race out to the middle, wire shaking, and hope for the best in a blind leap for the net below.

But there was no net.

"You know who I'm talking about. I'm talking about the person to whom belongs a bed to the side of which was placed your notebook last night. Late last night. That's who!" Michael shook the retrieved notebook in the air.

"Oh, thanks. My notebook." Jim reached up, hoping to deflect the heat with a simple acknowledgment of a returned item.

"Not so fast. *Who* is she?!" Michael screeched, ruining any possibility for a loving exchange of truth and feelings.

"She's, uh . . ."

"And what were you doing with your notebook by her bed . . . taking notes I presume?"

"Well, I was working on . . ."

"Were they good notes? Something I might be interested in reading? Or were the notes mere distractions for something else that preoccupied your mind as you vi-si-ted her bedside?" Mike punctuated each word knowing for sure this was either an episode of *All My Children* or *General Hospital*.

"I was getting to know . . ."

"Oh, I bet you were. You were getting to know her pretty damn well, weren't you. I'll wager my pot of chili you know how many moles are on her"—Michael paused to consider —"*tit*." The word rang out hard, dry and mean, but Mike liked it. It's not every day one gets to play Bette Davis.

"Alright. You want to know." Jim tried to hold it in a second too long and it boiled out in all the wrong ways. "I slept with her. We were going at it like Tarzan and Jane. It was great. I loved every minute of it. Does that make you happy?"

Michael recoiled, smitten. "I'm so happy I could lick the damn alley clean of all its filth. I'm so damn happy I could stick my foot through this door and pull what hair I have left out by the roots and weave a rope to hang myself. Am I happy? Fuck yes, I'm happy. I'm so happy I'm going to fly outta here." And out the door flew Michael Monk as he raged up the alley, fuming out of the ears, cursing at the broad smiles and happy dispositions of sidewalk strollers, leaving a trail of chili in his wake.

Jim followed the trail of chili down by the lake, under a bridge and found Mike chasing ducks in the water, fully dressed, blabbering incoherently to a picnicking crowd of rollerbladers perched on the wall.

"Mike. Mike. Come on, get out. You don't have to be such a drama queen."

"Yeah, get him outta there. He's polluting the lake," yelled a rollerblader.

Mike spit a funnel of water toward Jim. The heat was still blazing in his Leonine furnace.

"I'm outta here," Mike declared, pulling himself up on the bank, refusing Jim's hand.

Jim was in a major pickle.

He stood there, deep in Gemini thought, hopelessly attempting to unearth an answer. In rapid-fire succession he began to ask himself the core yuppie questions everyone else in the previous generation had asked, but which he'd postponed after meeting Mike and embarking on a life of Monkhood.

"What's so bad about an open relationship?" he finally asked Mike, who was drying off in the grass.

"Yeah, what's so wrong with it?" echoed the rollerbladers.

Mike didn't answer as he shot a poisonous mental dart toward the neighboring crew. "Keep out of it, dudes!" he growled.

"Come on, buddy, we can work this one out," pleaded Jim.

"There's no working it out. Apparently that little astronauts-in-training ceremony didn't mean squat. I suppose I'm just fun and games. When it comes time to really get your rocks off, you go where you please."

"Astronauts in training? That wasn't real. You said so yourself. It was just a symbol of our friendship. I never said I wanted to commit to you. You've known from the start of this trip where I'm coming from."

"Well, where are you coming from?"

"Yeah, where you coming from guy?" The rollerbladers were all perched up on their haunches now, paying rapt attention to every word.

"Either you people butt those blades to the tarmac or I'm going to personally roll those suckers down your throat." Mike stood his six-three, thin-as-a-stick frame erect as the four muscled dudes and dudettes in their color-coordinated skating outfits suddenly realized they were dealing with a potentially dangerous psychomonk and hastily retreated off the lawn, down the sidewalk.

"We're still a team. The Monk unit. I'm just really confused, that's all. I mean, I haven't been with a woman in *ten years*. It's all conditioning I know, but sometimes you need to go with the conditioning to see what's at the root of it. You're my soul mate, Mike. I know that. But I can't expect you to wait around either. That's not fair. I just need this experimental phase to get it out of my system. You had your dating period at my age, why can't I?"

Mike was softened a bit by Jim's heartfelt honesty, but still had to dig his two cents in.

"I personally think you're having a premature midlife crisis, exacerbated by unresolved heterosexual tendencies coupled with unresolved animosity toward your Republican upbringing, which barely cloaks your passive-aggressive agenda to own the world," Mike gritted through his pearly white post-Freudian, neo-Reichian smile.

"Cut the crap, he just needs to get laid by a good-looking babe!" chided the last of the rollerbladers as he sped down the walk. This remark retriggered Mike's latent Bette Davis sector.

"Okay. You want a babe. I'm sorry I stood in your way. I can take a hint. You want to have a few flings. Have 'em on me. I'm going home!" Mike yelled.

"Home? The Bounder?"

"No. *Home*." Michael paused a second, momentarily grasping the emptiness of that statement.

"We have no home," Jim reminded softly.

"Well, then I'm going. Somewhere. I don't care. You can make up your mind on which side of the zendo you're sitting and let me know. I'm just not waiting around to find out." Mike was growing increasingly disaffected with his good friend Jim's chronic decision anxiety. Jim's wavering back and forth. *To be or not to be a Monk, that was the question.*

"Space, that's what he needs." Mike's audible thought lingered in the air like a kite on a string.

"Space," a passing punker nodded.

"Space," said the original Space Monk.

Northwest
Airlines Flight 122
was boarding for
San Francisco as Mike and
Nurse's Aide gave an emotional
good-bye to Jim. Countless miles under

their belt, yet neither Mike nor Aide had strayed more than a few miles from the Monkmobile since leaving California. And now they were reluctantly stretching their umbilical cord toward the gate. Mike, notoriously afraid of flying, was doing his courageous Monk best to hold down his morning meal of two butter-drenched bagels, smoked herring, boiled egg, turkey jerky, oat-bran muffin, cottage cheese and a tall glass of V-8, while a brooding Aide sunk into his own private fears of returning to earthquake-prone Baghdad by the Bay.

"Cheer up, Aide. He wants space, so he got it. You and me, we're going to have a fabulous time. San Jose, Oakland, Fresno, Bakersfield, Tijuana, San Fernando—we're going to have a Monk white-trash blast. Only the best for us!"

But Aide wasn't licking it. Looking out from between the bars of his kitty carrying case, Aide pressed up against the cage reaching out with what seemed like a final paw toward a confused and hurting Jim. His little kitty whiskers softly brushed against Jim's cheek, delivering a delicate kitty tear on Jim's face, sending a slightly shaken Mike onto the plane wondering if this was a sign of things to come.

As the plane ascended into the sun, the Monkmobile glistened in a sea of cars in the airport parking lot, while a waving Jim disappeared below into the twinkling lights of the Twin Cities.

Yes, the Monks had spent three days of marathon processing trying to *work it out* . . . to no avail.

"You want me to be the rock while you go out and sow your oats? So what does that mean? I stay parked in this alley like a kept person, waiting? And how long am I supposed to wait? A week? A month? A couple of years?" Michael was fast learning about his newfound limits and his capacity for jealousy, the great leveler of relationships, large and small.

"It's not a bad alley. You can see other people too," reasoned Jim, intent on working it out.

"I'm just not into other people. I'm a one-person-at-a-time sort of guy. If you can't handle we being a *we*, that's okay. I was coping as long as we were just *brothers*. But as soon as we crossed over the line, there's no coming back. I can't take it all back and be a complacent second fiddle while you play the big brass." Michael was serious.

"Mike, it's just a phase. I need to exorcise this straight thing out of my system, that's all. I just need a little break. I'll go somewhere. You shouldn't have to leave the Monkmobile," Jim offered.

"But maybe *I* need a break from this pressure cooker," Mike finally confessed. "You're not the only one that feels trapped inside here." *And to think I just refused Jack's offer of a job and a place to live.* Michael was inwardly kicking himself. "I'm leaving. We both need a break, and a simple day trip isn't going to cut it. We both need to think about what exactly we're doing together."

Round and round the Monks processed, day after painstaking day, through the pros and cons, ups and downs, highways and byways, to separate or not to separate. Every possible option, every possible solution was offered and analyzed, consumed and regurgitated until the trail of emotional debris was like a tangled mass of mangled used tires in the steaming jungle of the Monk subconscious.

Aries-moon Mike finally declared an end to it all, being the deterministic soul that he was. Taking Nurse's Aide as his only share of the spoils, he left Jim with the rest.

"And you can have the computer too."

Now Jim, the original Space Monk, could have all the space he could handle, as Mike and Aide flew off into an ocean of clouds, heading west for the promised land of California.

"Well, that's the end of him for a while," sniffed Mike. "I hate teary good-byes."

Mike scoped out the plane. "Time for a martini or a stogie, or how 'bout a dirty movie, Aide. Would you like that? What do ya think of that, buddy?" Michael cradled Aide in his arms as he blotted a wet kitty tear off Aide's whiskers. "Now, Aide, don't start going off the deep end."

But by the time they hit San Francisco, the deep end had come to them.

While Michael stood waiting for the five pieces of kitty luggage, an announcement came over the loudspeaker: "Michael Monk, please pick up the nearest white courtesy telephone. Michael Monk, courtesy phone."

Carting five pieces of mismatched luggage, the pink cat-carrying case, the pressure cooker, two brown sacks of dirty clothes and a box of books to read, Michael found his way to the nearest white phone in the mezzanine of the San Francisco International Airport.

"Mr. Monk, you have an important telegram. Please come by the traveler's information booth," chimed the sweet mechanical voice.

"Who could that be?"

"Who's calling at this ungodly hour?" Aide dittoed as he propped open an eye, then slammed the curtains shut in his kitty cage, passing out for the night.

Michael marched toward the booth expectantly. "Michael, we've received urgent news. We must make contact. Please call as soon as you get this. We need to hear from you. . . . Mom."

Michael held the message in his trembling hand while the counter clerk busily completed a signature form. She was painfully slow, causing Michael's blood pressure to rise as he counted seconds on the clock.

He was already anticipating the call he would place at the phone booth outside, the hassle of punching in all of those calling-card numbers and the agonizing wait for Mom to pick up the phone.

He knew it must be bad. He could feel it in his intestines, in his throat, in his fragile heart. Mom never, ever, sent urgent messages, unless, of course, it was something incredibly grave . . . a terrible accident . . . a death . . . an arrest . . . an impending earthquake? His mind was spinning with possibilities. Maybe it was Jim. Maybe Jim went off the deep end. Maybe Jim got married to a *real* woman.

Outside, Mike was immediately assaulted by a busload of

kids invading the airport wearing Fisherman's Wharf caps, speaking in loud, excited German. While Michael stood at the phone booth, a tall, lanky kid with a wide mouth smacked headfirst into the Monk, knocking both of them to the sidewalk.

The message Mike held was caught by the wind and the kid bounded after it. The boy's hand was bleeding from the fall, his knuckles having scraped on the sidewalk, and in retrieving the piece of paper for Mike, his blood smeared on the paper.

This must be really bad, thought Mike as he finished dialing Mom's number in El Cajon. *This is going to be really, really bad. I can feel it.* Mike's stomach was an agitated washing machine of pure fear.

"Hi, Mom, it's Mike. What's going on? How did you know to send a telegram to this airport?"

"Oh, Michael, thank God you called. I got through to Jim in Minneapolis and he told me you'd left for San Francisco. What's going on with you two? He sounded really upset. Oh, never mind, I've got some really bad news, but I want to know if you're okay. Are you okay?" Her voice betrayed panic, and Mom never panicked.

"Yes, I'm fine. What's going on?"

"Well, listen, Michael, it's Jack. You've got to promise me that you're going to be okay."

"I'm okay, I'm okay, just tell me what it is!" Mike's heart was pounding from the suspense.

"We just got an urgent call last night. Jack is in a hospital in France."

"France!" Mike screamed in the mouthpiece. "That's impossible, I just saw him less than two weeks ago in Santa Fe."

"Really?" Mom paused for a second. "That's totally strange. Was he okay?"

"Well, yeah, sort of. Actually, no, he didn't look good. But he wouldn't talk about it. He seemed under stress. What's going on?" Michael replayed the scene in the restaurant and the driven look in Jack's eyes.

"We're trying to get through, but we can't find anyone there who speaks English. It doesn't sound very good, Michael. In fact . . . we're not even sure if he's still alive."

Michael's heart dropped to his knees. Uncle Jack? In a hospital? The mere thought of Jack in a hospital was almost an oxymoron. He could not picture Jack in a hospital, let alone a doctor's office.

"Michael. We're going over. It's the only way to find out what's going on."

"But what happened?" asked an incredulous Mike.

"All we know is that he's been in a coma. He might have had a stroke . . . but they were very guarded. Do you know what toxoplasmosis is?"

Mike dropped the phone.

Uncle Jack had AIDS.

"I'll be on the first plane down if you need me."

"Well, I don't want you to do that . . . yet. Me and Aunt Babe are going to catch the first flight to France. We've got to find him before it's too late. Just stay in touch, okay?" Mom sounded tired. Very tired.

Michael hung up the phone, feeling as if he'd just jumped from ten thousand feet and crashed into the Bay. Every joint in his body ached as he lugged the carload of luggage into the back of a rent-a-heap and headed off for Oakland to visit Charles and Mary David, sobbing uncontrollably all the way.

Jack had seemed unusually thin in Santa Fe, but he passed it off to stress. And this whole business about buying property in Santa Fe. Did Jack know he was sick then? Of course he did. Then why wouldn't he tell me?

Michael remembered how evasive Jack had been about his health, circumventing the questions. Jack never was one for sharing the intimate details of his life.

Upon arriving at Charles and Mary David's, Mike was ready to collapse from the stress of the day and, absentmindedly thinking he was still traveling in the Aide-scented Monkmobile, opened the door to Aide's kitty carrier, allowing Aide to bolt out of the car and scamper around the side of Charles and Mary David's house.

"Oh, well, Aide always comes back. I'll see him in the morning."

The next morning there was no trace of Nurse's Aide. And Mom had called to report she was at the airport boarding for France.

Michael felt somber that morning looking for Aide. In Oakland there were as many cats as people, and in this particular block over a hundred cats prowled the alley at night, most of them male, most of them very territorial. Aide had been released into a virtual combat zone, the Beirut of the feline world.

"What have I done?" moaned Michael as he spent the morning combing the alleys. Knocking on every door, he only reaffirmed the truth that every house had an array of territorial male cats.

With Nurse's Aide abandoned in the wilds of Oakland and Jack ill in France, Michael felt double cursed.

Mike took up residence in the alley behind Charles and Mary David's. For four days he kept a nightly vigil looking for signs of Aide. All the cats came out for their nightly cruise of the turf around midnight, and Mike was there waiting.

Thirty calicoes, ten tiger stripes, three Siamese, twelve black cats, nine white tomcats, several raccoons, an ugly possum and countless stray dogs later, a determined Mike still waited, but still no sign of Aide.

That is, until the fourth night. Driving down the street after a meal at Ay Caramba, Mike saw him.

Michael bounded out of the car chasing down the fleeing feline. Over a Cadillac, through a garage, under a fence, racing through the backyards, patios and hedges of countless homes, over hot tubs, clawing through wisteria vines, pulling through rose bushes . . . Always one step ahead, "Aide" avoided the expert chase of Michael, until finally, exhausted and empty-handed, Michael returned to the stalled car.

Five police squad cars were soon hot on Mike's tail, summoned by a neighbor. Mike was on his stomach, handcuffs to his back, facing the dirt, trying to explain why a wild romp through the backyards of Oakland at three A.M. was not really an act of aggression, nor an attempt to burglarize, but was in fact the most perfectly normal thing to do when trying to sequester the great, one and only, Nurse's Aide.

The cops weren't amused. But neither was Mike, who, when released, spent a final, sleepless night in the alley, empty-handed.

The next morning a neighbor directed Mike up the street where she was convinced a cat of Aide's description now resided. Mike leaned on the buzzer, summoning an older woman to the door, who held yet another gray and white tabby.

"No, I've had my Peaches for nine years. She's a girl anyhow. Sorry."

In a final attempt, Mike sequestered animal retrieval expert Sherlock Bones and posted reward posters around the block. All to no avail, save one threatening hand-scrawled note reading: *Die yuppie scum, your cats are being sold to animal researchers where they are being tortured and tested for scientific research.*

Mike held his head in his hands.

"Jack has AIDS, and now I've lost Aide. Why is this all happening at once?"

That night Mom called from France with the solemn news that only one hour before she arrived, following a transatlantic flight, a harrowing trip through Paris, negotiating her way to Nice not knowing a word of French, Jack died in the hospital.

Mike had no choice but to leave Oakland and Aide and board the next flight to San Diego to await Mom's return. He called Jim to relate the news.

"Jim, I'm going to have to leave Aide in the alley. He's gone for good. And now Jack. He's gone too."

Jim's heart sank.

"Oh, Mike, I'm really sorry to hear about Jack. I should fly out to be with you," said Jim. But Michael knew this was something he had to face by himself, with his biological family.

The memorial service was held in a modest church outside El Cajon. Michael's family clutched hands during the final rites as the well-meaning pastor extolled Jack's "virtuous life."

If only Jack could hear this, he'd turn red! thought Mike.

Mom had a determined look on her face when she pulled Michael aside after the service.

"Listen, we have to talk about something."

"Look, Mom, don't worry about me, it's you I'm worried about, you're really stressed out. You've been through a horrible ordeal."

"No, Michael, you don't understand."

"Believe me, Mom, I totally understand. Let's both just take it easy. I don't have to go back."

"Michael, listen, listen, you don't understand. Just stop a second. Oh, I hope you can handle this."

"Handle what?"

"Well, it's about Jack. He's not exactly . . . well, gone yet."

"What?! He's still alive?" Michael's skin crawled.

"Well, no, but your aunt Babe, your cousin Linda, and I had a little problem in Nice. We couldn't uh, well . . . bring ourselves to do anything with the ashes. We still have them."

"You what?"

"I know it's crazy, but we tried for five days to do something with them. At first we thought it'd be as simple as just scattering them out on the water. But then we realized if we did that the ashes would just float back to shore on all the sunbathers. Then we learned that it was illegal anyhow. If we were going to take them out to sea, we would have to hire a boat to go far enough out to be in international waters. Then we found out we needed papers. On top of it all, none of us spoke a word of French. Besides, you wouldn't believe the bureaucracy in France. It was going to take a month to get the right permits. We just didn't have enough money, time or nerve."

"Nerve?" Michael asked.

"Yes, nerve. To open the box. We were scared to open the box. And then the three of us, well, we thought about just skipping the permit and renting ourselves a little rowboat. We were going to row far enough away from shore so as to not be obvious. We thought we'd bring a bottle of Jack's favorite wine and make a toast. But when it came right down to it . . . we just couldn't do it. Open the box that is!"

Michael looked at a curious burgundy bag that sat in the corner, which had caught his eye when he first arrived home. "You don't mean to say . . ."

"Yes, he's in there."

"His ashes?"

"Yes. You have no idea the ordeal we've been through. When we couldn't bring ourselves to, well, scatter them, we were afraid to leave Jack in the hotel room. Babe was afraid that someone might break in and steal the box thinking it was valuables. So we started carrying him around with us. Babe wouldn't let the box out of our sight.

"It was ridiculous. We carried him all over Nice, signing papers, in and out of restaurants, on and off the bus, going through the grocery store. It almost became a joke. When we'd go to eat, we'd get an extra seat. A few times we'd sit him right on the table. People thought we were crazy. One night we were sitting in the hotel when we suddenly heard gospel music coming out of a church."

"In French?"

"No, in English. Can you imagine? Here we were in the middle of Nice and you would have thought we were in Alabama. We grabbed Jack and tried to get into the church, but the place was packed. And there we stood with the bag, as this black gospel singer sang 'Ol' Man River.' We just fell apart. We knew it was for Jack. Babe lost it."

"The box?"

"No, her mind. We were all losing our mind. I really thought we had totally lost it when we started talking to the bag like he was still in there."

"Like what would you say?"

"Oh, we'd be sitting down to eat, looking at the menus and we'd start asking Jack what he recommended, or we'd be walking along asking Jack to interpret signs for us. He spoke French. Not us. Finally, we knew we'd have to bring him back to the States. I mean, we couldn't just leave him in the airport. So we went to the American consulate. They weren't even sure if it was legal. In fact, they just shook their heads and told us not to tell anyone what we were carrying, which made us even more paranoid.

"I thought Babe was going to have a fit on the plane. We wouldn't check it as luggage because we thought it would spill open, so we brought him on board and kept him right under our feet. The stewardess wouldn't let Babe hold it in her lap so she used it as a footrest after apologizing profusely to Jack. We were positive customs would stop us. But they just waved us on through.

"We were just praying we'd make it here in one piece. But now we don't know what to do. We thought maybe you could do something about it."

Mike eyed the burgundy bag. "Well, I guess I could take them up to San Francisco. He'd probably like that, to be scattered in the Bay."

That afternoon Mike was once again boarding a plane back to San Francisco.

"No, it won't be necessary to check this bag," he assured the ticket agent. "I'll carry it on."

Michael wondered if the scanners could pick up ashes. He didn't exactly have any certificates, and besides, what were you supposed to do about things like this? Notify the authorities? Get a police escort?

He obsessed on the box all the way up. The burgundy bag, and the sealed box inside, had become a thorn in his deep subconscious. *What exactly do these ashes look like? Are there bones in there?*

Mike was feeling nervous, so much so that by the time the plane landed in Oakland he was certain there would be a squad car waiting at the gate.

Instead he found his rental car waiting in the parking lot where he'd left it, packed to the roof with the five pieces of mismatched luggage, the pink, empty cat-carrying case, the unused pressure cooker, two brown bags of still-to-be-washed dirty clothes and the box of books, which had yet to be opened.

Feeling conspicuous, Michael carried the burgundy bag around to the passenger's side and opened the door for Jack.

He too had begun talking to the box as if Jack were still in there. "Okay, Jack, I'm going to just sit you right here in the passenger seat. I don't even mind if you smoke."

That first night Mike stayed in the car, feeling a little raw to begin calling up friends for a place to crash. Certainly cheap hotels were out of the question as Jack would never have allowed for that. Since Jack liked to travel, Mike spent the wee hours of the morning traveling around the Bay.

After a brief nap in the parking lot of Golden Gate Fields, Mike thought he heard Jack talking to him. Stunned by the reality of Jack's death, another virtual reality set in. Michael began asking the box what Jack wanted to see, and the box began to answer.

"Hey, Jack, where to next?" asked a deluded Michael as he hauled the burgundy bag around the Bay.

First stop, U.C. Berkeley, where Jack had been a student. Then City College, where Jack taught French. Out on the streets Michael carried Jack on his shoulder, carting his uncle around town, taking in the last sights and sounds of Jack's favorite city.

Down in Union Square, after two sleepless nights on the town, Michael sat on a bench facing Macy's, sporting a three-day beard and eating a bag of potato chips. The world seemed like an eerily small place when an acquaintance of Jack's happened by and, remembering Michael, asked how Jack was doing. Mike cordially declined to comment as he rested his hand on the burgundy bag.

As cable cars discharged their loads at the corner, the hustling throngs of San Francisco seemed like a vacuous circus of fools, with the fashionably hip racing through the doors of Macy's, I. Magnin's and Neiman-Marcus.

"Jack hated these places. I should take him to the San Francisco he really loved."

Michael Monk hopped a cable car making the sharp ascent to Nob Hill, only this time he sat down with Uncle Jack underneath. And as he contemplated the San Francisco Bay, the conductor's bell rang out for Jack's soul, clearing the way for his final tour of the city as a wall of thick fog threatened to engulf the tall, cold girders of downtown.

Mike carried the bag in his arms as if he were holding on to the last thread of memory to the great Uncle Jack.

"His heart may have stopped, but his life and his work still live, and what remains of him shines as a testimony to his existence," Mike muttered in the now empty cable car.

Jumping off the cable car at Jackson Street, Mike wandered North Beach taking Jack by all of the places he had loved. The Savoy Tivoli, Washington Square Bar and Grill, Coit Tower . . . Jack had brought Mike on this same tour in the midsixties when every evening Jack would proudly cart Mike around on the back of his Vespa to see the big-city lights from his favorite vantage points. And this was his favorite—only now it was Mike who carted Jack to the base of Coit Tower to view the vastly changed San Francisco landscape.

"It's a city for lovers," Jack used to say, "and if you're not careful, a city for losers."

What else had Jack seen on these streets over the course of his life? He'd arrived poor but passionate, and in his rise to fortune had given as much of himself back to the city as he'd taken. He'd known these streets during the days of Kerouac, Ginsberg, Ferlinghetti, and had put his own pen to prose when every well-traveled young man of intelligence held a secret desire to write the great American novel.

Always one for the great adventure, he believed in life on the edge, and taking risks. In fact, his savvy encouragement had encouraged the Monks to take to the road.

Walking across Grant Avenue through Chinatown, Michael turned up Sacramento to the park on Nob Hill where he sat on a bench watching the streams of tourists snap pictures of the Bay. He watched an aging grande dame feed the pigeons with a bag of popcorn and wondered what Jack would have to say about her oversize jewels.

"I wonder if he found his dreams here on the Bay or did he die searching?"

The cold San Francisco air bit at Mike's skin as he pulled Jack closer. There, at the top of Nob Hill where the cable cars stopped, in front of the Mark Hopkins and across from Grace Cathedral, sat Jack's old condo overlooking the Bay.

Mike rang the bell, but there were no answers. So he sneaked in through the door off the alley and climbed the back stairs to the roof where Jack had spent many late nights and afternoons entertaining the city's best and brightest.

Mike then escorted Jack from his Nob Hill condo down California Street to Polk Street and with hesitation walked into Q-T, one of Jack's favorite watering holes. He was certain that he'd meet some of Jack's young friends here, some of whom might have used Jack for his power or influence, or most likely, money.

Yes, a few were there. Mike recognized them from old parties. Sitting two stools down was Erik, a prissy beach-blond queen, looking every bit the twenty-one-year-old hustler, chain-smoking over his gin and tonic at two in the afternoon. Michael rested the burgundy bag on the stool between them.

"Hey, how's your uncle, haven't seen him around in ages. How's his car doing?" said Erik, blowing smoke above Michael's head, as affected as ever.

Michael shrugged, biting his lip in bitterness, daring to reveal what sat between them. *Might Erik have some part in this?* Mike wondered. *Who's to blame anyhow? We sit here with Jack between us. This cheap, jaded hustler probably took Jack for more than he was worth and could care less what's become of him. All he remembers is the Corvette and the connections he made off my uncle.*

"What's in the bag . . . no, let me guess. It's white, it's light, and I'll need a straw . . . right?" said a half-serious Erik.

Michael told him the truth.

Erik's face turned blue as steel as he backed away from the bar in horror.

"What the hell you bringing that around, are you crazy, isn't there a law against this?"

Erik quickly gathered his things and left the bar, afraid to feel, afraid to make the connection.

With a bit of remorse Mike had a drink and a toast with the burgundy bag. He asked for two glasses of French red wine, a pack of Camels and a candle. Jack's last smoke was lit by the light of the flame and its uninhaled draw extinguished by the wine. Jack wouldn't have approved. Jack didn't like needless sentiment or unorthodox behavior. At least not in public. But what the hell, Mike was treating Jack for a change.

He then took Jack up from Hyde Street to California by the old Chez Jacques, his popular cabaret, which brought the finest voices of Europe and America back to the city.

Mike took him to the Bay, by the wharf, up the Marina, across the Golden Gate, and on the ferry to and from Sausalito. He covered every mile of Jack's old stomping grounds and, then at long last, brought Uncle Jack down to the sea.

Michael called up his old friend Elizabeth in Berkeley. If ever there was a time he needed emotional support, it was now, as he pleaded with Elizabeth to join him at Baker Beach in the late afternoon, near the foot of the Golden Gate Bridge. Elizabeth and Mike had been on more than one shamanistic quest during the days when Mike lived in the city. So Mike asked his soul sister Elizabeth to help him bury Jack. She brought her infant son, Sam, as witness.

The day was menacingly cold as the walls of thick summer fog flogged the beaches like an assault from a Nordic winter. The walkway down the beach was littered with bottles, cans, wrappers and condoms. Lovesick sonnets, abandoned promises and forgotten vows were carved into the rocks, wood and railing lining the path. Mike walked ahead holding the box in his arms, coddling it like a baby, coddling it like Elizabeth held Sam, gripping so tight his veins were ready to burst in the frigid air.

Mike was feeling blood. Poisonous blood, angry blood, the blood of poets, of lovers, of teachers, of uncles. The blood from persons of meaning, of vision. Of sons and daughters filled with the joy of living, the desire to breathe, create, express and feel, struck down in midstride by a mystery assassin. A thief in the night that had entered through the door of passion and left poison in the lovers' cup.

The beach was desolate, save for a tribe of lone runners, pacing the surf, skimming the tide.

Mike traced the shore with his mind, envisioning the descent into the watery grave, into which depth he should deliver his charge. The towers of the Golden Gate stood fortress over the unforgiving mist, anchored deep into the rock, spanning the treacherous currents of the Bay.

Elizabeth, Michael and Sam sat in a circle near a fire. The box sat like a shrine against the foreboding sea, ominous in its message.

Death was inside.

Death to one man's journey well lived. Death striking a final stroke to another human light. A final bow before the curtain.

To the wind Mike sang Piaf, Jack's femme fatale. He lifted the box to the sky and prayed for the gods to release his soul, to ease pain, to forgive suffering.

The box was opened as a young Sam looked on. The beginning of life witnessing the end of life. Formation delivering cessation back to the elements.

Mike rose, carrying Uncle Jack to the sea. Each hesitating step condemning the last. Delaying release, delaying the truth that Jack was gone.

After an eternally long pause, he at long last swam into the ocean submerging himself and Jack deep under the water, deep beneath the sky, releasing the ashes into the strong currents moving out to sea.

Michael stayed long in the water, bathing with Jack, feeling Jack's life, feeling the fleeing brilliance of life, feeling Jack's soul as but a flicker in the grand scheme of things.
"He's free. What more could he want? He is finally free."

Uncle Jack.

Northwest
Airlines landed an empty-hearted Mike
at the Twin Cities airport

on a crisp, cool fall day. As the jet approached the airfield, Mike could see the Monkmobile in the parking lot, just the way he'd left it with Jim a month earlier.

Mike carried with him a photo of Jack and a small tuft of kitty hair from the missing Nurse's Aide. As he slowly walked out the boarding gate, his head hung low from the weight he carried in his mind. Like all things recent, he only assumed that this would be the end of the road with Jim. He'd returned, if only to see with his own eyes, that there was no hope in the Monks' continuing the journey together.

Suddenly a smiling Jim appeared out of the wings holding a bouquet of daffodils. Mike stood at the gate shaking his head at the sight of Jim in that old, tattered white jumpsuit, with a hand-lettered sign across a sheet of cardboard proclaiming, *Welcome Home, My Sweet Brown Rice. To Know You Is to Chew You Well.*

Mike stood stunned.

Jim's deep foray into Midwestern matrimonial madness had awakened him to his true Monkhood, to the beauty and unheralded importance of the road well traveled, and more than anything in the world, more than a wife, kids, more than a corporate job with a cushy salary, more than a normal life played by normal rules, more than social acceptance, he wanted Mike back on board. Back before he lost his true life direction. Back before the Sirens of Conformity swallowed up another free-spirited prince of possibility. Back before Jim could change his mind.

"I think that maybe it's time for you and me to *hit the road*. What do you say, honey?"

Mike *hoped* it was time.

Jim *knew* it was time.

Jim led Mike out to the Monkmobile, which stood radiant and clean. It's shiny tan exterior was expertly polished. Each window sparkled in the low setting sun. It smelled like jasmine.

"Smells like angels have been here!" Michael's eyes widened.

"Yeah, angels with jasmine incense," replied a smiling Jim. "I'm ready for your *brotherly love*, Mike. Everything about you, me, this journey, it all seems right somehow. It's crazy, sad, absurd, fun, challenging . . . it's everything I want. It's exactly who I really am."

"So who are you?" asked Mike.

"I'm a traveler on a journey. So are you. And journeys take you to unexpected places, both in the heart and in the world. This journey *is* a search for ourselves. It's not just about finding family. It's about being family for each other, and that means starting with you, Mike. I'm going to be family for you from now on. I don't care what it's called— gay or straight, bi or try. I'm your family and I'm not going to be afraid anymore. I'm not going to hold back the passion and the love. I want our life to sing with excitement. We've got to live every day open to the world around us. That's what being a Monk is all about. Being receptive to what is in front of you. You know, beginner's mind."

Michael stood shaking his head. Feeling Jim's words course through his veins. Feeling truth.

"No, it really doesn't matter how you define what we are to each other," Mike agreed. "I'm not one for labels either, you know."

"Life is too short to run from what is real," added Jim.

"Does that mean I can throw out my gloves and scarves?"

"Yes!"

"And my lipstick and earrings?"

"If you want!"

"And the wigs and skirts?"

"I'll take you just the way you are."

Mike stood with his mouth open letting it all sink in, having absolutely no intention of throwing out *anything*. But to be accepted just the way he was . . . He could feel it coming. Those hot, wet tears welling up the inside of his eyes. That rumbling, tumbling commotion in the pit of his stomach. That churning release of built-up tension and expectation. He let his head sink back, then dropped to his knees, spread open his arms, opened his mouth wide and let her fly at the top of his lungs . . . "I . . . love . . . you . . . Jim! You're the best! You're the fucking best! You take my heart away." Mike's eyes rained with tears as he stretched out his arms to his soul brother, giving him a big kiss and a long hug.

"Just when I was prepared to give the whole thing up, you pull me back on board. Oh, my God, am I relieved. Coast to coast, you're my partner. An astronaut in training. You're my kind of Monk. I love you so much!" After all that he'd been through, Mike was beside himself with happiness. He'd emerged from the darkness back into the light.

Mike was home.

Now safely back inside the mobile monastery, carrying an empty kitty case and a wide, warm smile, Mike joyously hollered, "God, am I glad to be here!"

He stepped into the driver's seat like a king returned to his throne. Jim took shotgun as Mike turned the key, pumping gas through the bowels and jowls of the Bounder. The Monkmobile revved up, Mike slapped her in gear, strapped on seat belts, took out the map, and the Monks charged out of that parking lot with the freedom of two doves on a breeze, charged with a mission, fueled by love. Onward and forward. The final frontier.

"Coast to coast, coast to coast." The Monks chanted down the road leaving Minneapolis and its memories far behind. "Coast to coast, coast to coast." The rolling, flat landscape stretched far toward the sky, soothing the pain, healing the wounds. Yes, coast to coast, the Monks were back in gear. The road was our medicine. The road was queen.

A week later, after a flip of the coin, the Monks arrived in the Ozark's Ouachita Mountains. Mike was determined to pay a friendly visit to the land of his birth before heading farther east.

Undoubtedly one of the best campgrounds in all of Arkansas, Lake Ouachita came with hot showers, ample wood-

All roads lead to Monk.

lands, fantastic trails, swimming, boating on "the second-cleanest lake in America" and was within an hour of Crystal Country and the coveted diamond mines of Murfreesboro.

As Jim spent the evening reading up on the crystal and diamond mines, Mike loaded up on the natural spring water pouring out of McFadden's 3 Sisters Springs. According to folklore, each spring was thought to have curative powers for different ailments. Mike filled up from spigot #3. Interestingly, as he carried the water back to the Monkmobile, he heard the whining of a cat, but dismissed it, thinking it was just his fever.

Suddenly a loud, piercing whine shattered his ears, chilling him to the bone.

"Nurse? Nurse's Aide?" he called into the dark forest.

Michael went running to the Bounder to fetch a flashlight and to grab Jim. The two Monks bolted out the door, circling the campground in a frenzied search for the fading sound of a distressed feline. After an hour of searching we put out Alley Cat brand food in the old Nurse kitty bowl and fell exhausted into bed, fading into a deep deserved sleep.

That night Mike dreamed he was in a big pit with a pile of crystals and naked savages roasting whale blubber over hot diamond coals with a mysterious man standing on the side of the road furiously scratching his balls, holding the talking head of Elvis as a chorus of screaming sex goddesses threw water on the fire bowing to a crowned feline sitting on a throne.

Phew. What in the hell was that? Mike tossed in his sleep.

The next morning there she was. Just like in the dream. Not Nurse. Not Aide. But another cat.

She was nervous at first, and rightly so, sensing our history with cats. We offered her food, but she split into the woods. This poor little babe was abandoned, thin and undernourished. Finally, by midafternoon she came around for some leftover catfish, and before long she was asking for more catfish and more. And then without warning she suddenly hopped into the Monkmobile and immediately went to the back and picked out her place.

When she started to suck Mike's sweater, we knew this was providence. The third in the Nurse lineage had arrived.

Preacher Jim crowned our newest arrival "the great Dolly Lama, a country and western mystical cat . . .

"We praise Bob this evening that Nurse has sent us his

only begotten daughter to wash away the inequities of the Monks. Have kitty fur on us. . . ."

Interestingly, she acted as if she understood her calling right from the start. Once fed, she immediately nestled into our queen-size bed, perched high on the lotus seat from where she could reflect on the busy happenings in the next room. As one would do with any true-blue avatar, we moved all our belongings to the front of the Monkmobile and gave her the best room in the house.

"O Lord, O Michael, O Mom, this *is* the Dolly Lama. This is another gift from the gods, the long prophesied . . . Registered Nurse!" Jim broke down into Jimmy Swaggart–style tears.

"It's an omen! Look at her. She's taken over right where Aide left off."

That evening the Monks saw God.

**Her Holiness, the Great Dolly Lama
(aka Registered Nurse).**

On the third day the Monks arose again and headed for Hot Springs. But on our way into town another great spiritual master hit the scene. There on the side of the road stood a mysterious, hitchhiking man holding a sign reading "Only Go Straight . . . Graceland" with a caricature of Elvis the King.

"Oh, my God. It's the man in my dream." Michael swerved to a stop.

Mr. Burris had traveled thousands of miles from Poona by way of Santa Fe, leaving behind his beautiful German wife, Telasmee, and his saxophonist stepdaughter, Johanna Herself, to pay homage at the shrine to Elvis. He was on his last leg to Memphis when we spotted him on the road, furiously scratching his balls. It seems that after a "most terrible night" in the woods the honorable Mr. Burris had surfaced with the worst case of poison ivy in the worst possible place.

"Hello, kind sir, need a lift?" Jim, ever the generous Monk, jumped out of the Monkmobile to help a struggling white-robed Mr. Burris haul his bags on board.

"Sheeet, man. My balls are on fire."

Michael Monk peered from around the steering wheel at Mr. Burris as he sheepishly stepped into the Bounder, desperately scratching his testicles.

"Where are you going, kind sir?" asked Mike.

"To a doctor. It is certainly a most pressing emergency. And then to the Holy Land of Memphis." He stood in his cutoffs, with the inside of his thighs oozing from the rash.

Offering his rare and exotic clay and herbal mud treatment, Michael was down on his knees spreading an herbal mud pack on those poor swollen balls. But that only made matters worse. Mr. Burris was begging, and we mean begging, to be put out of his misery.

"I want that magical American drug. I want the cortisone."

Jim, fresh out of his own cortisone daze from his recent bout with herbalholic dermatitis, warned Mr. Burris of the dire consequences. But to no avail.

Mr. Burris was mainlining that cortisone in the emergency room by noon.

"We'll get you to the highway and you can catch a ride from there," Michael offered.

Mr. Burris hopped back in the Monkmobile, which was bursting at the seams with bags of soybeans, brain machines, cases of herbal supplements, Jim's half ton of scrapbooks and those river rocks.

"Gentlemen, what might be in these burlap bags?" asked

Mr. Burris in that affected Hindi accent he had acquired from years in Poona.

"Cow skulls! From Santa Fe," Jim said proudly.

"Is that so? We've been contemplating where all our cow skulls had vanished. I'm afraid the desert's been picked clean."

Mr. Burris surveyed the well-appointed Monkmobile, its mountains of material karma, and smiled a knowing smile to the back where Dolly Lama sat in meditative silence. "Oh, Doll Face. Here you are again!"

"You know our cat?"

"But yes, this is the great wandering Buddha cat. Look at her orange and golden fur. She appears wherever I go! She's a *sanyassin*. A holy wanderer." Mr. Burris climbed on the bed settling down with the Doll. "Where're you kind gentlemen heading?"

"The mines," Mike replied.

"Take me with you. Doll and I have some catching up to do. I'm in no hurry anyhow."

The Monks shrugged and took off down the road with yet another Monk on board.

"Gentlemen, let me explain myself. I recently sold my million-peso-a-year business, the Reefer man. I was tired of delivering salsa and tofu to natural-food stores and very unappreciative oriental restaurants. I am now on a pilgrimage to scramble my brain a little. I created a choice: either I go to Chicago and stay with my weight-lifting pappa or hit the holy road. Of course, as a holy man, I chose the latter."

The Monks could relate.

Mr. Burris was a gentle, friendly Aries bodhisattva love spirit. He stretched out his long, thin frame on the Monk bed, cuddling up to Dolly, whispering in her ear.

"Dolly, we are fellow travelers, moving in the same way."

Dolly was not interested.

"Oh, Dolly, let me tell you about one of your previous nine lives and maybe then you'll understand why I must stay."

Dolly yawned.

"Dolly, you at that time were very tired of life in skunkmobile. Too much commotion. So, Dolly, you packed your yarn and secret stash of curried cat food and caught the next ricksha to Bombay. So began your quest for the Mystic Nose."

Dolly's ears picked up.

"For days and days, Dolly, you sniffed through the Indian

countryside stumbling upon swindler money changers and others wanting to end one of your nine lives and spread your ashes into the stinking Holy Ganges in Benares."

Dolly turned.

"But, Dolly, you escaped. 'The nose knows,' you would say. And onward you sniffed. One day while dreaming of curried mice underneath the very sacred Bodhi Tree Animal Shelter, you smelled the filthy socks of Zorba the Buddha, the Enlightened One. And you looked up at the morning star and knew, at long last, whom you never wanted to be.

" 'Meow!' you cried. 'I must find these stinking, smelling, putrid, god-awful, ancient Indian-guru feet!' You turned and turned and then . . . you stopped turning. And took a nap.

"That evening you woke to the sound of one leper's hand clawing. You said, 'I've heard that sound before . . . and I don't like it!' So, Dolly, at that auspicious moment you agreed to respond to each distraction of mind with a simple mantra: 'Just say nose!' "

By the time we reached Royal on Highway 270, Mr. Burris had so persuaded Dolly with fantastic tall tales of her past lives that she agreed to keep him on board. In celebration and gratitude Mr. Burris then promptly volunteered to be the Monks' itinerant gofer, cook, mechanic, and part-time

That wise and silly pundit, Mr. Burris.

live-in celibate. Finally someone who knew how to prepare more than your Basic Apricot Duck Fat Gravy recipe #3.

Stopping in at the local café in Mount Ida to get directions to "the sacred crystal mines," the Monks half-expected to meet their very own guide. You know, the type who'd been expecting us for years now, posing as a gum-chewin' waitress until the day we arrived. Instead, our sweet little Shirleen blurted out, "Katrina who? Wrote what? . . . I'm a Christian, honey. I put my faith in my Lord and Savior Jesus Christ. I don't need a durn rock!"

Our *guide* was clearly more interested in taking our order than in telling us where the best gems lay.

Up the road a spell we finally encountered our first mine. But again, something didn't feel right. Maybe it was the hefty fee for digging through some overpicked tailing pile or maybe it was the cool commercial vibe. After a quick call to a local crystal expert, an hour later the Monks were paying a visit to one of the best mines in all of Arkansas.

The drive to the second mine took us nearly ten miles down a treacherous dirt road. Old Bounder was barely making it under the trees when we finally arrived at the top of one of the most beautiful mesas in all of Arkansas, just in time to catch a spectacular show of thunderheads moving in from the distance.

Oh, it was a mine to be certain. Huge canyons raped out of the earth with Caterpillar tractor tracks running up the walls. The call of the quartz was strong, bordering on greed. So with screwdrivers, shovels and picks in hand, off we went in search of our rocks.

Within minutes Mike was seriously picking away at a hard wall of dirt, crumbling the clay in his hands, looking for a vein of wealth.

Mr. Burris, meanwhile, sat leisurely on the edge of a pit, blissing out on cortisone with Doll at his side. "Oh, Dolly, now that I am nearing the end of my long journey, I want to give you my last and greatest gift. There is nothing in life to which it can be compared. So bright, so pure, so solid. If you ever have a little speck of it, it is enough to transform your life forever. . . . A little to the left, gentlemen. Looks like that's been dug out already."

After an hour of fruitless digging, finding nothing bigger than what Mr. Burris termed "Barbie crystal dildos," we began noticing the off-limits signs to the lower forty.

"Aha! So that's where they keep the real stuff!" Mike snorted.

"Yes, gentlemen, that's the direction!"

Mike, the miner's son, diggin' up the largest durn rock you ever did see. (M. Burris)

Seconds later ole Mike, the miner's son, had jump-started an old backhoe from the mine.

"What the heck are you doing!" Jim screamed.

"I know there's treasure under these rocks. I'm going to make us rich!"

Mike rammed the backhoe down the valley scooping out veins as big as your house. Something took over. It must have been in his blood because we couldn't get Michael out of that earth for the next four hours. He insisted that he'd find the biggest diamond the world had ever seen.

"Look, I got something. Get over here!" Mike shouted at the top of his lungs, jerking Mr. Burris out of deep satori.

Mike was jockeying the backhoe into position, straining its pistons against the weight of a ton of earth. He had a gleaming rock on the tip of the shovel and was jerking the hoe up and down trying to loosen it from the dirt.

Mr. Burris pitched in with a long pole, as Jim raced to the other side to pick away at the backside. The three Monketeers groaned in the struggle to free the rock from its roots.

"Just pull it like a molar. Yank it out, Mr. Monk!" yelled Mr. Burris.

With that, Michael Monk throttled the backhoe, and up the rock jerked with the spring of a launching rocket as a massive heave of dirt fell to the ground around us. The stone itself flew through the air for a couple feet and landed on a pile of rocks, shattering upon impact.

The Monks stood speechless.

As thousands of tiny flakes of rocky quartz fell to the side, there in the center of the unearthed treasure stood a blazing jewel.

"Holy quartz. It's my dream. Look at that!" Mike exclaimed.

"Yeehaw! We've struck it rich! I don't believe it! Quick, get the camera!" yelled Jim.

The Monks and Mr. Burris were running to the side of the rock and began scraping away the shards of quartz to reveal a blinding surface of pure-as-liquid, glassy crystal.

"Om shanti. Look at the size of that bugger! Gentlemen, this is the biggest rock I have ever had the pleasure to encounter," stated Mr. Burris.

"This thing must be worth a fortune!" Jim was already calculating how to drag it out of the pit.

The Monks stood back as the brilliant surface reflected the setting sun, sending darting light prisms around the red clay pit.

Michael got down on his knees and ran his fingers around its sides trying to reach his arm around the rock. Streaks of light cut a grid of sunbeams through the building clouds, across the turquoise sky, lighting the huge crystal from inside.

"That must be the first time in aeons since light has shown on this rock," said Mike.

The Monks and Mr. Burris sat down, exhausted, around the mammoth stone, staring deep into its watery core, deep into the beckoning jewel, deep into the ethereal glow.

"Where the hell we going to put this thing?"

Jim's words sank into the heavy earth.

The big rock

sat on the Monk bed in the back of the Monkmobile, adding another three hundred pounds to the rear axle. After considerable effort the Monks and Mr. Burris had conquered the stone with the backhoe's assistance and delivered it through the back window of the Bounder.

Kaplunk. It rocked the tires as we pulled off the mountain to find shelter for the night. Back at Denby Point we felt as if we were in Crystal Heaven with our big giant quartz sage in back.

"So what are we going to do with it, sell it to one of these roadside gentlemen?" Mr. Burris was already planning an early retirement back to New Mexico.

"Heck, I don't know. I sort of like it back there. It's very grounding," said Gemini Jim, smiling.

"My God. Do you realize how much this thing must be worth? We'd better keep our mouths shut or we're going to have every dealer in the world hot on our tail," Michael Monk added. Besides, Mike had other plans. *Maybe this big rock will fetch a nice price from the museums.*

The next morning, we decided to hit the road for Memphis and take Mr. Burris to see the King. If anything, we knew we'd better get outta town before the news spread.

Despite ourselves, we knew we'd feel compelled to gab about our big find.

As we drove Bounder out of the safe refuge of Denby Point campground, the Monks decided to go for a drive down to the lake. But Michael Monk, a little waterlogged from a morning swim, misjudged the turn. Bounder was soon resting across a ditch, wheels wedged into the culvert, blocking the road.

One by one over the next few hours most of the town strolled by to take a look and offer their two cents worth of advice. It was the general consensus that something "ought be done 'bout that turn." It was also the general consensus that it'd take a "purty big rig" to haul Bounder out.

Just then, while the Monks were in heated debate about how to get a tow, up drove a local mechanic. His name was Elroy and he pulled up alongside in his oversize tow truck, chewing on a straw. He leaned back shaking his head and yelled in a dry, throaty cackle from across the road, "Well, if that don't beat all. Looks like you fellers got yourself in a pickle. Where'n da hell ya'll learn to drive?"

After tugging the Bounder out of the ditch, Elroy had us shove her in park, so he could detach the load from his truck. "What in the hell are ya'll dragging around in thar? A pile of rocks?"

"How'd you know?" Jim volunteered.

Mike cast a furtive look toward Jim, but it was too late. The Mouth was about to *blab*.

"We found the biggest piece of quartz you ever seen!"

"Oh, you did?" Elroy squinted from Mike to Jim.

Jim was about to show Elroy to the door when Michael Monk interjected, "But there wasn't a thing we could do, so we just left it on—"

"The bed. It's sitting right back there." Jim could never tell a lie and led Elroy around the side and pointed through the window.

Elroy's eyes popped when he saw it. His stereotypical good ole boy disposition suddenly changed as he muscled his way past Mike and walked to his truck, took out his CB and radioed a friend. "Hell, Fred, I got me a bunch of Northerners out here, they got them one of the biggest durn rocks you ever seen. You git yourself down here with some boys and we'll see if we can't help these fellas out with it, heh, heh."

Mike pulled Jim inside as Elroy hung up the CB. Mike was starting the Bounder when Elroy raced to the side and hollered, "I think one good turn deserves another. I'd say this little tow job here ought to cost you a nice-size rock. Maybe something about the size of what you have sitting right there in the back of your rig."

"No thanks. We appreciate your help. But we have the Good Sam Emergency Road Service. They'll be glad to pay you." Michael took out his Good Sam card.

Elroy's eyes flared. "That's not what *I* had in mind."

"Well, uh, no? Then how about this?" And Michael stuck out two crisp twenty-dollar bills.

But Elroy violently shook his head and locked his mean eyes onto the Monks. "I don't think you heard me quite right. I said that rock would do fine, and if I have to bring in some boys to convince you otherwise, then that's just what we'll have to do."

Michael jammed on the accelerator.

"You try moving this rig one foot and I'll—"

The Bounder jumped forward, lunging past a startled Elroy, who leapt out of the way as the slow-moving RV picked up speed, turned a sharp right, swerved around the tow truck, scraping the Monkmobile down its side, and charged for the road with Elroy cursing right behind.

"What the hell are you doing, Mike?"

"I don't know what I'm doing. What *am* I doing?"

"You're going to hit that tree—watch out!"

Mike swerved to the left narrowly missing the tree with the Monkmobile rocking on the road, grinding its gears, the accelerator pushed to the floor.

"We're picking up speed. Where is he?" Mike yelled.

"Oh, my God, he's on the back!" Jim hollered with his head leaning out the passenger window.

Elroy was hanging on the ladder, ascending toward the roof of the motor home.

"Get him off of there!" yelled Mike.

"What am I supposed to do?" Jim pulled himself inside.

"Throw something at him. He'll break our roof in."

Elroy was now up on the roof with his heavy boots, stomping madly on the thin frame, cursing his lungs out. The roof was bowing with each kick as the madman marched forward toward the front.

Jim ran to the cupboards and started to grab some dishes.

"No, not our new dishes, something heavy."

Jim grabbed a couple of books and arched out the window, tossing them up at Elroy, but they simply crashed down on the front windshield.

"No! You're throwing them the wrong way." Mike could

see Elroy's foot above the air vent. Then Elroy popped open the vent with the heel of his boots exposing six inches of his mad-as-hell red face through the vent screen.

"You fuckers. Pull this thing off the road or I'm going to kill ya." His voice crackled with rage.

Jim started frantically pulling out the drawers throwing everything he could lay his hands on out the window, but not once hitting Elroy.

Mike opened his window and started heaving river rocks from the Monks' stash. He could here them cracking on the roof bouncing along the edge and rolling off the side.

Boom!

Elroy's boot crashed through the other vent, leaving a gaping hole. He was putting his face down to the screen.

"Dadgumit! I'm goin' to git you little shits!"

Mike picked up speed on the country road driving like a maniac, swerving from side to side as he tried to dump the raging monster on top. Elroy rolled to the front. The low-hanging trees were brushing across the roof and Elroy stayed low to the Bounder.

Jim opened the fridge and started tossing long daikon radishes, lotus roots, giant Hokkaido pumpkins, beet juice, any food he could find.

"No, not the pie, that's for tonight!" The pie splattered on the top of the motor home.

Mike continued a constant spray of rocks. He threw a bottle of water and then resorted to throwing pennies.

Elroy was back at the vent. Jim grabbed the bug spray and dosed Elroy's face through the vent, but that didn't stop him. He was so mean, he was beginning to tear at the roof.

"Stop him, he's going to tear our roof open!"

Jim took a bottle of dishwashing soap and started squirting it up on the roof.

Elroy was pounding, sending shock waves through the speeding Monkmobile. Dolly was darting back and forth meowing frantically in the aisle.

"Quick. Give me something to heave!"

Elroy was back dangling over the front windshield.

"He's going to break the damn windshield. Give me that fucking brain machine!"

Mike heaved the brain machine in an arc around the side just missing red-faced, raging Elroy, who now stood up and marched back toward the vent ready to crash through in one final kick and kill.

"Do something!" Mike screamed.

"What! *What?*" Jim panicked.

The Monks scanned the Monkmobile and spotted the case of soy milk.

Jim ran for the box, ripped it open and started hurling cartons of soy milk through the screen. A solid barrage of soy milk flew through the air. Carton after carton, bouncing off the roof leaving a trail of soy down the road until suddenly Mike put on the brakes to slow for a low-hanging tree, hit a huge bump, and Elroy came sliding across the roof as Jim heaved four more cartons, which splattered on a falling Elroy, who gyrated wildly in the air, as he grabbed for a branch and crashed to the hard ground.

The Monks jammed down the road heading another three miles out to the highway, passing a red pickup filled with country boys coming in just before Mike turned west.

Mike went another fifty yards and then did a wide loop in the road, coming back east.

"What are you doing?" screamed Jim.

"If that red pickup was his friends, when they find Elroy, they'll tell him we headed west."

"Smart thinking, Mike!" Jim was proud.

The Monks were panting, afraid to move a muscle, as the Bounder sped down the highway. Jim was frozen in a squat position by the passenger window where he'd been heaving, with Mike arched over the wheel with his knuckles white as ice.

"Soy milk. We got him with the soy milk." Jim dared to laugh.

After five miles the Monks took another detour down a side road into Hot Springs and a mile later turned back onto 70 heading to Little Rock. Then we finally took a sigh of relief. Mike kept looking in the rearview mirror for a sign of Elroy, but knew that by the time Elroy and his friends figured out which way the Monks had gone, there would be no trace.

Jim was recounting the escape, blow by blow, when all of a sudden Michael screamed out, "Oh, my God, Mr. Burris!"

The Monks' hearts stopped with visions of Mr. Burris, a hostage back in the campground, tortured at the hands of Elroy and his henchmen.

"We've got to turn back!"

Mike was just about to turn back when a tall, thin man stumbled forward, rubbing his eyes out of a cortisone daze, waking from his blissed-out nap in the back.

"Gentlemen, what has happened?" He smiled a goofy, sleepy smile.

"Oh, just a little adventure on our way outta Dodge."

Riding on that midnight RV to Graceland. Destination: Memphis, Tennessee. Well, this train we call the Monkmobile, and it'll be gone five hundred miles before the day is done.

Ole Woody couldn't have been more prophetic. The Monks hightailed it to Memphis. The Monks and Mr. Burris had a meeting with the King, and we best not be late.

Rumor had it that Elvis was alive and well somewhere in the gaudy catacombs of Graceland. Another rumor had it the King wouldn't come out until he met the Monks. Seems Elvis had recently taken an interest in the finer aspects of Buddha dharma and wanted Jim Monk to help him brush up a bit on the meaning of the Heart Rock Sutra.

Never ones to leave an errant bodhisattva in distress, the Monks kicked ole Bounder into high gear and headed east with an ever-watchful eye in the rearview mirror. Maybe Elvis could give us a few tips on loosening up our pelvic lock. Seemed like a meeting made in rock 'n' roll heaven.

There was only one problem.

Elvis was dead.

But the Monks and Mr. Burris decided to visit Graceland anyway.

Mike reluctantly agreed. "But *God*, was he sleazy."

Mike had lived through the Elvis heyday, when his mom used to stand outside Graceland praying for an autograph. Mike felt Elvis was a stupid redneck, and he never forgave him for sucking up to Tricky Dick during the heat of the Vietnam War. Even still, Mike had enough of the tourist bug left in him to still be a little curious. And besides, maybe the Monks could unload the Rock for a solid piece of Elvis gold.

The Monkmobile shimmied up Elvis Presley Boulevard to Graceland at about ten A.M. We parked a mile down the road, rather than pay the parking fee for motor homes. We hiked back to Graceland where we found ourselves in the company of dozens of fawning tourists, most of whom seemed either to be British art students or American fundamentalist Christians, perhaps one of the few places on the planet where these two came together.

Mr. Cortisone Burris was in Elvis ecstasy, as he realized he'd finally reached his destination. But for the Monks there was a different reaction. Once inside, it immediately hit us. Graceland was just a poor cousin to the Hearst Castle, but far more popular because it's exactly what most Americans dream of when they think of opulence: a pink Cadillac, a dune buggy, a Hell's Angels–style motorbike, and an extensive gun and badge collection. Elvis had pedestrian tastes to say the least, but because he was so faithful to them, the Graceland estate struck as true and pure campy Americana.

Jim was busily engaged in deciphering cryptic messages left by the King in the downstairs billiard room, while Mike approached the estate manager proposing they buy a three-hundred-pound piece of quartz to go with the Meditation Garden. The management declined.

Somewhat miffed, Michael carefully studied the Elvis wardrobe for clues in planning the Monks' next fashion statement.

"Lavender polyester bell-bottomed cuffed jumpsuit, cut to the belly button with silver lamé cape, orange Nehru collar and gold, glass-beaded trim. . . . Pink pigskin leather harem pants with green tassels and a wickedly cut green velvet cape on the bias with virgin white lace and chartreuse studs. . . . Did this queen have an eye for color or what?" muttered Mike.

Graceland was a shrine not so much to Elvis, but to what can be bought when millions of dollars filter through the hungry heart of a poor white Southern greaseball. And the Monks were taking copious notes, just in case they ever had a spare million to revamp the skunkmobile.

"Let's see . . . I'd put purple velvet drapes over the sacred windows." Mr. Burris was getting into the swing of things. "Gold-leaf the steering apparatus, hot pink brocade upholstery on *all* the chairs, six-inch lime green shag, glass beads over the doors, baby blue metallic on the wheels, a miniature Taj Mahal next to the yoga room, a row of Greek columns and a statue of Dollface with a most holy fountain in the bathroom."

Burris was on Elvis overload. And the Monks were pulling our silly cortisone-infested pundit out the door when we spotted the Elvis shrine. Jim was the first to feel an ominous throbbing presence as we stood next to the tomb of the King. Jim, the Channeling Overlord of Sedona, was beginning to have hot revelatory flashes that someone was near. Someone the Monks knew but not well.

"Hey, guys, I'm getting this funny feeling in the pit of my stomach," said Jim.

Mr. Burris stood at the foot of the shrine staring at the inscribed words on the stone. Michael could feel it too. We stood there sensing an approaching energy. Something bigger than the three of us together.

"What do you think it is?"

"Maybe it's a message from the other side. Maybe it's the spirit of Elvis. Maybe the King still—"

"*Lives!*" A low, grungy Southern voice boomed from behind them.

The Monks jerked around. And there stood . . .

"*Elroy!*" we screamed. "How the hell did you get here!"

"I have your fucking license. Every trucker in this country has their eyes out for you turkeys!" He chuckled his low, sadistic, mean-ass laugh.

Yep, there he was again, Elroy and his two ugly bubba men towering from behind.

"Ya'll's up shit crick without a paddle, aren't ya?"

Just then Elroy and his boys charged for the Monks and Mr. Burris as we took off sprinting for Elvis Presley Boulevard.

Fortunately for the Monks, Elroy and his gorillas were no match for the lightning speed of Mike, Jim and the cheetah-fast Burris.

"Dadgumit!"

The Monks charged across the lawn, weaved through traffic and caught a cab just as Elroy rushed out onto the street in front of a Memphis bus.

We could hear the rubber screeching and then a loud bang. But we didn't look back as the cab raced up the Boulevard to the waiting Bounder.

"Gentlemen, I think it would be a most appropriate moment to leave your fine company," stated a dazed and disheveled Mr. Burris. "It's been most enjoyable, but you can keep my piece of the Rock. I'm heading back to Santa Fe. Dollface, we shall meet again. . . ."

After pit stops to drop off Mr. Burris at the nearest bus terminal . . . "I leave you my dream, my dream I leave you" . . . and to see the waddling ducks at the Peabody Hotel, the Monks hightailed it east.

The spirit of Old Elroy was haunting the Monks as we fled Memphis. We wanted to get as far east of the Mississippi as we could. So far east that only an ocean would stop us.

"Let's do it, Mike. Just get the hell to the East Coast."

"But where?"

"Hell, I don't know!" The Monks looked at the map. *Baltimore, Richmond, Boston, D.C., New York.*

"New York!" the Monks shouted.

"Let's *do* New York! No one will ever find us there."

From the
New Jersey Turnpike
across the Hudson
River, New York looked
like just another town. But once

on the George Washington Bridge the buildings stacked up like dominoes as far as the eye could see.

Jim decided to jump out and ride topside to get a better view, one of his more dangerous habits. But before he could jump up, the New Jersey Port Authority was on our tail.

"Get down from there," the officer bellowed on his bullhorn.

Expecting a confrontation, we stopped to talk.

"Whaddya doin'! Don't talk to me. I said get down and get outta here!"

We obliged and crossed into Manhattan.

Dolly Lama's kitty fur stood on end as we hit our first pothole. Dishes and books went flying before we could slow our pace, and then the holes widened.

The Monkmobile careened off the side and grazed an island, but another hole put us on track again as we barreled down the West Side Highway looking for trouble. Everyone but the Monks seemed to know the rules—turn signals were optional, clearly marked lanes were ignored entirely. It was a frantic dance of trucks and cars, buggies and bikers, making a mad dash for the water's edge.

What seemed like an eternity of high-rise apartments suddenly gave way to even taller sky-rise buildings. We were beginning to move at a snail's pace around the Seventies, and by the time we passed that big tugboat *Intrepid*, we could count the dead rats on the highway.

"Nice," Dolly purred.

Yes, it was a *perfect* day for motoring in Manhattan. The sun sparkled over the Hudson, and the Empire State Building glistened from the morning rays. Well equipped with our trusty street maps and compass, a handy guide to landmarks, and a naive sense of maladventure, the Monks prepared for the Avenues.

Traveling coast to coast had taught us the accepted courtesies of the road. We were, after all, Good Sam members. And as gentleman motorists we also know the unwritten rules of decency: look out for speed traps, step on it when the light turns yellow and don't back into parked police cars. Yet deep in the heart of the asphalt jungle another fate awaited the amiable, well-mannered Monks.

One good turn across the West Side Highway and off we sped down Ninth Avenue. A pothole at Forty-second Street put Jim in the sink, and it was time for some petro.

"Where do you find gas on this island?" Mike screamed, his hands bracing the wheel.

"Ask a cabby," yelled Jim.

Jamming back up Tenth, Mike soon learned the rule of the Avenues: step on it when the light turns *red* or you'll have ten limos up your back. Another pothole and . . .

"Jim, the blinkers just went out." Mike freaked.

"Big deal. Who needs blinkers when you have the horn. Let me tell you something, Mike. I've lived in this town. In Manhattan you signal with your horn. You brake with your horn. You pass with your horn. You *are* your horn. It's you, the horn, the road . . . nirvana. Get it?"

Mike got it . . . sort of.

A trucker edged up to us at the light. "Is that how they teach you to drive in Nebraska?"

"Get outta here!" Jim retorted.

Mike was amazed. *That Jim. He picks up fast. He don't take nothing from nobody . . . yo!*

Back again past Forty-second Street and the Bounder sputtered, coughed, gagged, and once again . . . "Hey, I think we're running outta gas."

"Well, we've run out of gas in every state of the union, so why not New York City, right?" Jim was clearly not fazed.

"Yeah, let's make it fun and run out of gas in the middle of the busiest intersection," Mike said sardonically, clearly annoyed.

The Monkmobile chugged to a stop at a major artery out of the Lincoln Tunnel during rush hour. Mike was stunned by his self-fulfilling prophesy.

Jim trudged the three blocks to retrieve five gallons. Mike nervously watched as every third truck sideswiped the pristine RV.

They must be friends of Elroy's!

Back on track we fueled up at the Hess pit stop. A hundred cabs, three limos and a very conspicuous Monkmobile jockeyed for position. They even had a cop directing traffic in and out.

"Now that's a busy gas station," noted Jim.

We then took a tour of Central Park. The people didn't want us there. They were shaking their fists as we passed. We eyed the undeveloped land. It looked good enough for a Monk KOΛ.

"It's not just camp, it's kamping!"

Mike kept his eyes on the road, clutching the steering wheel. Right next to the reservoir Jim laid plans for installing full-hookup RV pads.

"Yeah, build a little service and supply store with chain-smoking attendants. Install cable TV and a launderette. Bus shuttles to Times Square. We'd make a killing, Mike. Central *RV Park!*" Jim was full of schemes.

But the men of blue chased us off. No stopping, no parking and definitely no camping.

It was noon and we were hungry. A cabby told us to drive down to St. Marks Place.

"Lots of cheap places to eat."

There were.

"But where do you park a twenty-six-foot motor home?" Mike whined.

"Don't worry about it," Jim proclaimed confidently.

The Monkmobile made the turn from Third Avenue as a tall, thin homeless man with a goatee and a radio strapped to his back rushed the Monkmobile pushing a shopping cart filled with Cabbage Patch dolls, his hair shooting skyward in a towering assemblage of curls and ribbons. The wild man honked on a squawky bike horn hanging from the shopping cart and sang out in a deep, raspy wail, "It's Howdy Doody time, it's Howdy Doody time, it's Howdy Doody time, c'mon, white folks, take a lookee here!" a big crazy smile coming across his face as he whirled in his own cosmic orbit, gesturing wildly, poetically, bobbing up and down St. Marks Place.

In the middle of the block a truck had double-parked, lights flashing. Cars stacked up behind us, horns blaring. Jim ran out to ask the trucker to move. But there was no trucker to be found. Traffic was backed up onto Third Avenue when Mike got the bright idea to squeeze by. It was a *learning experience*. With half an inch to spare Mike learned his first rule of the streets: *Drive it like you don't own it*. Besides, what are a few battle scars.

By now, Mike was getting a little frazzled. Still a gentleman at the wheel, he would slow down for jaywalkers. But that proved fatal. Pedestrians had gall. Don't Walk meant Walk Fast. Wait meant Run If You Can. Pedestrians didn't stop for nobody or no light. They stood inches from speeding traffic and they dared Mike to claim his right of way.

Our handy Parking Angel hung on our dash. It took a few circles around the block before we realized the first rule of parking: *Just stop where you are . . . you've found your parking space*. Otherwise known as double, if not triple parking. No one cared.

It was approaching noon. The radio announced gridlock conditions for Midtown around one.

"Jim, can we do it? We wouldn't want to miss a gridlock, would we?" Jim looked at Mike as if he were possessed.

"Whatever you say, boss."

With fresh boxed lunches from Eat and two cups of miso soup from Dojo, the Monks raced toward Trump Plaza in search of a traffic jam.

At first, traffic was too easy. So we headed over to Sixth. Still a piece of cake. Thirty-fourth was a breeze. The Forties and we were worried. Traffic was moving. But at Fifty-second we found it. Traffic stuck against the green light.

"Gridlock for days!" Mike hollered.

Nothing was moving for blocks and blocks. The Monkmobile edged into the intersection, but the light changed and we were caught.

"Yippee!"

Cross traffic and pedestrians swarmed around. A midget went underneath. The cops came on horse.

"Out of the box. Out of the box!"

Expecting a confrontation, the Monks began to disembark from the Monkmobile.

"Whaddya doin'? Don't talk to me. I said get in there and get out of the box!"

We were in the box . . . the intersection that is . . . a cardinal sin on gridlock day.

The Monkmobile inched back down Fifth.

"Downtown," Dolly purred.

By the time we hit SoHo a completely transformed Mike had lost touch with the courtesies of the road. He took lanes at will and turned on a whim. He charged through mobs of jaywalkers with reckless abandon. He began to talk like a cabby, but with a Southern drawl. Streetwise and quick to the draw, Mike's modest Monkmobile was fast becoming . . . *The RV FROM HELL!*

At Canal some fool tried to pass while Michael took a left. The blue Buick snagged on our front bumper and was dragged half a block before losing its door. Michael calmly pulled over. With insurance papers in hand he surveyed the damage. Our fender pointed ninety degrees forward, the side badly scraped. The Buick was even worse, its front right badly damaged.

But no one was hurt.

So they took off at top speed, dragging their door behind them.

A stolen car? Or did they know? . . . The RV FROM HELL!

Downtown Wall Street proved a scene. Too many brokers clogging the streets. The corners were tight and an impatient sedan took the right fender and bent it forward. This time the Monks sauntered out confident. *We might be Monks and we might be sweet, but watch out, Bud, cause . . .*

"Fifty bucks and we'll forget about it," Jim demanded in the best goodfella pose he could muster.

"Whaddaya mean fifty bucks, I don't have fifty bucks," the sedan owner replied.

"How about thirty?" Jim feebly rebounded.

"Gedouttahere. Where's a cop?"

"Okay, look it. We'll let it go if you let *us* go."

And without further adieu, off he sped, revving the engine extra hard for emphasis.

"Hey, you fuckhead, I'll fuckin' kill ya if I get my fuckin' hands on ya!" Mike screamed out the window.

"Mike, Mike, my God, take it easy," Jim replied.

The Monkmobile now drove with forked tongue. Both ends of the bumper stuck straight forward. Both sides were bleeding from countless sideswipes. A trucker put a heavy dent in the back, and the horn, lights and signals had long since given out. The Monkmobile rounded the bottom of

Manhattan and headed back up. It was a mad rush for the water up the FDR.

"Mike, I think you're definitely gettin' the hang of it."

Turning over toward Park Avenue, heading up to the Pan Am Building, the cars, the people, the police, the cabbies . . . they all stared in amazement . . . stunned by what they saw. Afraid to venture ahead of us, the streets were ours for the taking. No more Mr. Nice Guys; good-bye, Good Sam. The Monks had learned what it takes to drive . . . *The RV FROM HELL!*

Ten minutes later it all came rolling to an abrupt stop. The corner of Park Avenue and East Twenty-ninth was a dismal scene. With that last right turn the Monkmobile had plowed right up over a rolling Dumpster in the middle of the street, gutting out the bottom of the Bounder.

Half the block came out to look, as the newly acclimated Monks stood on the corner watching a river of oil roll down the street into the gutter.

The RV from hell! *(Mark Trunz)*

Mike held Dolly in his arms as the firemen prowled around inside checking for gas leaks. The Monks were ticketed for double-parking!

Jim was at the phone dialing the Good Sam Emergency Road Service when Mike sauntered into a Korean market to find something to soothe his shattered nerves.

He was fondling the chocolate chip cookies, absorbed in the dozens of choices, when he bumped head-on into a woman who was likewise working her way through the chocolate looking for comfort food.

"Oh!" She was startled. Then, eyeing Dolly: "Well, pretty kitty. What a doll you are!"

"That's her name, Dolly." Michael smiled through his distraught eyes at the friendly stranger.

"Does she live around here?"

"Well, you might say so. We're sort of stranded now. Our home was just totally trashed out there!" Mike pointed to the corner.

"That's yours?" She gasped staring at the smoldering mess of Bounder.

"Yes. Or it *was* ours. It looks like it's the end of the Monkmobile."

"Monkmobile!" She gasped again. "Are you the Monks?"

Michael looked at her carefully. *Millions of people on the streets of Manhattan. And whom have I run into?*

"I'm sort of a Monk. I've been on the road traveling with my friend and —"

"The Monks! I don't believe this! I sent you a letter. I'm Annie Sprinkle!"

Michael's face dropped as Dolly clambered on top of his shoulder. Now people were staring at the threesome hunched over the cookies exchanging astonished yelps.

"*Annie Sprinkle!* You *did* write us a letter when we were in Colorado."

"*The Monks. I've been wanting to meet you forever!*"

It was all coming back. Annie Sprinkle, the self-proclaimed postporn modernist, and her glowing letter to the Monks and her unlimited offer of a *free* place to crash if *ever* in the Big Apple.

"You *are* Annie Sprinkle!"

"You *are* the Monks! I've been reading your newsletter."

"You have?"

"Oh, God, I'm so honored to meet you. I'd be sooooo thrilled if you stayed in my salon and meditation center. It's right around the corner!"

Mike looked out toward the demolished Bounder as the

last drops of oil burped out onto the street. The firemen were leaving, and he could see Jim at the phone frantically working out a deal, looking for a place to stay.

"Hey, Freddie, remember me? We roomed together at Northwestern." Click. "Macadoo. Hi, guy . . . Oh, right, sure. . . . Yeah, a bit spur of the moment. Yeah, need at least two years' warning. . . . Okay, well, maybe . . . for lunch. . . . Okay, great." Click. "Sister Carol. Yo, babe, it's Jimmy, burrrrn! . . . Need your space. . . . Getin' your act together. . . . Know what you mean, gotta work on your stuff. Yeah, distance from the family. No problem, I understand." Click.

"You mean you have room?" Michael asked Annie hopefully.

"There's always room at the Sprinkle Salon."

Michael breathed a sigh of relief.

As Ames Truck and Towing carted a severely damaged Monkmobile off toward Queens, the Monks stood on the corner of East Twenty-ninth and Park surrounded by boxes. The mechanic had said, "If you plan to ever see this thing again, you're gonna have to come up with some serious dinero. *Capisce?* This piece of shit belongs in the junkyard!"

"Just take her to the garage. We'll work out a way." Jim

The Good Sam Emergency Road Service will tow you anywhere, anytime.

Annie Sprinkle, postporn modernist.
(James Styles)

was determined not to lose another monastery on wheels to the junkyard, no matter what the damage.

"What'd you do with the big Rock?" Mike whispered.

"I covered it with our tent and put the cat box underneath. No one will come near it. The smell's atrocious!"

"How're we going to get all this stuff up to your place?" Mike said to Annie as he surveyed the streetside contents of their former home.

"Simple. We'll all chip in."

Hours later, nearing sunset, after dozens of trips, the Monks hauled the last brain machine off the streets of New York to the awaiting Sprinkle Salon and Meditation Center.

"Gee, for Monks you sure do have a lot of stuff!" Annie said, smiling.

. . .

Annie Sprinkle lived on the eleventh floor of an apartment building in the Little India section of Manhattan. Quite appropriate we felt for a tantric sex devotee. Annie gave us a tour of the apartment. Her walls were pink and lavender, dusted with silver sparkles and stars. Her master bedroom was both living room and photo studio, with the satin-covered bed taking up a good deal of the corner with a view of the glimmering skyline.

Up in the Sprinkle Salon the city spread out before us. To the north of us was the Chrysler Building and the great Empire State. To the west the Crown Building. A steady stream of moonlight shimmered through the windows as traffic streaked down the avenues. It was our first time up off the street and our mouths hung to the floor as we absorbed the city lights.

We were perched far above the noise of the concrete valleys, like cliff dwellers straining to see the mobs below. As far as the eye could see, giant monoliths crowded the horizon, each adding its personal mark to the collective skyline. An eternity of living on the road and here we had landed, two homeless waifs in the city of dreams.

Annie was now barefoot, wearing a loose-fitting smock. "So the Monks have finally made it to New York." Her voice was like warm milk, a soft, cuddly come-on, throaty and strong, but veiled in softness and sensual splendor.

"Would you like some Cafix?" As was her civilized custom, Annie shared her favorite brew after dinner. We were seated at her black dining-room table.

"Where'd you get the name Annie Sprinkle?" Jim began verbally probing.

"Oh, it came to me while I was making *Teenage Deviate*, one of my first porno films." She said with a proud smile and a playfully devious giggle. "They had to know what credit I wanted. And the name Sprinkle came to me. It was like a gift from God. Water sports was only five percent of it. I love sprinkles. When I bake cakes, I like to use sprinkles. I like sprinkles on ice cream. I like rain. Sexually I like anything wet—whether it be spit, rain, sweat, cum, tears, or clear sparkling waterfalls. Want some more Cafix?"

"Yeah, ah . . . sure," answered Jim cautiously.

"I'm fine," answered Mike.

"So what do you really do?" Jim continued probing.

"Well"—Annie pulled in her cheeks, her eyes circling the room—"I guess I'm a researcher. That's what I am. I research sex. I research my own sexuality, other people's sexuality and sex in our society. That's really what I do and that's what I've always done, it's just that I do it in a nontraditional way. I don't just go to college and read books. I've gone into prostitution and pornography and kinky sex clubs or whatever. But also I've been in ashrams, I've been on top of mountains."

As Annie went back into the kitchen, the Monks scanned the walls looking for pieces of the Annie Sprinkle puzzle. More than an apartment, this was a gallery of her life. On one wall was a poster of Annie as a fairy slutmother; on another, a small cabbage patch quilt entitled *Pornografica*. Nearby were two handwritten diplomas from Annie's trip to Sister Rosita's Summer Saint Camp, adjoining a bulletin board with dozens of before and after snapshots of people who had been "liberated" in the Transformation Salon.

Next to the bulletin board was "The Sprinkle Sexual Resource Center," with every book, magazine, newsletter, and video imaginable on sexuality. And on a thin strip of wall behind the front door were framed photos of Annie in a variety of her favorite poses.

Annie brought out the Cafix. "That shot is me, my dear friend Veronica Vera and Little Mike at the gay pride rally. We're holding a sign that says 'Bisexual Exhibitionists Into Midgets and Proud,' and that photo is me with members of Club 90, my feminist porn-star support group. That's Linda Montano, my favorite artist and lifeist. And Jwala, my tantric teacher. Have you heard of Joseph Kramer?" She moved back into the kitchen. "He teaches tantric sex for gay men!"

The Monks looked at each other.

"Aren't you lovers?"

"We're soul mates!" Jim affirmed.

"Well, I mean . . . are you two monogamous? Or do you see other people?"

"I'd like to see other people!" Jim answered.

Mike didn't answer, but sat quietly brooding.

Above the dining table a fish tank was presided over by a statue of Kwan-yin. Nearby was an altar with rocks, shells, photos of spiritual teachers and the ubiquitous smell of sandalwood incense, which gave Annie's Salon a kind of bright, sensuous temple atmosphere that was unmistakably her own.

"Would you like some chocolate chip cookies?" Annie asked with a devilish smile, just peeking out of the kitchen.

"You bet," said Mike.

"I'm fine," answered Jim.

Annie delivered the cookies to the table with a wink,

as Mike pondered where the Monks might be sleeping that evening. Mike suspiciously eyed the big bed at the front of the Salon and then the huge dildo that hung from the fridge.

"Now, whenever we're tired, we can all just sleep in my bed," Annie said coyly.

"Isn't it a little early for bed?" Mike looked at the clock. But the clock said ten. *No wonder I'm tired.*

Annie smiled.

Annie was a deceptively sleepy Leo, her speech languid and easy like a humid summer day.

"I just love sex. And I see everything in terms of sex. One way or another, everything. It's my primary interest. Well, I guess there are a few other interests, but if I had to make a choice, I'd choose sex." Jim hung on every word. Right then he felt a very long way from the nuns at Christ the King grade school.

"I use sex for healing, meditation and as my path to enlightenment. You know, I've learned that sex is a lot like food," said Annie, taking a sensual, satisfying bite of cookie, humming with satisfaction. "There is junk sex, health sex, and gourmet sex. Junk sex is very fast, not always nourishing, and very genitally focused. Health sex is using sex as a healing tool. And gourmet sex takes some skill and knowledge and a lot of time to prepare and needs to be savored very slowly. Mostly we are a junk-sex society. I've had a lot of junk sex. Now I'm more interested in health sex and gourmet sex."

Jim sat transfixed.

"I want to be in a constant state of orgasm. I want to see how much ecstasy I'm capable of, if I can achieve enlightenment through sex. I really think I'm getting there."

Annie slipped into the bathroom to prepare for bed as Mike decided to get a head start, slipping between the covers with clothes *on*. Jim eventually wandered over and fell in on the far side with clothes *off*. The two sets of Monk eyes wandered around the room, noticing the tall black boots with the six-inch heels, the photos of a contortionist in drag, tattoo freaks, pierced nipples, lips, cheeks and tongues, endless porn videos, sex books, sex magazines, whips and chains, a box of sex toys . . . *I'm not sure if I'm ready for this*, Mike thought. Here at last was someone who clearly outdid even Mike's wildest, kinkiest fantasies.

When Annie came out of the bathroom, Mike closed his eyes feigning sleep, nearly holding his breath. Annie giggled at Jim. Jim giggled back. The lights were lowered, a candle lit.

Annie slipped into bed between the Monks. Jim cuddled, Mike lay stiff, waiting . . .

Only to hear Annie say a prayer, turn out the light and fall fast asleep in her flannel nightgown.

Next morning Annie began her day with a tantric aerobic workout, leading the Monks from Jane Fonda stretches to Native American dancing, concluding with a wild, frenzied breath of fire. The phone rang, but Annie didn't answer.

"Hi, you've reached the Annie Sprinkle Temple and Meditation Center. Sorry, I'm busy attaining enlightenment and can't come to the phone. Please leave a *cosmic* message."

She had a different message every half hour it seemed.

"Hi, you've reached the Annie Sprinkle Center for Lesbian Studies." Annie was feeling feminist.

"Hi, you've reached the Annie Sprinkle Diet and Fitness Center." She was feeling remorse over one too many chocolate chip cookies.

Finally, after a final set of stretches, Annie was ready to let in the world. She dialed her triple Gemini boyfriend, Les, for the tenth time in two days. He hadn't picked up even one of her friendly phone calls. So today Annie decided to take a different tack.

"Hiiiiiii, Les, it's Annie. Pick up the phone, you worthless piece of shit, hee hee!" And right on cue Les interrupted the message machine to talk. "Do you want to meet the Monks? Come on over, I'll lock you in the closet!" she offered coquettishly.

"You'll love Les. He's a female-to-male transsexual." She turned, abruptly cutting off Les. "He'll go into an installation and cum ten times from that one abusive phone call. He's so appreciative of S and M."

Twenty minutes later the front-door buzzer rang. It was Les. Hairy, well built, slightly unshaven, with small eyes that didn't seem to match his frame, Les, dressed in boots and leather, was slightly drunk.

"Les, I want you to meet the Monks."

"Happy to meet you, Les."

"Hi," Les said quietly, bashful before all the attention.

After this quick introduction, Les went straight to the mirror and began carefully examining himself.

"Do you think I look macho?" he asked forthrightly, turning toward Jim.

"Sure," said Jim. "Real macho."

Les returned to the mirror, looking closer to see for himself if there was any trace of femininity, if any blemish had shown through, seeing if the transformation was complete.

"Do I look strong to you?" Les asked with a shade of self-doubt.

"Well, that's more of an inside thing. You'd know better than I," said Jim.

Then Les did something strange. He turned abruptly to the Monks and asked, "Do you want to see my penis?"

The Monks looked at each other.

"Oh, you have to see Les's penis," said Annie in a motherly voice. "He's so proud of it." Les let out a big smile.

And soon Les was playing show-and-tell, proudly showing off his new improved body. "I take testosterone pills to generate all the hair and to lose the plumpness in my breasts." His shirt opened and under a chest full of hair were the scars from rounds of surgery.

"Les is one of only a handful of people to have a man-made penis, hee hee," Annie interjected, as Les dropped his drawers.

"Do you want to see my tattoos?"

It was clear Les only came alive when talking about his body.

"Oh, sure, yeah, well . . ." Jim could stomach practically anything, except pierced nipples and huge tattoos.

"Let's see them!" Mike was mesmerized and shook his head in amazement as Les removed his shirt and revealed more than a dozen tattoos expanding across his rosy flesh. Mike was holding on to the wall as Jim peered around the corner to steal a glance. The Monks had seen it all, *until now*.

Les had come by to fool around a bit and was getting impatient for Annie, who was now busy giving phone.

"I was a woman just a few years ago." He had a halting way of talking.

"Why'd you change?"

"Because nobody respected me," the former lesbian said with a slow, husky voice that still had the ring of femininity in the background. "I was treated like a second-class citizen. Like shit. Now I can get anything I want. Just because I'm a man. It's amazing."

"Okay. I'm ready." Annie put down the receiver.

"No vanilla sex," he insisted as Annie came over to give him a big juicy insult.

What Les means is "nothing normal, don't nurture," explained Annie. "Isn't that right, you worthless piece of shit?"

As the Monks quietly exited to the back room, Les crawled under Annie's bed.

"It's the only way he'll do it!" she said in the distance.

After a few restless nights adjusting to the indoors, the steam heat, the street traffic, the pedestrians and the heavy smell of incense, we decided

to hit the streets of Manhattan to "meet the public."

And the public was waiting. In fact, right outside the door. Three startled teenagers, two Hispanic boys and a girl with a wall of lacquered hair were conducting some *business* by the building. A professional dog walker with five dogs on leashes was curbing his canines, and a stream of yups clogged single file up the sidewalk with Wall Street stamped on their foreheads.

At first it was glorious walking around *our* neighborhood. We were surrounded by bright yellow cabs, high-rise apartment buildings, brick flats with marbled entries, intricate fire escapes, tilting light poles, and streets that looked to have been paved a hundred times over . . . to no avail. Kids were darting back and forth to school, and bright young cannibals worked the pavement toward the subway grabbing coffee, pastries, and papers at the hundreds of streetside newsstands and greengrocers.

Our neighborhood also had its share of pharmaceutical professionals. But the drugs didn't shock us. We'd been warned. What did shock us were the people wandering

Jim at the vast corporate headquarters of *Monk*, the mobile magazine. (*Ari Mintz*/New York Newsday)

about who didn't have a place to live, whose main profession was holding out an I LOVE NEW YORK coffee cup and hoping some coins would drop in.

Outside a twenty-four-hour Korean grocer, a beaten, world-weary woman held out her styrofoam cup. She was silent. On the way into the market Jim passed her by. The doubts, as always, echoed in the brain—*she doesn't deserve it, she's not even trying, what good does it do?* As if a person must be entertaining to deserve help.

On the way out he passed her again, thinking again about the futility of giving. The standard judgments: *She's a drunk, she'll just spend it on drink. She's a nut, why can't she get a job? What's so hard about getting a job?* Any *job.*

Jim turned around just before we hit the corner. He turned back and gave her a dime.

"I was so quiet you didn't even notice me," she said.

Jim thanked her for preserving the quiet.

"A lousy dime, Mike. Only one-twenty-fourth the cost of this liter of soy milk I just bought. That's nothing, maaan. I don't care where it goes. She deserves it."

The Monks headed toward the Empire State Building as Jim taught Mike how to walk a crowded street.

"Mike, you got to pick it up, man. You're walking too slow! This isn't Arkansas."

"How am I supposed to walk?" Mike hated to be corrected.

"You go for open space. Keep your eyes forward, hands out, and the minute you see a space, close in."

Jim was a pro. He kept his hands out wide, knees bent and eyes locked on the ground. He got more space than he needed, and Mike followed in his wake.

Manhattan is a walking town, and the Monks took that literally. Five hundred blocks, eight hours, seven blisters and umpteen street scenes later, the Monks dragged themselves back to the Sprinkle Salon with severely swollen feet.

"Hiiii, Monks." Annie smiled her wide-eyed, over-the-top smile. "Meet my good friend Veronica!"

"Heeeellllooo, Monks," said Veronica with a seductive smile and a delightful chuckle that was tinged with knowing humor. The Monks exchanged air kisses with the dark and alluring Vee.

"Enchanted. I'm so honored to be meeting the Monks." She spoke with a deep feminine power, her words lingering languidly after each . . . carefully . . . pronounced . . . syllable.

Ms. Sprinkle and Ms. Vee assured us if we wanted to see the *real* Manhattan, we would have to let go of our Monk habits and see the city by night.

Then Vee advised, "Show Palace, Thomas is working tonight. He's *so* fabulous!"

"Oh, I don't know. The Monks might not like the Show Palace." Annie modestly grinned. "It gets a little raunchy!"

"Let's go!" Mike brightened up. With Annie and Vee, anything would be ultrafab. The Monks were free from the mobile monastic digs. Life was changing, fast and furious.

Across the red carpet and through the bright, glitzy lights, the Monks stumbled into the Show Palace, which offered practically anything for practically every sexual taste. Jim's virginal eyes were wild with excitement.

"The Show Palace has New York's finest exotic dancers!" pointed out Annie, the proud and enthusiastic tour guide.

Jim nodded his head as he lingered at the glass booth that displayed all the stars for the night. Mike was afraid to say anything.

"This is my friend Bruno, the doorman."

"Hi, Annie, welcome home."

"Thanks, Bruno." She extended her arm for a kiss on the wrist.

"And these are the enclosed booths where gentlemen can dial up women and see them on the other side. Aren't the rooms neat?" It was if she were showing off a new condominium.

Annie was filled with fond memories.

"You know, Monksters, why don't you both have a little fun in New York. Both of you ought to meet other people, hee hee!"

Mike was getting increasingly irritated.

"And here's the magazine section," Annie continued, showing it off like Vanna White on *The Wheel of Fortune.* "They have magazines on every fetish from lesbian bondage to transvestite porn." Annie described it so matter-of-factly, so free of judgment, it was as if she were a White House tour guide for a group of Iowa farm wives.

"This place was part of my sexual nursery school, my playground, my wonder years." She sighed. "I learned so much about people and their sexual fantasies from working here. Now I feel like I have a Ph.D." Annie paused. "Gosh, you know, in my commercial sex career I figure I've had about three thousand men sexually. And, you know, because I've had so many partners, I've really learned where people are at. It's just like face reading. I can watch someone walking and tell you everything they're into."

Annie noticed Jim eyeing a nearly nude stripper making her way into one of the other show rooms. "Monkster, we have to get you a woman, hee hee." Jim perked up, but then glanced at Mike, who was clearly not approving, and his spirits sagged.

Just then Vee hurried us up the stairs to a small theater where Thomas was about to perform.

We crowded into the posh red theater as a male stripper was winding down his act for the final tips. The theater was softly lit and full of older men, single and alone in various rows. The music died and the stripper walked off into the wings.

Suddenly the music blared on again and a new dancer, a tall, muscular, totally provocative and intense Adonis danced toward the stage, ascending the stairs wearing only a G-string and a Santa Claus hat, moving to the pulsating rhythms of "Jingle Bells." It was the day after Thanksgiving and Thomas was doing his damnedest to get the lonely crowd into the holiday spirit.

Mike's eyes widened as Thomas took to the floor in pounding, wet, erotic moves, his black body glistening with oil. Every twist and turn of his pelvis arched his firm back up into the air. His veins popped under the pink lights, pulsing with blood.

Mike was sinking into fantasy. *Why don't you have a little fun in New York? Both of you ought to meet other people!* Annie's words were suddenly hitting home. Annie was watching Mike. But Jim was watching Vee.

Vee went wild as her demure personality suddenly shifted into a wild, ecstatic Scorpio in heat. She lifted her skirt and began crazily jingling a small bell she was wearing between her legs. Thomas suddenly smiled, quickly flung his G-string on the floor and came toward Vee with a ravenous grin on his face as he dangled his dong at her jingling bell.

Several patrons got up to leave. The hot music continued as Thomas sweated away in the eros of the night. Mike felt sad watching Thomas furiously flirt with Vee.

Why are all the great men taken?

The pink lights filtered through the dark room. Other men joylessly sank in their chairs devouring the dancer with their stares. Les was on the floor licking Annie's toes. Thomas worked the floor dirty and hard, pulling the crowd into his seductive gaze, gyrating his hips around the room, filling the men with his lust. Finally, in an amazing leap, he brought the house down with his finale, as he twisted, throbbed, and spastically contorted to the beat, moaning with the music of Christmas.

Then suddenly the lights came on.

As the Monks and Monkettes huddled around Thomas, management quickly intervened, asking the Monkettes to leave the show room because it was "upsetting the gay male clientele," who didn't take kindly to women breaking in on their fantasy.

Jim was outside checking out the all-girl revue that was coming up later that evening.

"Oh, no. I feel like I'm corrupting the Monks!" Annie teased.

Jim stared intently at one female dancer who was beaming back at Jim. Mike came up to Jim's side, but Jim didn't notice. Annie came up to his other side, and still his eyes locked onto the dancer, who teased Jim with her seductive eyes until finally she brushed him off, running into the theater, her music calling.

"Oh, don't get hung up on her. I have a friend who looks

just like her. You'd love her. She'd probably like you too. I'll introduce you!" Annie giggled.

Mike look puzzled.

"Oh, but only if it doesn't cause any problems." Annie looked apologetically at Mike. "Maybe I can find someone for you too! I think Jim needs to sow some oats."

Jim nodded his head.

Mike hung his head. "Ah, look, you guys, I think I'm going to split."

"Why, Michael? Don't you like the Show Palace?" Annie asked innocently.

"No, that's not it. I just feel like walking alone. I'll see you later back at the Salon," Mike said solemnly. Mike was always discreet and polite, never letting on what was really bothering him.

"Michael, are you okay?" Annie was genuinely concerned.

"No, I'm fine. Jim, you go back with Annie, alright?" Mike was businesslike.

"Oh, no," Annie moaned, "I feel like I started something."

"No, Annie. You definitely didn't start anything that wasn't incubating long before we rolled into New York." Mike answered with a bit more bitterness than he wanted to let out. Then, turning to Jim: "I just need to take a long walk."

Mike spoke firmly, attempting to sound positive.

Jim's mind was already absorbed. Jim flushed red, his thoughts on fire.

"Come on, Michael, you don't have to go." Jim spoke above the rumbling passion in his brain.

"Believe me, I have to." Then, looking at Annie: "Just make sure he finds what he's looking for."

Mike gave everyone a quick kiss and took off.

"Is he alright?" Annie asked. "I think I offended him. Oh, I feel so bad."

"No, it's alright, Annie. He'll be okay. He just needs to be on his own," Jim halfheartedly reassured.

"Okay, but I just feel so bad."

Jim, Les and the gals headed back downtown in Les's BMW, dropping off Vee in Chelsea and then driving over to Annie's in Little India.

Mike did not return that evening.

Instead, he walked in the cold night air, resigning himself

to the fact that he'd invested heavily in the Astronauts-in-Training Concept, and now the concept had finally crash-landed.

Can't keep a rein on him. Sisterly love. That's what he wants.

Off into the night, his Leo pride aching, Mike strolled past the street hustlers on Forty-second, past the crack trade in Hell's Kitchen. Down at the Hudson he braced for the winter chill, but didn't feel a thing as his memories were seized with the trip across the country and the nonending battle with brotherly love. He felt alone. So near to Christmas. Colored lights were already strung in apartment windows. The lights of the Empire State Building were aglow in red and green.

Farther down the river he walked, listening to the boats bellow in the night air. The lights of the Twin Towers beckoned in the distance like two giant overlords of the night.

A journey full of wild dreams, strange encounters and the earnest search for family. A journey deepened by unexpected obstacles and the great unknown. A journey with no physical destination save the coast. And now the other shore had been reached.

Through the Village he wandered, past Christopher Street, past Two Potato, past Boots and Saddles and The Monster. Crossing Broadway, Michael ventured into the East Village where all true night crawlers scurried in the cold, clothed in the regimental black.

Walking up Fifth Street, he passed a sign: "Palms Read, No Questions Asked . . . Five Dollars."

Mike liked that. *No questions asked* was always a good selling point.

Peeking through the door, he saw a baby lying on the floor and a table with crystals and a deck of tarot cards. The baby was suckling on a bottle, and in the back a woman was digging through a trash can looking for yesterday's race results. Her walls were covered with pictures of Mother Mary and charts illustrating the palms.

Michael walked in and took the liberty to sit down. Katrina was startled when she returned to the front of the shop. She stood staring down her nose for the longest time sorting out what she saw and finally said, "You're a mess. What happened to you?"

" 'No questions asked.' Can you read my palm? I'm very poor and . . ." Off Mike went into his sob story until even the baby was bawling her head off.

"Sure, sure," Katrina finally said, motioning. "But do the

cards. Shuffle them and cut them three times, then lay them out."

Mike did as he was told. Katrina took a long, hard look at the deck and an equally long, hard look at Michael's face and, putting her hands to her head, began shaking back and forth. "My God . . . my God."

Michael leaned forward.

Katrina began to whisper.

Michael strained to listen.

"You're aura is very, very dark. You've taken on some very dark energy. I see a lot of pain. A lot of suffering. There is something very dark around you. It is very very bad."

"Oh, God." Michael was afraid. "So what should I do?"

"Oh, this is very very difficult. It will take a lot of time, but I can do it. I will have to clean your aura. It is very very dark. It will take a lot of work. But first you will have to take this crystal with you for several days and wear it wherever you go. Then when you come back, I will be able to see who is troubling you and what I must do to cleanse your aura. But it will take time. A lot of time. I will have to charge you two hundred dollars. Can you pay me now?"

Michael fell forward, and the table collapsed, sending cards and crystals flying. He had been leaning so far toward her, taking in every word, that the punch line caught him off guard.

"Two hundred dollars?" he choked. "But I told you I'm low on cash!"

"Yes, two hundred dollars. It's a very good rate. Especially for Manhattan. I take MasterCard and Visa."

Outside, Michael studied himself in the window of the neighboring store. Homeless, broke, and now an old dirty aura. Mike stumbled deeper into the East Village.

Why don't you have a little fun in New York? Both of you ought to meet other people!

Annie's words were fast becoming gospel. *Maybe a little roll in the hay might clean that aura up nice and fine. Maybe just a little debauchery and I'll have the cleanest aura in the Empire State.* Mike tried to amuse himself.

He walked into The Bar. The mood was dark and foreboding. He stayed only a second. Then he moved on, venturing farther east until arriving at the Pyramid near Tompkins Square Park. But the boys had attitude. Then in the Wonder Bar the men were so hip, so casually trendy, so bare bones, that they didn't even notice a real bare-bones minimalist walking in their midst.

Finally at the Tunnel, Mike stopped in and ordered a

beer, the first beer he'd had in ten years, and hung out with the boys. He was in the mood to totally drown himself in beer when his eyes settled on a pair of shoes at the stool next to him. Then the nylons, then the legs, and more legs, and more legs, and finally the skirt and the carefully arranged gloves, coat and long hairy arms and the narrow face and the painted lips and long lashes, blue eyes and the hands frantically rummaging through the purse, but the hands were long and narrow and big and . . .

"Excuse me. Do you have a pen I could borrow? I've got to write something down before I forget it." It was a man's voice beneath the makeup.

Mike turned, facing the man in drag.

"Oh, my God, you're a man! I really thought you were a woman."

"Oh, you did? I'm flattered."

"I mean, I would never have thought you were a drag queen."

"Well, dear, I'm not actually. I guess you would say I'm a TV . . . a transvestite. Though I'm not really sure if that fits either. It's a confusing issue. I'm not really into glam at all. I just feel like putting on a dress whenever the mood hits."

"Are you a transsexual?"

"Oh, God no. I'm not trying to be a woman. I'm just letting that part of me out who likes putting on a nice dress and a face. I wouldn't put myself in that league at all. Now don't take me wrong. I have nothing against any of it."

Mike was holding out his pen transfixed by the *she* who was a *he*.

"You mean you don't even pretend to be a woman?"

"No, why should I? I know some guys that go to great lengths to shave everything. You know, they want to go for the whole fem look . . . 'cunt realness' they call it. I say, 'Hey, who's got the time, doll. I'm a busy girl.' I'm into transvestite lib. You aren't going to find me slaving away for six hours shaving my legs and tweezing. God, I've got better things to do with my time. You miss all the men and get lost in a vacuum in front of the mirror. No, I just throw myself together and hit the street. Gotta keep it fresh you know. Nothing worse than a tired glam queen who's spent the night putting it together. Then there's nothing left for the boys." She/he smiled.

"What's your name?" Michael finally asked.

"Oh, I'm sorry. Ms. Kim." She reached over and took Mike's hand and squeezed a firm, warm welcome. "So, do you live in the Village?"

"No, I actually, well, I live, or I used to live on the road."

"The road. You mean the street. How fun. That's where I should be living. I bet you find them there."

"Find who?"

"The men!"

"Well, I didn't mean the streets, like these streets. I was traveling across the country, but I guess I've hit the end of the road."

"So where are you staying?" Ms. Kim was intrigued. Finally something more than the average East Village clone.

"Well, I was staying with a new friend, but it's getting complicated." Mike went into his life, taking total liberty to tell the whole story in stunning detail to his new friend Ms. Kim.

Ms. Kim took the pen and started taking notes, nodding approval, shaking her disapproval, astonished, disbelieving, amused and ultimately floored. "So do you still have the cowgirl outfit? What happened to your other dresses? What about your cat? Where's she?"

"Well, Dolly's at Annie's. I just left my dresses in the motor home. I didn't think I'd need them here."

"Oh, my God! Whatever possessed you to think *that*." Ms. Kim was horrified. "The girl doesn't have her dresses. No wonder she's so depressed. I would be too. You've been dumped, you lost your home, you're a stranger in town and you don't have a *thing to wear!* Well, there's always space where I'm staying if you can bear the late callers. And you can certainly borrow something of mine."

"But I'm not a transvestite."

"Well, neither am I. Like I said, I just like to throw on a dress now and then. We'll step out together. It's a new movement—TV lib. No more shaving, no more plucking. Hell, we may not even do the face. Just a little eyeliner and lipstick. We'll even do away with the heels. Sneakers and nylons. Just like Wall Street." Ms. Kim was bending over in restrained laughter, gasping at her thought.

Mike arched back in amazement. The second stranger he'd met in New York and now he'd been offered another place to stay.

Ms. Kim helped herself to another beer, delighting in her new TV lib sidekick. She sucked on that beer, writing copious notes to herself for her ongoing play in progress, before hailing a ride with Mike for the long journey back to the Upper East Side.

The next morning Annie and Jim sat talking at the kitchen table.

"Guess Michael must have found a hot boy, eh, Monkster?"

"Maybe." Jim was preoccupied. He never worried nearly as much about Mike as Mike did about him. *Mike always returns.*

"Jim, we've gotta get you a woman. Look at that hot ass of yours. Women will just die for you. You need to sow your wild oats, Monkster."

"I know, I've had about two sexual encounters with women in about ten years. It's been a while. I'm way out of practice."

"Look, why don't I give this friend of mine a call. She's a masseuse. She'd be perfect for you. She's *very pretty.*"

Jim's eyes lit up.

"She gives about eight massages a day, but she never has anyone give back what she gives out. I'll bet she'll even pay you."

Jim went downstairs to buy a fix of soy.

"Hi, Roxanne, this is Annie. I think I've found a perfect boy for you. He's so cute and really smart."

"Can he come over tonight?"

"I'm sure."

"Tell him to arrive around eight. I have clients until then."

"Great, Roxanne. Coming to my Sluts and Goddesses workshop? . . . Wonderful! Oh, gotta go, I hear him coming up the hallway."

Jim walked back into the Salon, the Tibetan bells jangling from the doorknob.

"Jim, she wants you to come over tonight at eight. Here's her address on the Upper West Side. Now, Monkster, I have to tell you a few things. You know how you can talk in that deep husky voice. She'll like that. She kind of goes for the strong silent type, so don't get too animated. Be strong and confident, okay?"

"Got it."

"She's going to pay you for a massage. I'm sure you'll do quite well. You give great massages I hear, hee hee."

Annie had actually heard wrong—Mike gave the great massages, but Jim could fake it.

"I'm going out to work on my video all day. If you'd like, you can use my club pass. Maybe take a sauna, go for a swim. It's so beautiful up there, Monkster."

"Yeah, I think I will. Thank you so much Sprinkeeee."

"Oh, no problem. It's a great honor to help a Monk."

All afternoon Jim worked out at Annie's club. Pumping, lifting, stretching, building, Building, BUILDING, desperate to forge in a matter of eight hours a strong silent type out of his hyperactive personality and flaccid physique.

By late afternoon Jim ran over to the Chogye Zen Center for an hour's worth of silence, followed by a yanged-out macroneurotic dinner at Angelika's Kitchen, finally popping by the Prana health-food store to pick up some yohimbé root. Then after taking the subway uptown for a bit of reflection in Strawberry Fields, Jim walked to the intersection of Seventy-second and Broadway, in the heart of Yuppieville, only a short walk from Roxanne's apartment.

Jim popped three hits of the yohimbé root, designed to strengthen and improve sexual endurance, and made his way up Broadway. Before turning down Roxanne's street, Jim stepped into the Fairway Market to buy some bread—
never know how long I'll stay.

Jim glanced at the Fairway clock.

"Oh, shit!" he blurted loud enough for all the yuppie mothers to hear.

In all his frantic preparation, Jim had forgot to consider time. Grandfather time! It was eight forty-five.

"I don't believe it," Jim sank into despair. "I don't believe it. How could I have done this? I should have skipped Strawberry Fields. Oh, well, no regrets. Old subconscious desire to be punished I guess."

Jim ran with trepidation down the street toward Columbus. It was near nine when he reached Roxanne's door. He buzzed and was let into a foyer. He buzzed again and was let into another foyer.

A door opened.

"Well, you took your time, didn't you?"

"I'm sorry I'm so late, I completely lost track of . . . "

"Well, next time . . . "

Next time?

"Next time at least call me. I had a client who would have gone for another hour, if I'd known you'd be so late. Okay, take your shoes off here."

She was more of a dominatrix than a kitten, but was definitely pretty. Tall and pretty, slightly Rubenesque, with dark, curly hair, a strong upright posture and bright red lipstick. Jim was intrigued, but embarrassed. It felt as if a battle of wills was impending, and Roxanne already had the upper hand.

"You can change in there. I've put out a robe for you." It was more of a directive than an invitation, though her voice did have a soft, sensual, if a bit twangy, appeal to it.

Jim changed nervously. All the bodybuilding and the last-minute rushing had made him a bit jittery. His hands were shaking when he walked into the massage room.

She lay flat on her back on a massage table with a white towel over her upper body. She looked up and watched Jim's every move with penetrating curiosity.

"Be sure not to touch my big right toe, okay? I broke it at my karate class and it's almost totally healed."

"Não problema," answered Jim, trying to gather confidence.

"It's *no problema*." Roxanne was clearly not of Portuguese descent.

This woman is tough, but beautiful. Jim turned his back, fiddling at some table, trying to conjure up that strong-silent-type persona. It was starting to come through.

"Okay, Roxanne, I want you to close your eyes."

"No, I'd like to keep them open, if you don't mind. I want to see you move."

She is *a difficult one.*

"Very well," Jim reassured in some archetypal doctor's voice he pulled in from the ethers. "I'd like you to take three deep breaths." Jim remembered this trick from the Bates Eye Improvement cassettes. "That's it. Okay, now take three more deep breaths." Jim needed some time to figure out his next move. "Very good." *She's still looking at me!*

"Okay, now I want you to repeat after me: 'Om, om, om.' " *A little Buddhist mumbo jumbo should chill her out.*

"Aren't you going to touch me?" she whined.

Damn, she's feisty!

"We're getting to that, darling. You just relax. This is your treat now. You've worked hard all day. Just let go, let Jim the Mad Monk work his magic."

"Why do you call yourself the Mad Monk?"

"We'll talk all about that later. You just relax."

Jim put his hands on her legs and began to knead and pinch and squeeze and rub.

"Don't you want to use some oil?"

"Oh, I was getting to that. I like to touch the bare skin before putting anything on it. It's part of my technique." *The oil. Forgot the damn oil. Jeez!*

"Why don't you turn over now, Roxanne."

"But then I can't see you."

"Oh, we'll put you back on your back in no time."

She obeyed!

Jim pulled up the white towel to reveal her soft, tan back legs. He began squirting the oil all over her legs. Jim then took the towel off and squirted oil all over her back. Suddenly the cap flew off and oil spilled all over her hair, all over her front, all over the massage table and toward the floor.

"There's some towels in the kitchen." Roxanne rose to go fetch them. *He had her. She was starting to relax. Then the bottle breaks!*

She returned from the kitchen without even a look at Jim and lay back down on the table.

"You gotta be careful not to squeeze the bottle too hard or it will burst," said the perfectly modulated voice of the professional masseuse.

"Sorry." *Strong silent types never say sorry.* Another point for Roxanne.

After wiping up the mess, Jim started The Massage. The sounds of Pachelbel played in the background. *Now maybe things will work out.* Roxanne lay on her stomach, unable to peer at Jim, who worked each section of flesh as if it were his own. She was beautiful. Stunning. The oil gleamed on her perfectly tan skin.

Jim worked quietly, diligently. The day's workout had

given him enormous strength, the yohimbé was starting to kick in as he felt a tug in his underwear. He was putting manly strength behind each stroke. Remembering aspects of Michael's more refined technique, Jim was employing a motley Swedish-Monk-shiatsu stew. He was into it. And maybe *she* was into it. *Everything's gonna be alright.*

"*Ouch! Ouch!* Don't you see that bandage on my big toe? *Don't touch my big toe!*"

"I'm so sorry. I forgot about that. I'll be more careful." *Pay attention, Jim!*

Jim stayed focused now, no more drifting into massage reverie. Roxanne had him on pins and needles.

"What do you do for a living?"

More questions!

"We'll answer that later. You just relax."

"I wanna get to know you. Where did you grow up?"

What a control freak!

"Nebraska." *Strong silent types come from Nebraska, don't they?*

"How do you know Annie? Have you ever done this before? *Ouch! Ouch!* That's my big toe. *Don't touch my big toe!*"

Jim was a nervous wreck. Roxanne had him against the ropes. He took a deep breath.

"You have a friend you travel with? What do you do for enjoyment? Do you like your work?" Each question was like a jab to the rib section or a left hook to the jaw.

Two hours later and Jim felt he'd been through a bizarre S&M massage ritual. Roxanne hadn't closed her eyes once. And considering how many times Jim had touched her big toe, he couldn't blame her. Jim was visibly shaken.

Roxanne handed him $300.

"What? You sure? Thank you." Jim was blown away. *Three hundred dollars for what I did? I feel like Richard Gere without the credentials.*

"Now, I have a big day ahead. Your clothes are in the bathroom. I'm sorry I have to ask you to leave. Thank you."

Jim hobbled into the bathroom. He threw on his clothes, thanked Roxanne profusely and shuffled out the door with his yohimbé root bulging out of his unzipped pants.

Roxanne the Scorpio Masseuse had scored a tenth-round TKO.

When Jim walked into the Sprinkle Salon the next morning, Annie was lying in bed with a blond woman in mousy glasses, who was

dressed entirely in orange.

"So, Monkster, how was it?"

"Painful."

"Oh, no. What happened, Jim?"

"I don't know. I don't understand women like that. She cut me down into small chunks and then ate me as a snack. I think I need a Robert Bly workshop. Maybe I *am* gay."

"Oh, Monkster, you're taking it too seriously."

"I don't know. Maybe I'm too Catholic. Get too wound up in the emotions and the romance. I know it's all conditioning."

"You want a cookie? I just bought some Health Valley prune-walnut cookies. They're delicious. Why don't you relax. I'll pour you some Cafix and you can have a cookie, okay?"

Jim took a seat at the dining room table as Annie brewed the Cafix.

"Aren't cookies great?" she called from the kitchen.

"Yeah, where'd you get these? Mike and I used to make these back in San Francisco. Did I ever tell you about that? We had so much fun together baking cookies."

"Say, Monkster. Speaking of San Francisco, I've got great news for you."

"Yeah?" Jim's eyes lit up.

"I think I've found the perfect woman for you."

"I don't know, Sprinkler." Jim's eyes sulked back down. "I've had it with women for a while. Too much confusion and disappointment. I think I'll go back to being celibate. As the swami says, 'Sell a bit here, sell a bit there.' "

"Oh, c'mon, Monkster," Annie began in a motherly voice, "when you least expect it, the person of your deepest, most soulful dreams can suddenly appear. I know it's been tough. But three's the charm, just you watch."

"Oh, Annie, you're so sweet for trying. I really appreciate it. But I think you can't grab for lovers, they have to come to you."

"Well, this one came to you."

"What do you mean?"

"Well, I got this call today from a woman who heard through Veronica that you were staying at my apartment. I guess she had heard a lot about you from Veronica and *really* wants to meet you. She's a little older than you, but maybe you'll do better with the older type. Oh, and Veronica says she has a lot of money. She's from San Francisco, hee hee."

"Money?" Jim had never considered *that* possibility. A woman with a *lot of money* who wanted to meet the Monkster?

"Yeah, money. And she's very straight, very spiritual and *very beautiful*. Not uptight at all. She wants to meet you soon."

"How soon?"

"Well, if you're interested, she's going to go to a club with Vee tonight called Edelweiss."

"Hum, never heard of it."

"I hadn't either, but here's the address. You should meet her there around midnight."

"Midnight?"

"Yeah. Maybe I'll even come down later. Isn't this great?"

"Well, yeah. Maybe I should check in with Michael though. He might be wondering about me."

Annie the yenta gave Jim Mike's new number as she fed her two cats, Linda and Tuttles. Jim took the silver-and-blue-speckled phone into the back room. Ten minutes later he emerged in a quiet mood.

"Michael says he's fine. He wanted to know if I was still

seeing other people. He sounded so fragile. So hurt. I really want to see him."

"Why don't you see him then?"

"He didn't want to yet. He said, 'If it's meant to be, we'll come back together, but until then, be patient.' "

"Maybe he's found another lover."

Jim didn't like that thought. "He wished me luck in finding what I'm looking for. He's so noble and sweet."

Annie agreed.

That night at midnight Jim arrived at Edelweiss "on time," which for Jim is forty-five minutes past the promised hour. At the entrance, things seemed pretty confusing. First, the ten-dollar cover charge. Jim only had a fiver. Secondly, the loud, pounding disco in the background. *How could we talk amidst this?* thought our Monk. *Oh, well, maybe we won't have much to say. We'll just keep it casual tonight. The financial details of our relationship can be sorted out later.* Finally, the straight, leather-faced goodfellas congregating at the doorway. The vibe felt more like a cross between a tacky nightclub and a strip joint. Not a likely place for a rich, self-respecting woman of hip to be spending a Saturday night.

Jim persuaded Robin at the door to accept his five while he prowled inside searching for Vee and the fabulous woman from San Francisco. As he rushed in, Jim passed right by the crowded bar heading toward the dance floor. It was another virtual babefest, but these babes were *really* decked out. Jim felt conspicuous in his K Mart suit and tie, donned especially for the occasion, but he pressed on. His mind was on finding *that girl,* and no amount of hairspray, girl talk, giant bouffants or big-breasted, red-dress come-ons were going to distract him from his appointed aim.

Jim moved to the center of the bar.

Where are all the men? Jim wondered. The bar was packed with gorgeous large-breasted stereotypes of 1950s femininity, but there was hardly a guy in sight. *Maybe it's a lesbian bar. But why'd she want to meet me here?* Jim was puzzled by the lack of males—that is, until he finally noticed in a far corner a gathering of men.

My God. Look at those blokes. I'm the best-looking one of the lot. In the corner were the dregs of Long Giland and New Joisey holding up the particleboard walls. Cheezy-looking, leather-faced sleazeballs, the type he'd expect to see in Atlantic City, with the requisite gaudy gold chains.

Jim stood gawking at the spectacle as a few ladies danced out on the floor with their shorter dates. *God, these are tall women.* Jim was just now noticing that at six feet tall he was almost the shortest person in the room.

Jim looked from side to particleboard side in the bar. It had the air of decadent Weimar Germany as shot through the lens of Rainer Fassbinder. And to complete the picture, Jim suddenly spotted Ms. Vee in her trademark, ravishing gown, looking unfazed and as happy as ever.

"Ms. Vee!" Jim explained, happy at last to see someone he knew.

"Heeeellllo, Mr. Monk." Vee smiled coyly, but then immediately turned back to chatting with a man. *Where've I seen that man before?*

Around Ms. Vee were a few more whom Jim recognized. But no one was saying hello, which made sociable Jim insecure. Jim stood in his K Mart suit, his smile slightly fading. With the loud disco music and the whole weird bar scene, this was the last place he wanted to meet "the woman of his dreams."

But everyone seemed quite at home except for the Mad Monk, who stood waiting for some kind of introduction. Maybe that was the uncool thing to expect. *Maybe she's watching me right at this moment to see how I perform.*

Jim took the initiative and broke into conversation with Vee and her circle of friends. Suddenly he caught some movement behind him. But it was just another tall brunette prancing on the floor. He turned again. But this time it was Annie Sprinkle waltzing toward the group.

"Annie!" Jim waved excitedly, relieved at the sight of his new friend, yet torn by a nagging anxiety that something wasn't quite right.

Annie smiled graciously, working her way around the high-heeled dancers with Les groveling at her feet. "So did you meet her yet?" Annie asked breathlessly.

"No, I don't know who she is. And no one's introduced me!" said a frustrated Jim.

"Oh, that's rude. Here, let me introduce you. . . . Let's see, *there* she is." Annie pointed.

Jim turned.

And sure enough, there she was alright, wearing a bright multicolored petticoat with red panty hose, perfectly accentuated by a big fur coat. The Woman of His Dreams was a slender, tall brunette, with deep blue eyes, shoulder-length hair, a low, shoulderless blouse with ample cleavage, a huge ring on her left hand, and a short black skirt revealing long, really long, legs. She smiled a pearly smile toward Jim as Jim felt himself falling into some deep deep hole. She was munching on a cookie and offered Jim one as she stuck out her hand for the introduction.

"Petunia, this is Jim the Mad Monk." Annie beamed.

Petunia. My God. Poor woman.

Jim bolstered up his best glad-to-meet-you smile and took the cookie in one hand and the bony hand in the other. Petunia gazed long and deep into Jim's monk eyes, so deep that Jim momentarily forgot to speak.

"You're ravishing," Jim complimented. *She's a dog. God, what a freak of nature. Look at all that makeup. She must use a shovel to get it on.*

Petunia smiled. Jim smiled back. No matter how grotesquely odd she seemed, there was something unbelievably compelling about her face and her strong but kind touch. Jim began to wonder if he was feeling attracted despite himself. "So, Petunia, what do you like to do?" Jim yelled above the din.

Petunia mouthed something, but Jim couldn't hear. Jim was falling deeper, deeper under her spell. Jim couldn't take his eyes off her.

Everyone around seemed to have stopped talking and stared at the exchange. Jim suddenly began feeling as if he'd entered some clandestine witches' coven.

Petunia was wearing huge, sparkling earrings, her lips painted siren red, and she wore a chiffon scarf over her head. As she slowly took another bite out of her cookie, she coyly winked.

Jim stared at her bony frame, her hairless arms, and her white neck and shoulders that looked as soft as a newborn. She was the pinnacle of femininity, despite her awkward height and crooked, toothy smile. Where had he seen a woman like this before? What movie was it? He felt such a pull toward her.

The dance floor was crowded now, and so Jim asked Petunia for a dance. He gingerly took her in his arms and began two-stepping around the floor while the other dancers danced the latest moves, staring, if not chuckling, at this odd couple.

Jim started to talk, but was once more mesmerized by her compassionate eyes, held captive by the sinking feeling that he was losing control of the situation. Another *powerful woman.* But she was so soft inside. So magnetic. So deep and compassionate. He tried focusing on her grotesqueness, which was easy to do. The gobs of makeup piled on the skin. The artificial, rosy cheeks. The penciled brows. The perfume. It all nauseated him. But still. He found her . . . well . . . strangely attractive. *She's as weird as me. She's a basket case!*

Finally the music ended, and Jim led Petunia back into the admiring circle of friends.

"What kind of cookie is this?" Jim asked as he nervously bit into it. It had a familiar taste. "What kind of cookie is this?" he asked again.

Suddenly the music stopped. The bar talk hushed between tapes. All the eyes near Jim watched him chew as he asked one more time, "What sort of cookie is this?"

And in a low, deafening voice, everyone nearby began slowly, delightfully, chanting in unison, *"Prune . . . walnut . . . square. Prune . . . walnut . . . square!"*

Jim's face began to turn white.

"Prune . . . walnut . . . square!"

An ever-growing fire began to rise in the Mad Monk.

"Prune . . . walnut . . . square!"

Everyone around him was smiling.

The slow-moving, evolving brain was waking up to a deep memory.

"Prune walnut square!"

Her blue eyes were staring from beneath a mask. Her lips chanted the answer to his deepest question. The words reverberated through the millions of synapses in his brain. The cookie was coming alive. The cookie was growing through the room. The cookie was taking over life. . . .

"Prune walnut square!"
"Prune walnut square!"
"Prune walnut square!"

And the heat rose through the throat, sweat dripped over his brow and . . .

"Prune walnut square!"
"Prune walnut square!"
"Prune walnut square!"
"Prune walnut square!"

. . . he felt it coming. Coming from the deepest fiber within his soul. Her eyes were big and bright now. Her mouth chewed lovingly on the monster cookie. Jim's vocal cords tightened at the edge. The Cookie flooded his soul. And he screamed at the top of his powerful lungs, sending shock waves through the crowd. *"Michael! Michael! Holy holy fuck! Michael, it's you! I don't fucking believe this. It's you!"*

The music resumed and the world began spinning around

Jim as he screamed, falling backward, blanking out to the smiling Michael and the circle of friends. Michael caught Jim on the fall and helped him back to his feet.

Club Edelweiss suddenly seemed like a nineties *Cabaret*. Jim was sure Joel Grey would appear any second on some hidden stage to sing "Willkommen."

But then suddenly the room came into mind-twisting focus for Jim, as everyone smiled. The bar was swimming with transvestites, transsexuals, and a few "real women." And behind Michael stood Ms. Kim, nodding TV approval toward this crowning achievement.

And just as Jim's addled Gemini brain was short-circuiting, Michael, in a grand bow, flipped off his wig, revealing his shiny dome, and welcomed Jim with a hug, a kiss and a familiar refrain: "Coast to coast. Brotherly love. The astronauts have landed."

The Monks

were reunited at the Sprinkle Salon, but on Wednesday got the word that paraplegic performance artist Frank Moore

and his tribe of Rainbow groupies would be arriving soon.

"You're welcome to sleep on the floor," Annie offered.

But the Monks knew they'd hit the peak of the fun curve. Annie's place was starting to feel like home, which was precisely the problem. It was time to move on.

Jim left Mike to the arduous chore of packing it all up, while Jim went out to scrounge up a new Monk pad. "Don't worry, the Mad Monk will find us a new monastery. You just load up everything and get it down to the street."

Hour by painstaking hour Mike disassembled our high life, saving the mementos from our excursions out to the street. Oh, what careless days we'd been living high on the hog in the Sprinkle Salon. All the parties, the late-night dancing, the cavorting, the teasing, the dining, and especially the gawking at the eccentric parade of call boys, call girls, strippers, porn stars, transvestites, transsexuals, photographers and tantrikas who made their way through the "Sprinkle Arms Hotel," all the while paying nightly homage to Annie's *Bare Bosom Ballet* hanging on the south wall. We were somebodies, we were contenders. Or at least had been.

And now, dragging two tons of junk out to the street, Mike and Dolly stood out on the curb feeling quite conspicuous. The Pakistani doorman asked when we'd be back.

Mike choked out, "Probably never."

At that moment a hysterically gleeful Jim came wheeling around the corner in his Yankees hat with a giddy smile, whooping it up, honking the horn of . . . you got it . . . the Monkmobile.

"*The Monkmobile!* How the hell did you get that?" screamed Mike.

"I had them repair it. We're getting the hell outta Dodge. Yeehaw! Load 'em up and move 'em out! Let's go sell this shit on St. Marks Place."

"You're fucking outta your mind. How'd you pay to fix this?!" said a skeptical Mike.

"The big Rock, dude. They took the big crystal as payment. You should of seen their eyes pop. They were the only New Age mechanics in all of Queens. We just rolled the rock out of the Bounder, and they handed me the keys. It's ours. All paid for, guy."

Mike stood in disbelief.

"C'mon, Space Monk, you want to get out of here, don't you? We're selling everything we own and hittin' the road," said a wide-eyed Jim.

"The road?" Mike yelled.

"You betcha, partner, that's where we belong . . . out on the open road, chasing windmills, seeing where the horizon ends, meeting our extended family."

Mike was in shock. The intensity of New York had left him dazed and confused. *The road? What road?*

"Mike, Mike, we're losing it here. We're getting sucked in. Gotta leave before we forget why we came."

"But how are we going to support ourselves? Where are we going to live?"

"Mike! We've gotta go."

Mike gave a zombielike nod.

The Monks squeezed every last box into the restored Bounder, strapped a few burlap bags on the side, and sped across town to St. Marks Place. The day was getting late and a full-moon night was fast approaching.

Jim pulled up alongside the Gem Spa newsstand at Second Avenue and St. Marks. Mike stumbled out and set up shop.

"C'mon, man, you're crowding my space," said a thin, homeless junkie, hunched over his stolen loot of women's dresses, leather jackets and alarm clocks.

"Yeah, go somewhere else, you're blocking the way,

maaan," said another homeless retailer, hovering over his specialty, new CDs and cassettes.

The street vendors were getting nervous at the mountain of debris spilling out from the Monkmobile heading toward their fenced goods, but the Monks were on a mission from Nurse and weren't letting anyone get in their way.

"It's fresh, it's used, it's hot, it's fenced, just in from the Upper East Side . . . get it now. It's yours, and yes, it's yet Another Space Monk Production. Yes, Another Space Monk Production: The Final Sale. Get it here, New York. Get it here." Jim was using his powerful lungs for what they do best: kibitzing, schmoozing, outrageous salesmanship.

"Hey, I'll take those ten bags of soybeans," said a passing blond photographer. "I know some guys who just love that stuff. . . . Organic, right? . . . Wait a minute, don't I know you?"

"John Deming?" the Monks rang in unison. "What are you doing here?"

"On my way to Yugoslavia. Big croquet tournament. I don't believe you guys . . . what happened to your van?"

"Oh, God, John, it's a long story, maaan. How you been?" said Mike, giving his soul brother a big hug.

"So this is the new Monkmobile I've been reading about."

"Monks," a soft, quivering voice spoke up. It was a man dressed as a nun, wearing lipstick and rouge. "I want you to have these," he said, handing the Monks a jar of figs.

"Phillip?"

"Phyllis. I switched orders."

"I don't believe it!" shouted Jim.

"I'm sorry to interrupt you, Phyllis, but Michael . . . Michael . . . are those fifteen cases of herbs sold by multilevel? I think there might be some good business potential in that."

"*Mom?!*" screamed a shocked Mike. "How the hell did you find me?" Mike stood glaring at his mother, Roberta.

"In-cre-dee-ble, in-cre-dee-ble. How . . . do . . . you . . . boys do it? It's incredible!"

"Bighearted Jay!" screamed Jim.

"That's right, pilgrim," said Jay, letting out a gargantuan chortle that shocked half the street vendors on Second Avenue.

"Yo! Monks!" a familiar youthful voice rang out. "How much for these whatchamacallits, these boxes of soy milk," a handsome man in white said with a big goofy grin.

"*Pi?*" The Monks turned.

"No, silly, Apple Pi," he said with that characteristic Pi giggle.

"Yo, Monks, like *This Is Your Life*. I was just thinking if there's ever someplace I'd run into the Monks again, it'd be on St. Marks. So how much for those cases of soy, dude?" Pi giggled his trademark laugh again.

"Pi, Pi, how are you?" said Jim, giving *his* soul brother a big bear hug.

"Remind me to tell you about my Vagueness Concept and the Macintosh program that goes with it. It's awesome."

"What is going on here?" Mike smiled, deliriously happy yet completely wigged out. "Did you all just simultaneously get into town? This is crazy!"

"Hi, guys, I've got my credit card . . . what's for sale?" A woman laughed a little too forcefully. "How 'bout those piles of papers?" she blurted out in between those big laughs. "And will you throw in the pile of river rocks?"

"Cheryl . . . Cheryl Wagner? You're back in New York?"

"On my way to Harvard. Landscape architecture. I might need some scratch paper this winter. Might need some rocks too!" she said as she broke into a long, hysterical guffaw.

"Honey, I brought you this new seersucker suit and some miso soup from that nice restaurant on Twelfth Street. You know, Dad and I are macrobiotic now."

"*Bev!*" Jim yelled. "What are you and Dick doing here? Oh, but I don't eat fermented foods anymore, Bev. I'm sorry. I'm on the caveman diet. It's the latest rage. I only eat red meat."

"Oh, I see. Well, Dad wants to be sure we buy that Michio Kushi book, honey, and anything you have on holistic health. Ever since that Zen retreat he's really gotten into herbs and acupuncture."

Dr. Dick was busy gettin' it sorted all out with Michael Monk.

"Ho, ho, ho, pretty good for you, Mike!" the doctor roared. "Yeah, let's see, Bev and I took 80 in from Chicago. Guess if you fellas were headin' west, gosh, you could just hook up with 80 there and see ole Boler out there in . . . where is Doc Boler now, Bev?"

"Oh, gad, my memory's so bad. Here, Dick, can you come over here? I want you to pose with Jimmy next to this nice homeless man. Say 'Enterprise zone.' "

"Enterprise zone!"

"Great!" Bev's camera clicked and flashed. . . . "It *worked!*"

"Those scrapbooks, zay burn vell, don't zay?" came a distinctly German accent. "Would you Monks care to join us in a fire?" It was the Germans!

"Down in zee, er, Tompkins Square, of course," they added matter-of-factly.

"Wait a second, where did all you come from? How'd you know we were—"

"Woof, woof, woooooooofeeee!"

"Girl Doggie?"

"How much for those dozen chili *ristras*," said a girlish voice.

"Leapin' lizards, holy kachinas . . . Girl Carol! I don't believe this," said Michael.

"It is not a matter of belief, it is a matter of apricot duck gravy, isn't that right, Doll Face?" The distinguished Mr. Burris bent down to pet Dolly Lama, who was on her leash attached to a telephone pole. "It has always been a great moment in the lives of disciples when a monk leaves the holy city."

"Mr. Burris?"

"At your service, gentlemen."

"We thought you went back to Santa Fe to build solar adobes."

"Well, I was detoured and went back to India. Oh, but that stinking Ganges was too much. So happy now to see my Doll Face. Oh, I think I will purchase those rose quartz crystals. Only good karma can come from financially supporting a Monk at such an auspicious moment."

"And while you're at it, dawlings, I want those cow skulls . . . pronto *pleeeeasssee*," said a stunning Chuck Yma Sumac. "What a dump! Is this your corner now?"

And for the next hour from all four directions poured the Monk family—haggling, schmoozing and finally coughing up the dough to put the Monks back on the road to Damascus.

John Deming, Phillip the Hermit, Momma-ka-poo, Big-hearted Jay, Pi, Cheryl Wagner, Bev and Dick, the Germans, Chuck Yma Sumac, Mr. Burris, Girl Doggie and Carol . . . and in a final coup, Annie Sprinkle, who arrived by cab in a giant pink tutu dress and agreed to pay for the parking ticket. "With pleasure," she purred. "My very own Monk parking ticket."

Free from possessions, with a little money to boot, an exhausted and excited duo, the Monks, Mike and Jim, loaded up their computer, waffle iron and her holiness the great Dolly Lama. And to the deafening cheers from the Monketeers, the exalted Monkmobile pulled away from the curb and back onto the open road.

"All roads lead to home!" shouted Dick.

Happy tales! *(J. Deming)*

"Don't forget to write!" trailed Momma-ka-poo.

"If you land in jail, you know my number," whispered Uncle Jack.

Speeding uptown dodging streams of cabs and trucks, buggies and bikes, dodging potholes and barricades, Jim and Mike took a wistful look at the crowds and garbage they were leaving behind. Past A&S Plaza and Macy's, past Port Authority and the street trade on Forty-second, past *Intrepid*, past Elroy lying in a gutter.

Faster and faster they drove. Up the West Side Highway, Dolly and the Monks sat focused and still.

Slowly the tall buildings gave way to high-rise apartments as the road cleared. The Monks and Dolly turned and looked back at the city of dreams.

And in the twilight hours and in the aftermath, as the naked city came to light, the two lone Monks, and the great Dolly Lama, breathed a big sigh of relief.

The Monks had crossed America and lived to tell the story.

The journey Continues!! If you enjoyed

Mad Monks on the Road,

you will run around and go

naked over *Monk,* the mobile magazine.

Each spellbinding episode features a unique city or region. We encourage you to dramatically improve your karma by becoming a *Monk* subscriber today. Subscriptions are available at the following rates: $10/4 episodes; $18/8 episodes; $100/For a Lifetime After Lifetime of Episodes (guaranteeing you a *Monk* subscription next time you come around). Subscriptions can be ordered by calling 1-800-GET-MONK or by sending a check, money order, or MC/Visa information (card number and expiration date) to our vast corporate headquarters: Monk, 175 Fifth Avenue, Suite 2322, New York, NY 10010. We also receive love mail at this address.

Happy Tales!

The Monks

And Her Holiness, The Great Dolly Lama
Nurse, Where are you?!!